Confederate Admiral

LIBRARY OF NAVAL BIOGRAPHY

CONFEDERATE ADMIRAL

THE
Life AND *Wars*
OF
FRANKLIN BUCHANAN

Craig L. Symonds

BLUEJACKET BOOKS

NAVAL INSTITUTE PRESS
Annapolis, Maryland

Naval Institute Press
291 Wood Road
Annapolis, MD 21402

First Naval Institute Press paperback edition published in 2008.

ISBN-13 978-1-59114-846-3 (paperback)

Library of Congress Cataloging-in-Publication Data
Symonds, Craig L.;
            Confederate admiral : the life and wars of Franklin Buchanan /
Craig L. Symonds.
            p.   cm. — (Library of naval biography)
Includes bibliographical references (p.   ) and index.
ISBN 1-55750-844-5 (alk. paper)
1. Buchanan, Franklin, 1800–1874. 2. Admirals—Confederate States
of America Biography. 3. Confederate States of America. Navy
Biography. 4. United States— History—Civil War, 1861–1865—Naval
operations. 5. United States. Navy Biography. I. Title.
II. Series.
E461.1.B773S96 1999
359'.0092—dc21   99-15202
[B]

Printed in the United States of America on acid-free paper

14 13 12 11 10 09 08   9 8 7 6 5 4 3 2
First printing

Frontispiece courtesy of U.S. Navy

For Marylou, again

ᴐ Contents ᴐ

Foreword xi
Acknowledgments xiii
Chronology xv
Prologue: Resignation 1

PART ONE. NAVY BLUE

1 A Mid in the Med 7
2 Chasing Pirates and Other Adventures 22
3 Nannie Lloyd 37
4 Command: The USS *Vincennes* 51
5 The Naval School 67
6 War and Diplomacy 83
7 The Mysterious Orient 99
8 The Immortal Fifteen 115
9 War Clouds 128

PART TWO. REBEL GRAY

10 The Confederate Navy 143
11 Iron against Wood: The Battle of Hampton Roads 156
12 Confederate Admiral 172
13 The CSS *Tennessee* 189
14 The Battle of Mobile Bay 203
15 Home from the Sea 220

Epilogue: Retrospective 233
Notes 235
Bibliography 257
Further Reading 265
Index 269

~❧ Foreword ❧~

Franklin Buchanan served during one of the great transitional eras of naval warfare. He entered the U.S. Navy in 1815 when sailing warships reached their highest state of development after three centuries of evolution. By the end of Buchanan's naval service fifty years later, propulsion was changing from sail to steam, the hulls of ships from wood to iron, ordnance from muzzle-loading smoothbore cannon to breech-loading rifled guns, and projectiles from solid shot to exploding shells. Buchanan, a leader in naval reform, played a significant role in all those developments. Serving as Matthew C. Perry's flag captain during the expedition to Japan, he was in the vanguard of America's emergence as a transoceanic power. As the superintendent of the new Naval Academy he influenced not only the midshipmen who attended Annapolis during his tenure, but those of subsequent generations by laying the foundation of a curriculum and training regime that characterized the institution for much of the nineteenth century.

Buchanan was affected by his times as much as he influenced the navy of the era. His vacillation between loyalty to his service and the United States and allegiance to his home state and its institutions reflected the agonizing decisions faced by thousands of Americans as the nation drifted toward civil war. When Buchanan chose the Confederacy and joined its navy in 1861, he immediately assumed positions of great responsibility. As chief of its Bureau of Orders and Detail, Buchanan both recommended assignment of other officers to various positions and participated in the design of defenses along the Potomac and James Rivers in Virginia, and at Savannah, Georgia. While directing the naval defense of the James River, Buchanan commanded the ironclad *Virginia* in its initial combat against wooden vessels of his old service. Wounded during the battle, he stepped down as captain, but three years later commanded the ironclad *Tennessee* in its doomed engagement with Union forces at the Battle of Mobile Bay.

Craig Symonds has the perfect combination of experience and knowledge to write this, the first scholarly biography of Franklin Buchanan. An award-winning scholar and teacher of both Civil War and naval history, Symonds gives us an excellent study of U.S. naval policy in the early years of the republic as well as a gripping account of Civil War naval combat. The biographer of Generals Joseph E. Johnston and Patrick Cleburne, Symonds understands the Confederacy and its leaders, as well as the art of biography. His illuminating study captures the life of Franklin Buchanan, the revolution in naval affairs of the mid-nineteenth century, and the strains that tore apart the United States.

The Library of Naval Biography provides accurate, informative, and interpretive biographies of influential naval figures—men and women who have shaped or reflected the naval affairs of their time. Each volume will explain the forces that acted upon its subject as well as the significance of that person in history. Some volumes will explore the lives of individuals who have not previously been the subject of a modern, full-scale biography, while others will reexamine the lives of better-known individuals, adding new information, a differing perspective, or a fresh interpretation. The series is international in scope and spans several centuries. All volumes are based on solid research and written to be of interest to general readers as well as useful to specialists.

With these goals in mind, the length of each volume has been limited, the notes restricted primarily to attributing direct quotations, and a Further Reading section added to assess previous biographies and to direct readers to the most important studies of the subject. It is the intention that this combination of clear writing, fresh interpretation, and solid historical context will result in volumes that not only are enjoyable to read, but that restore the all-important human dimension to naval history.

James C. Bradford
Series Editor

❧ *Acknowledgments* ❦

Every book is a collaboration, and as usual I am indebted to a number of individuals who aided me in the completion of this work. It was James C. Bradford, the editor of this new series of naval biographies, who convinced me that Franklin Buchanan needed a modern biography. He then labored mightily to compel my adherence to the prescribed length. Though the process of expurgation was painful for me, the book is no doubt better for it. Paul Wilderson at the Naval Institute Press was Jim's willing collaborator and a supportive editor.

I am much indebted to the many archivists and librarians around the country who made it possible for me to gain access to materials that might otherwise have escaped me. Close to home, Alice Creighton and Mary Catalfamo of Special Collections at the Naval Academy's Nimitz Library were always extremely helpful; and also at Nimitz Library, I am indebted once again to Barbara Manvel and Barbara Breeden, and to Florence Todd, the interlibrary loan coordinator, who cheerfully put up with my many requests.

The Naval Academy Research Council provided a grant that enabled me to visit a number of distant archives. John Coski and his wife, Ruth Ann, of the Museum of the Confederacy in Richmond not only made available to me the collections there, but also directed me to other important collections. Marjorie G. McNinch, the reference archivist at the Hagley Museum and Library in Wilmington, Delaware, graciously allowed my wife and me full access to the Du Pont Letters. Scottie Oliver, librarian at the Talbot County Library in Easton, Maryland, tolerated our regular visits to the Lloyd Family Papers. Rick Peuser at the National Archives not only guided me to a number of important sources, he took it as a personal mission to track down a pristine copy of the 1862

Confederate Navy Register. Frances Pollard welcomed our visits to the Virginia Historical Society in Richmond. Ruth Simmons at Rutgers University Library personally copied the Perry-Buchanan correspondence for me. John E. White at the Wilson Library of the University of North Carolina was invaluable in helping me to obtain materials, including the Mallory diary. James Cusick, curator of the P. K. Yonge Collection in the George C. Smathers Library at the University of Florida, helped me track down Stephen Mallory's letters.

Linda Crist of the Davis Papers project and Nat Hughes of Chattanooga each sent materials about Buchanan that they had discovered in their own research. Others to whom I owe a debt include Brig. Gen. Hank Morris (Ret.) of Portsmouth, Virginia, who helped me verify the Eugenius Jack manuscript. That manuscript was provided to me by Alan C. Porter of Washington, D.C., who also introduced my wife and me to Michael and Mary Tilghman, the current occupants of Wye House and the eleventh generation of the Lloyd family to occupy that home in an unbroken line that dates back to the seventeenth century. They not only welcomed us to their home, but also offered a personal tour of the house and grounds, which includes Buchanan's gravesite. We also enjoyed the generous help and warm hospitality of Oliver Reeder and of Nancy Reeder, Buchanan's great-great granddaughter.

Several colleagues read parts of the manuscript and offered advice and corrections. This included Tom Campbell of West Chester, Pennsylvania; Fred Harrod, my friend and colleague at the Naval Academy; and Bill Still, now in what he calls retirement in Hawaii but still very much an active scholar.

Finally, I am indebted most of all to my wife, Marylou, who accompanied me on all my research trips, helped transcribe seemingly indecipherable letters, and remained my most reliable sounding board and critic.

~ Chronology ~

17 Sept. 1800	Born at Auchentorlie, near Baltimore, Maryland
28 Jan. 1815	Receives warrant as a midshipman, U.S. Navy
1815–17	Service on frigate *Java* in Mediterranean
1817–20	Service on ship of the line *Franklin* in Mediterranean
1821–22	Mate on merchant vessel *Dorothea* to Hong Kong
Feb.–June 1823	Service on schooner *Weasel* in Caribbean
1824–25	Acting lieutenant on sloop *Hornet* in Caribbean
13 Jan. 1825	Promoted to lieutenant, U.S. Navy
1826–27	Delivers frigate *Baltimore* to Brazilian navy
1827–28	Service on sloop *Natchez* in Caribbean
1829–31	First lieutenant on frigate *Constellation* in Mediterranean
1833–34	First lieutenant on ship of the line *Delaware* in Mediterranean
Apr.–Dec. 1834	First lieutenant on frigate *United States* in Mediterranean
19 Feb. 1835	Marries Ann Catherine (Nannie) Lloyd in Annapolis
18 Dec. 1835	Sallie Lloyd Buchanan, first of nine children, born
1836–39	Commanding officer of receiving ship in Baltimore
1839–41	Flag lieutenant on frigate *Constitution* in Pacific
8 Sept. 1841	Promoted to commander, U.S. Navy
1842–44	Commanding officer of sloop *Vincennes* in Gulf of Mexico
1845–47	First superintendent, U.S. Naval Academy
1847–48	Commanding officer of sloop *Germantown* during war with Mexico
18 Apr. 1847	Leads assault on Mexican fort at Tuxpan
1851–55	Commanding officer of steam frigate *Susquehanna* in the Far East

14 July 1853	First American to land at Tokyo Bay
May–June 1854	Ascends Yangtze River in *Susquehanna*
June–July 1855	Service on the Navy Retirement Board
14 Dec. 1855	Promoted to captain, U.S. Navy (promotion delayed until 1 Aug. 1856)
1859–61	Commanding officer of Washington Navy Yard
22 Apr. 1861	Resigns from U.S. Navy
4 Sept. 1861	Reports to Richmond for duty in C.S. Navy; commissioned captain and named chief of Bureau of Orders and Detail
24 Feb. 1862	Appointed to command of ironclad CSS *Virginia*
8 Mar. 1862	*Virginia* sinks *Cumberland* and *Congress* in Hampton Roads; wounded
6 May 1862	Leaves Norfolk hospital for Greensboro, N.C.
June–July 1862	Member of court martial for Josiah Tattnall
26 Aug. 1862	Promoted to admiral, C.S. Navy
Feb. 1863	CSS *Tennessee* launched in Selma
18 May 1864	*Tennessee* crosses the Dog River Bar
5 Aug. 1864	Battle of Mobile Bay; wounded
1864–65	Prisoner of war in Fort Lafayette, New York
4 Mar. 1865	Exchanged
Apr. 1865	Returns to Mobile Bay
1868–69	President, Maryland Agricultural College
1870–71	Secretary, Life Association of America, Mobile
11 May 1874	Dies at the Rest on Maryland's Eastern Shore

Confederate Admiral

~✹ *Prologue* ✹~

RESIGNATION

. . . the most unpleasant duty I ever performed.

On Monday morning, 22 April 1861, navy captain Franklin Buchanan walked into the office of the new secretary of the navy, Gideon Welles, in the Navy Department building next to the White House. Welles had been in the job for less than six weeks, but he knew Buchanan to be an important visitor, and he rose from his desk to greet him. His visitor was of medium height, with dark blue eyes and white hair that was receding noticeably above what polite individuals would call a high forehead. A few years earlier when he had been asked to provide a physical description of himself, Buchanan had described his nose as "rather large," his complexion as "florid," and his face as "nothing remarkable." Indeed, his features were dominated by that prominent nose, and by the deep creases extending downward from it to the corners of his mouth that seemed to give him a perpetual frown. His gloomy physiognomy was especially apparent this morning, for he had come to see Welles for a special purpose, and not a happy one.[1]

On the previous Friday, 19 April, blood had been shed in the streets of Baltimore when the Sixth Massachusetts regiment, en route to defend the national capital in the expectation of imminent civil war, had been assailed by an angry mob of civilians. The Massachusetts men had arrived in Baltimore from Philadelphia at the President Street Station, and had to cross the town to the B&O station for the trip to Washington. During their brief passage through Baltimore, a mob had hurled epithets at them, then stones and bricks; finally, a few pistol shots had rung out: several soldiers fell to the ground, stunned or wounded. The crowd closed in, and the panicky troops returned fire. When it was over, four soldiers and twelve citizens lay dead, and many more were wounded.

The news of the "Pratt Street massacre" had hit Buchanan like a thunderclap. Born in Baltimore nearly sixty-one years earlier, he had called Maryland home for most of his life. Of course, the navy was his home, too. He had a forty-five-year record of distinguished service: as founding superintendent of the Naval Academy at Annapolis, as second in command of Matthew Perry's expedition to Japan, and now as the commanding officer of the Washington Navy Yard. But Buchanan was a man of prompt decision with a stern and uncompromising sense of right and wrong. To him issues were almost never ambiguous. Men were either completely meritorious or entirely worthless; ideas were either manifestly correct or utterly without merit. After hearing and reading about the bloodshed on Pratt Street, he decided that Maryland had been ravaged by the hirelings of a hostile and malevolent administration. There were rumors in the streets that Baltimore was about to be shelled by the guns of Fort McHenry. The state, he believed, was sure to leave the Union and join the eleven other states that had already seceded. He did not wait for the fulfillment of this expectation. On Monday morning he handed his resignation to the secretary, saying as he did so that "it was the most unpleasant duty I ever performed."[2]

Welles did not try to dissuade him, saying only that he regretted Buchanan's decision; but Buchanan apparently felt the need to explain himself. He was a Marylander, he told Welles, and "under the present circumstances it was the duty of every Marylander to assist his state when the blood was flowing in the streets." He had a sister and several nieces and nephews who lived in Baltimore. If he could serve his state, it was his duty to share the fate of his fellow Marylanders. He assured Welles that he had done his full duty to the last: the defenses of the Washington Navy Yard were in order, the guns were in good repair, and arrangements had been made for the defense of the Ordnance Building should it be attacked. He had even given orders to blow up the magazine rather than let the arms that were stored there fall into the hands of insurrectionists.

If Buchanan expected some expression of gratitude for doing his duty, or sympathy for his moral dilemma, he got neither from Welles. The secretary only repeated that he regretted Buchanan's decision. It was, he said, something that "every man has to judge for himself." There appeared to be nothing else to say. Buchanan turned and left, returning to his office at the navy yard to turn the command over to John A. Dahlgren before departing for his home on Maryland's Eastern Shore.

But Maryland did not secede. And within days, Buchanan realized that he had acted too hastily. Not for the first or last time in his long career, Old Buck had acted on instinct and emotion. He tried to recall his resignation, writing to a friend that it was "tendered under peculiar circumstances." Peculiar or not, Welles was not inclined to reconsider; he wanted no halfhearted patriots in his navy. He responded to Buchanan's request with a curt note: "By direction of the president, your name has been stricken from the rolls of the Navy."

Characteristically, Buchanan saw himself as the victim in this drama. "Thus I am for ever separated from a service in which I have felt such pride," he wrote to a friend, "and in which I have spent so many happy years of my life in the *faithful* performance of my duty." Banished from the navy he had served for nearly half a century, he might have remained out of the war altogether. But that was not his nature either. He could not sit idly by while the great events of his age were determined by others. Instead he went south to Richmond to offer his services to the infant navy of the Confederacy. In the war that was tearing his country in half, Buchanan would do his "duty," as he understood it, not in the navy blue he had worn for forty-five years, but in rebel gray.

Part One

NAVY BLUE

❧ I ❧

A Mid in the Med

I am desirous of gaining as much experience as I possibly can.

Franklin Buchanan's fifty-year career as a naval officer began in the summer of 1815. From his point of view, the timing could not have been worse, for the nation was then celebrating the end of a war with Britain that had begun three years before in 1812. Although the United States had not exactly won the war, neither had it lost, and that was cause enough for celebration. In fact, news of the recent American success at New Orleans and the lingering memory of several early victories by American frigates over their British counterparts led many Americans to conclude that they had achieved, if not victory, at least a kind of respectability. Never mind that British forces had sailed boldly into the Chesapeake Bay the year before, landed on Maryland's western shore, and marched to Washington, where they had burned many of the public buildings. With the news of a negotiated peace in this "second war of American independence," a surge of nationalism and patriotism took hold of the country.

At age fourteen, Franklin Buchanan shared in the popular mood, but his joy was muted by disappointment that he had missed an opportunity to share in the glory of America's David versus Goliath struggle against England. He had obtained a midshipman's warrant in the last week of January 1815 while the war was still under way—indeed, while the British were retreating from their bloody repulse at New Orleans. Then, only days later, in the second week of February, news arrived that a peace agreement had been reached in Ghent. Ratification came quickly, the Senate voting 35 to 0 on 16 February to accept the treaty. The orders Buchanan received two months later to report to Capt. Oliver Hazard Perry aboard the frigate *Java* were thus somewhat anticlimactic. That sense of anticlimax increased when Buchanan reached Baltimore and discovered that the *Java*, a new-construction frigate named to commemorate the victory of "Old Ironsides" over the British *Java* in 1812, was not yet ready for sea. Instead of waiting the two months it was likely to take to finish fitting out the *Java*, Buchanan requested and received a furlough from the secretary of the navy in order to sign on as a crewman aboard the merchant ship *Acme* bound for the West Indies. He may have missed the war, but he was determined to seize any opportunity to get started on his great adventure. He was a young man in a hurry, and that spirit of impatient eagerness would be a lifelong characteristic.

Franklin Buchanan (pronounced *Buck-annon*), whose friends often called him "Buck," was born in Baltimore on 17 September 1800, the fifth child and third son of Dr. George Buchanan and Laetitia McKean Buchanan. Three other children born to the couple had died in childhood, a pattern of infant mortality not uncommon in the early nineteenth century. The family was well-to-do by the standards of the day, and Franklin's childhood was one of relative comfort. His father was a respected and successful surgeon, and his mother was the daughter of Thomas McKean (1734–1817), who was not only the governor of Pennsylvania, but also "a signer"—that is, one of those who had affixed his name to the Declaration of Independence in 1776. That distinction opened doors into the very best social circles of the early republic.

Young Franklin spent his first five years in Baltimore under the care of a governess. Three more siblings joined the family between 1802 and 1806, although one of them lived barely a month. Then, in 1806, Laetitia's father appointed his son-in-law to the position of attending surgeon at the Lazoretto Hospital half a dozen miles south of Philadelphia. It was a controversial appointment not only because it invited charges of nepotism, but also because Dr. Buchanan was not even a resident of the state at the time. Nevertheless, Governor McKean made the appointment stick, and the family moved to Philadelphia. At the Lazoretto Hospital,

Dr. Buchanan treated patients suffering from communicable diseases, and there (inevitably, perhaps) he contracted yellow fever from one of them and died in July 1808, leaving behind seven children ranging in age from fifteen to one.

Only seven years old when his father died, Franklin no doubt wept for his loss, but his father had been a rather distant presence in his life. Both physically and emotionally, Franklin Buchanan resembled his mother far more than he did his martyred father. Physically, he bore his mother's rounded chin and wide-set eyes rather than the sharper features of his father, and emotionally he was significantly more mercurial than his father, whose obituary remarked on his "mildness of temper" and "amiable" demeanor, characteristics little evident in his impatient and energetic third son.[1]

It is difficult to know which events helped to mold the perspective of young Franklin Buchanan, but the years of his youth were punctuated by milestone historic events that may have contributed to his later decision to embark on a life at sea. He was five when news reached America of the end of the war with Tripoli, in which the fledgling U.S. Navy had made its effective debut. He was six when the British boarded the American frigate *Chesapeake* just outside the bay of that name and removed some alleged deserters from its deck after firing several unanswered broadsides into the American vessel. He was eleven when Congress declared war on Britain. Whatever later historians might make of the motives for that declaration, young Franklin saw it as a noble—even a righteous—response to intolerable provocations. He was old enough to cheer the news of America's early frigate victories over the British, as well as later news of American successes on Lakes Erie and Champlain. He was thirteen when he read in the Philadelphia newspapers of the repulse of the British fleet at Baltimore, which he always thought of as his hometown. Such events doubtless contributed to his determination to seek a midshipman's warrant. His mother supported his ambition, and fourteen-year-old Franklin received his warrant on 28 January 1815.[2]

It was not unusual for aspiring naval officers to begin their careers as teenagers. Indeed, although an appointment as a midshipman set the bearer immeasurably above the hoi polloi of the lower deck and certified that with time, good performance, and luck he would someday be promoted to lieutenant, the designation defined an apprentice as much as it did an officer. The boys (average age seventeen) who accepted service under these circumstances were trained to become officers. Often called "young gentlemen," they had putative authority over the enlisted men who served "before the mast," but their own officers allowed them to exercise that authority only with significant oversight and discretion. Fourteen-year-old midshipmen soon appreciated that it was unwise to be too authoritative with a forty-year-old veteran who had been at sea since before they were born.[3]

Midshipman Buchanan joined the *Java* in August 1815 as it lay at anchor off Annapolis, Maryland. As a new-construction frigate, the *Java* had the clean lines and sheer bow characteristic of the large American frigates of the early nineteenth century. As he was rowed out to the ship from the Annapolis dock, Buchanan could hardly have avoided glancing upward at its three masts, towering to heights of 150 feet above the sea and held in place by a dizzying complex of cables, lines, and stays. After climbing aboard and saluting the officer of the deck, he would have been told to sling his hammock in the midshipmen's berth—traditionally called the gun room. Perhaps he was given over into the care of another midshipman who led him to his new home. Sailors would have been ordered to carry his dunnage and follow him as he scrambled down the stairs ("ladders," he would have been told to call them) to the dark passages belowdecks.

The midshipmen's mess was a crowded corner of the ship, but there were few places aboard a warship in the age of sail that were not. By the standards of the forecastle (which the old salts pronounced *foke-sul*), Buchanan's berthing space was generous, but for a young man accustomed to the luxuries of Baltimore or Philadelphia, the two or three feet of space where he was allowed to swing his hammock was crowded indeed. The food, too, must have been something of a shock. Salt beef, hard bread, and dollops of congealed rice formed the standard fare at sea, with occasional treats such as salt pork or bean soup (considered a particular delicacy). In spite of this spartan fare—or perhaps because of it—morale in the *Java*'s gun room was high. According to one of their number, the midshipmen aboard the *Java* were a disorderly and wayward lot, and earned a collective nickname as "the roaring Javas," a label "by which they became long after celebrated."[4]

Buchanan learned an infinite number of lessons during his initial year in the navy. Many of them were absorbed during formal classes held aboard ship specifically for the instruction of the midshipmen. But in addition, the practical curriculum of his sea education was dominated by three courses: learning the duties and routines of life aboard a man-of-war; experiencing and appreciating the navy's role in the development and execution of American foreign policy; and, of course, coming face-to-face with the dangers inherent in the very nature of life at sea.

The *Java* was delayed for two weeks by a westerly gale, but in early September it stood out past the Virginia capes into the Atlantic, bound up the coast for New York. Thanks to his two-month sojourn as a crewman aboard the *Acme*, Buchanan would already have been familiar with the rolling of a ship at sea; indeed the sixteen-hundred-ton *Java* was considerably more stable than the much smaller *Acme*. Nevertheless, there were many other things to get used to. There was always work to do—and always in a very prescribed way. Many of those who followed the sea found a comforting security in the routine of shipboard life; more than a few chose the life precisely because the reliable routine on a man-of-war provided a center and an anchor in their lives. At dawn—generally between 4:00 and 4:30 A.M.—the hands were called. They spilled out of their hammocks, lashing them up in tight rolls to the overhead to get them out of the way. Buchanan, too, lashed up his bedroll and took his place at divisions with the other midshipmen. Once the hands were mustered at quarters, they drew their morning rations—generally rice pudding and hardtack. After this spartan breakfast they set to work scrubbing the ship: swabbing the decks wet and then flogging them dry. In this, at least, Buchanan did not take part, for midshipmen did not do the cleaning and maintenance work assigned to sailors. Indeed, their specific duties were rather vague, for their primary function was to learn, not only in traditional classes aboard ship, but also by doing and seeing.

And there was plenty to see. At least once a day, the captain was likely to call for the exercise of the great guns. Like all midshipmen, Buchanan had a designated station for those exciting occasions when the ship cleared for action, when the long roll of drums provoked a frantic flurry of activity as the men broke down the portable bulkheads and cast loose the great guns to pantomime the actions of loading and firing. In light air, the hands might be called on to wet the sails to capture more wind, running up the ratlines like monkeys and passing buckets of salt water up the rigging to spill their contents against the canvas. In heavy weather, they would be called up by the boatswain's (pronounced *bo-sun's*) whistle to reduce sail. Indeed, the men were constantly adjusting the number and position of the sails according to the elements. Buchanan's careful journal, written in his near-perfect hand, carried endless variations of "made and shortened sail as required."[5]

During the run up to New York it became evident that much of the standing rigging on the *Java* was defective. After dropping anchor at Sandy Hook, Perry kept the ship there for three months while the rigging was replaced. Finally, in January of the new year, the *Java* sailed up the coast to Newport, Rhode Island, where it filled up its complement of officers and crew. One of the new arrivals onboard was the ship's senior lieutenant, Dulaney Forrest, who was something of a dandy and appeared nearly every day in full uniform with his coat buttoned up to the chin. Another new arrival was twelve-year-old Midn. Alexander Slidell Mackenzie, whose subsequent memoirs provide a firsthand view of life in the *Java*'s gun room. Finally, on 22 January, the *Java* left Newport for the Mediterranean.

The focus of American overseas interest for more than two decades, the Mediterranean remained a prime trouble spot. As an ardent student of American naval history, Buchanan would have been acutely aware that Algiers, Tunis, and Tripoli—the three city-states of the North African coast that were affiliated with the Ottoman Empire—made a practice of attacking the merchant shipping of any nation that declined to pay an annual fee to ensure the safety of its trade. Although they were called pirates by most Westerners, the Barbary States considered such raids legally justified because they took the trouble in each case to declare war, a declaration occasionally signaled by chopping down a nation's embassy flagpole. Moreover, the North Africans considered these raids morally justified as well by virtue of the fact that all of their victims were Christians, and therefore infidels.

Most European nations paid the tribute—it was simpler and generally cheaper than war. But in the United States the issue of whether to pay or to fight had been a running argument virtually from the moment of independence. For the first decade of its national history, the nation had paid the modest tributes demanded. Then, in the 1790s, the United States built a half dozen oversized frigates (designed principally by Joshua Humphreys and therefore called "Humphreys frigates") for the purpose of suppressing the Barbary States. A successful war against Tripoli in 1803–5 had compelled that city-state to reduce the tribute it demanded, and after the end of the war with Britain, the United States had sent not one but two squadrons to Algiers to settle with that city as well. The first squadron, under Stephen Decatur, had arrived in June 1816 while Buchanan was in the West Indies on the *Acme*. Decatur had captured the Algerine flagship at sea, and then compelled a peace with Algiers that was dictated "at the cannon's mouth." The *Java's* mission was to carry that signed treaty, which Lieutenant Forrest had brought aboard at Newport, back to Algiers for confirmation.[6]

En route to the Mediterranean, the dozen or so midshipmen on the *Java* gathered each day in a makeshift classroom behind a canvas screen "under the half deck on the larboard side." There they sat cross-legged on the deck as one or another of the ship's lieutenants conducted classes on mathematics and navigation. There was also formal instruction in Spanish and French, and there was even "a good swordsman to render them skilful in the use of arms." Captain Perry took a particular interest in the education of his midshipmen. The victor of Lake Erie was only thirty years old in 1815, elevated to the command of a frigate as a reward for his heroics in the late war, but no doubt he seemed ancient to a fifteen-year-old midshipman. Perry not only required his midshipmen to study their profession, he also emphasized such social refinements as proper etiquette at the table and dancing. Very likely, there were occasions on the *Java* when Buchanan had to pair up with another midshipman to practice his dance steps under the critical scrutiny of his captain.

The *Java* made a swift crossing. Only eight days out of Newport, it was already within a hundred miles of Cape St. Vincent on the Spanish coast. Buchanan and the other midshipmen were attending to their lessons, sitting between the guns and taking notes, when a wild shriek reached their ears. Looking outboard, they saw a seaman flailing desperately in the water as the ship swept past him. The class dissolved at once as the midshipmen ran onto the deck crying, "Man overboard!" Later, Buchanan learned that the seaman had been attempting to wash his blanket by "towing" it over the bow of the ship. It had become snagged in the chains, and he had climbed over the side in an attempt to disengage it when a wave swept him away. Perry rushed to the quarterdeck and barked out orders designed to bring the ship about, but the *Java* was making better than ten knots, and despite the sailor's desperate attempts to keep up, he fell farther and farther behind. Buchanan witnessed his pathetic efforts until the man was lost to sight in the distance and the lookout called down that he was no longer visible. Reluctantly, Perry ordered the *Java* to resume its original course. The event left "a pervading sadness through the ship," and the midshipmen remembered for a long time the sailor's "terrible shrieks" as he passed "almost within an arm's length" of them.[7]

Five days later, an even more tragic event occurred. Ten men were spaced out on the main topgallant yard gathering in the sail, when the mainmast broke off below them and the entire structure came crashing to the deck in a tangle of rigging. Four of the ten men were killed outright, and a fifth died soon thereafter. A subsequent inspection proved that the main topmast, like the rigging that had been replaced in New York, was completely rotten. According to Midshipman Mackenzie, it was a long time before the ship was able to shake off "the gloom occasioned by this dreadful casualty."[8]

There was one light moment amid all this disaster. One of the topmen flung to the deck by the falling rigging, Dennis O'Dougherty, fell all the way through an open hatchway and into the midst of a work crew that was stowing cannonballs belowdeck. Improbably, he landed on his feet, flung out his arms, and cried, "Here's Dennis!" before walking away entirely uninjured. For the rest of the cruise, every unlikely event was heralded by the call of "Here's Dennis!"[9]

The *Java* limped into Gibraltar looking more like the loser of a naval battle than a new ship on its first deployment. After a refit, it moved on into the Mediterranean, making a brief stop at Málaga en route to Port Mahon on the Spanish island of Minorca, which the American squadron used as a winter base. Sailing into Mahon Harbor on 7 March, Buchanan saw a sight to stir his youthful patriotism. Four American warships—two frigates and two sloops—were lying in the roadstead, all flying the Stars and Stripes and with the broad pennant of Commo. John Shaw flying from the frigate *United States*. The *Java* cast loose its guns and fired a salute. Seventeen times the guns boomed out across the roadstead, the white smoke rolling across the surface of the water, to be answered by a salute of fifteen guns from the *United States*, aural evidence of America's growing naval power.[10]

The *Java* spent three weeks in Port Mahon completing repairs. In the evenings there was liberty by divisions, with the officers free to go ashore if they did not have duty. Port Mahon offered a number of attractions. On almost any given night there were sure to be theater parties and for-

mal dinners where American officers were welcome guests. As a mere
midshipman, and barely fifteen years old, Buchanan would not have
been a particularly noteworthy social catch at these dinner parties, but
no doubt he had some opportunity to sample the local cuisine.

On 5 April, Commodore Shaw ordered his command to get under way,
and the U.S. squadron sailed off to Algiers. When it arrived three days
later, a large British fleet consisting of half a dozen ships of the line was
already present. Lord Exmouth, the commander of that impressive
armada, was attempting to convince the dey of Algiers to grant Britain
the same terms he had conceded to America the year before. By now the
dey was regretting that he had ever made those concessions, for it was
clear that the other Western powers would demand similar terms.
Exmouth succeeded in getting the dey to release nearly twelve hundred
Neapolitan and Sicilian hostages in exchange for a ransom in excess of
$600,000, but the Englishman could not wrest a new treaty from him.
Very likely the hefty ransom reminded the dey of just how profitable the
Barbary system was. In any event, when Commodore Shaw presented
the dey with the newly ratified treaty brought from America, the dey
claimed that it was not what he had agreed to and declined to accept it.

Returning to his flagship full of anger and determination, Shaw
decided to launch a full-scale invasion of Algiers that very night. The
word spread quickly through the ships of the American squadron, and, like
the other midshipmen, Buchanan reveled in the thought that the next
twenty-four hours might give him a chance to duplicate the feats of
Decatur, Somers, and other heroes of the late Barbary wars. His messmate
Mackenzie wrote that "the squadron was in a fever of excitement . . . ,
every officer and man became a volunteer . . . , greater enthusiasm for
an enterprise never prevailed." But it was not to be. Shaw hesitated, concerned that the treaty's stipulation that three months' notice was required before resuming hostilities might be binding on him even though
the dey had refused the treaty. The question soon became moot, because
word of the American preparations leaked to the Algerines. Lacking the
advantage of surprise, Shaw calculated that an attack was too risky.[11]

The American squadron left Algiers and sailed on to Tripoli, then
westward back to Gibraltar, touching at Syracuse, Messina, Palermo,
and Tunis en route. In the interim, the public reaction in Britain to Lord
Exmouth's inability to obtain a new treaty prompted him to return to
Algiers with an even more powerful squadron, and this time he opened

fire and pounded the city into rubble. When the American squadron returned there in the late fall, the American negotiator, William Shaler, easily obtained approval of the new treaty from a much-chastened dey.

Buchanan left no record of his reaction to these events. The pattern of a lifetime, however, suggests that he would have disapproved of Shaw's decision to leave Algiers without making at least some effort to punish the dey for his faithlessness. All his life he abhorred the thought of relying on some other nation to fight his country's battles, and he almost certainly resented the fact that the British (those despised recent enemies) had acted with boldness after the American squadron had cravenly sailed away.

There was another topic of intense (though hushed) conversation in the midshipmen's mess that winter. It concerned a falling out between Perry and the commander of the marine contingent onboard, Capt. John Heath. Perry thought Heath lackadaisical and insufficiently devoted to his duty. Given Buchanan's lifelong commitment to rigid standards of deportment and discipline, the young midshipman probably shared that view. The confrontation between Perry and Heath was sparked by the desertion in September of two of Heath's marines, who jumped overboard and attempted to swim ashore while the *Java* was in the harbor at Messina. Perry called for Heath to report to him at once, but Heath declined, sending word that he was indisposed. Irritated by this response, Perry repeated his request as an order. When Heath finally presented himself, Perry was further irritated by the marine captain's surliness. In a fit of temper, Perry summarily relieved Heath of his duties. In doing so, he stepped beyond his authority, for Heath's commission came from the secretary of the navy. At the very least, Perry ought to have referred the case to the commodore.

Aware of this fact, Heath sent a message to Perry demanding to know the charges against him. Perry resented the confrontational tone of Heath's letter and again sent for him, this time demanding to know why Heath had written such an insulting letter. Unsatisfied with Heath's answer, Perry ordered him to be silent. Heath answered, "Yes, sir!" Perry, believing that Heath was deliberately challenging him, again ordered him to be silent. "Yes, sir!" Heath shouted back. At that, Perry advanced toward Heath and struck him. It was a shocking violation not only of navy regulations, but of the code of officers as well.[12]

Although Perry was unquestionably in the wrong, most of the ship's officers sided with their captain. Buchanan admired Perry greatly, and he very likely viewed Heath as one of that class of officers whom he would later describe as "worthless." Certainly he sympathized with Perry's predicament and saw him (as Mackenzie put it) as "the victim of uncontrolled passion."[13]

The next morning, in the light of day, Perry realized that he had made a horrible mistake and asked a group of officers from the squadron to approach Heath with his apology. Heath knew he had the advantage, however, and demanded a formal court martial. Perry thereupon presented the case to the commodore, including charges of misconduct against Heath. The solution was anticlimactic. Commo. Isaac Chauncey, who had succeeded Shaw in command, found both Heath and Perry guilty, but chose to punish each man with a private reprimand.

Heath would not let go of the issue, however, and later challenged Perry to a duel. Perry accepted the challenge but notified Heath (through his second) that he would not fire his weapon. At the duel, Heath fired and missed; Perry refused to fire, and there the dispute ended.

The episode provided Buchanan with a dramatic lesson in the limits of both power and discipline. A captain's authority on a ship of war was nearly—but not utterly—absolute. There were lines that could not be crossed. A man of rigorous personal standards himself, and as likely as anyone to become a "victim of uncontrolled passion," Buchanan nevertheless saw that giving way to such passions could lead to a career-ending gaffe. Perry survived this crisis, but only because Chauncey gave him a way out.

With the Heath situation resolved and a new treaty with Algiers in hand, the *Java* returned to America, arriving in the Chesapeake Bay on the last day of February 1817.

Buchanan's eighteen months on the *Java* had not cooled his ardor for adventure. On learning that Perry had been ordered to take command of the sloop *Ontario* and go immediately back to sea, he petitioned the Navy Department to be transferred to that ship, declaring, "I am desirous of gaining as much experience in my profession, and remaining in active service as long as I possibly can." For his part, Perry was willing to have him, saying of Buchanan and another midshipman that he did not know of "two more promising young men." Instead, however, Buchanan was ordered to the survey ship *Prometheus,* which had a crew made up primarily of midshipmen who performed most of the work of common sailors, including swabbing the deck and setting the sails. Finding such duty insufficiently challenging, if not outright demeaning, Buchanan renewed his request for more "active service" and was soon posted to a line-of-battle ship, the USS *Franklin*.[14]

The *Franklin* was a much larger ship than the *Java*. Although it was rated a 74, like many American warships in the age of sail, the *Franklin* carried many more guns than its official rating, and its crew of nearly seven hundred was twice the size of the *Java*'s. Like the *Java*, it was a new-construction vessel authorized by Congress in the heady aftermath of the end of the war with Britain. Master Commandant Henry E. Ballard was technically in command and oversaw the day-to-day working of the ship, but the *Franklin* also flew the broad pennant of Commo. Charles Stewart, who was en route to replace Commodore Chauncey in command of the Mediterranean Squadron. The *Franklin* also carried as a passenger the new American ambassador to England, Richard Rush.

The *Franklin* left Norfolk on 24 November 1817 in moderate weather and headed southeast, tacking into a gentle northeast breeze. Two-year veteran that he was, Midshipman Buchanan settled easily into the routine of life at sea, and his journal was soon filled with notes about taking in and letting out sails, gun drills by division, and experiments with the sextant and the compass. His formal lessons continued as well, as he and the other midshipmen were instructed not only by the lieutenants but also by the *Franklin*'s chaplain, Nathaniel Adams. Acting as schoolmaster for midshipmen was one of the primary responsibilities of navy chaplains, although only the largest warships, like the *Franklin*, carried them.

There were also a great many more midshipmen than had been on the *Java*—three times as many—and Buchanan made several new friends. Among them was thirteen-year-old Samuel Francis Du Pont, a tall, baby-faced scion of an aristocratic family. Like Buchanan, Du Pont was both intensely ambitious and intolerant of mediocrity. He and Buchanan became fast friends, and they remained close for more than forty years, often sharing opinions about ways to improve the navy. Another member of the gun room destined to be historically linked to Buchanan was sixteen-year-old David Glasgow Farragut.

After dropping Richard Rush off at Portsmouth, sending him on his way with a seventeen-gun salute, the *Franklin* sailed south to Gibraltar. From there the ship zigzagged its way across the western Mediterranean toward the Sicilian port of Syracuse, where it found the American squadron at anchor: the ship of the line *Washington,* the frigate *United States,* and the sloop *Erie.* After firing the requisite salutes, the *Franklin* then ignominiously grounded on a sandbar under the eyes of the whole squadron. Ballard called all hands to man the boats, and the crew spent two and a half hours kedging and towing the *Franklin* into deeper water. Two days later, Buchanan described the ceremony at which Stewart relieved Chauncey as commodore of the Mediterranean Squadron: "At 11:00 am mustered the crew and read the Articles of War. At 12 am Com. Chauncey hauled down the blue pennant and hoisted the red, Com. Stewart then taking command, all the ships at the same time firing a salute of 18 guns each."[15]

The squadron did not winter in Syracuse, but instead sailed north along the Sicilian coast to Messina, opposite the toe of the Italian boot. Arriving there in the second week of February, each vessel ran stout cables ashore and carefully warped inshore to nestle up to the stone mole. Then all the vessels were virtually emptied; everything that could be moved was taken ashore. The coopers checked the barrels, the boatswains looked to the spare lines and cables, and the unrated seamen were set to work scraping and painting. Spars and upper masts were sent down for inspection and reconditioning. Since almost all the work was conducted ashore, the crew camped there as well. There was a break on 22 February to celebrate Washington's birthday, but work resumed the next day. Then, in the first week of March, everything was put back again: the masts and spars swayed up and rerigged, the newly mended sails bent on, the hold restowed, and the entire ship painted.

By April, the Mediterranean Squadron was ready to begin its round of port visits. Its itinerary called for the squadron to show the flag along the hostile Barbary Coast, cruise west to Gibraltar, then cruise back to an Italian or Sicilian port for another refit. On 2 April 1818, Ballard called all hands, and the crew set to work unmooring the *Franklin.* Two days later the squadron left Messina and headed north through the Straits of Messina into the Tyrrhenian Sea, then south to Tunis. From there the squadron made a deliberate cruise along the Barbary Coast, stopping at each port as a visual reminder of America's naval presence. Off Algiers, the *Franklin* fired a twenty-one-gun salute, which was answered by the fort. Afterward, the *Franklin,* accompanied now only by the sloop *Peacock,* sailed past the Balearic Islands and Corsica to Leghorn (or

Livorno) just south of Pisa on the Italian coast, arriving on 18 April.

At Leghorn there was another round of visits: the ship's officers made visits ashore, and local Italian dignitaries made visits to the ship. One visitor was the duke of Modena, who was sufficiently exalted that Ballard ordered the crew to man the yards while the gunners fired a salute of fifteen guns. The *Franklin* remained in Leghorn for six weeks. On the last day of May, the anchor was finally drawn up and the *Franklin* sailed westward to British Gibraltar, where it spent another four weeks at anchor. Then the *Franklin* cruised slowly back to Leghorn, where it remained for the rest of the summer.

In the spring of 1819 the routine began all over again. The *Franklin* left Messina in April, leading the squadron on its rounds: north to Naples (where Buchanan practiced his piloting skills by taking careful bearings to Mounts Etna and Vesuvius), then south to Palermo for stores and fresh water, and back to Naples again. During this second visit, the emperor of Austria and the king of Naples visited the ship. These were exalted visitors by anyone's standards, and Commodore Stewart made a special effort to greet them. As Buchanan described the event, the Franklin's crew "hoisted the Austrian colors at the fore & the Neapolitan at the Mizzen mast head, fired 2 salutes of 21 guns each and manned the yards." The commodore greeted his royal guests and was conducting them about the ship when one of the entourage leaned against a taut wind sail, apparently thinking it a solid surface, and tumbled down an open hatch, breaking his leg. Bringing news of the incident to the officer of the deck, an irreverent American sailor reported, "One of them kings has fallen down a hatch, sir."[16]

In June the *Franklin* returned to its cruising ground along the North African coast. Off Tunis, Stewart ordered the squadron to conduct target practice. A target was heaved over the side, and the squadron sailed past in line, each ship firing a broadside; then the ships turned and passed again, this time firing by divisions. Then it was off to Algiers, Málaga, and Gibraltar.

Buchanan returned to America onboard the *Franklin* in the spring of 1820. His two and a half years in the Mediterranean had been mostly routine: showing the flag off the Barbary Coast, enjoying the hospitality of Italian and Sicilian ports of call, and making occasional stops in Gibraltar to exchange salutes with the British. But it was a routine that he had relished. When he arrived back in Philadelphia for an extended visit with his family, he was even more committed to a naval career than he had been when he first petitioned for a midshipman's warrant at age fourteen. Although still a midshipman, he was now a seasoned veteran of twenty. His long-term commitment to the navy was evident in his decision that summer to pay ten dollars—a substantial portion of his nineteen-dollar-a-month salary—to join the United States Naval Fraternal Association for the Relief of Families of Deceased Officers.[17]

He had decided that the navy would be his life, and he could hardly wait to get back to sea.

❧ 2 ❧

CHASING PIRATES AND
OTHER ADVENTURES

From her appearance I took her to be a pirate.

*B*uchanan spent the next decade accumulating experience and expertise at sea. It was not a passive undertaking, for he was not a man who was happy to wait for opportunities to come to him. When adventure was slow in coming, he set out to find it. His naval service in these years centered on the Caribbean Sea and the Gulf of Mexico, where U.S. warships carried on a nasty and often frustrating war with scores of small pirate craft that were raiding American merchant commerce. But in addition, he actively sought opportunities outside the navy that would broaden his base of professional knowledge.

It was quite common in the age of sail for aspiring young officers to take extended furloughs in order to accept assignments on merchant ships; fully 40 percent of midshipmen left the navy at some point for just that purpose. Their motive was at least as much professional as financial. Whereas a twenty-year-old midshipman might be tenth or eleventh in command on a sloop-of-war and never have the opportunity to exercise the responsibilities of a deck officer, he would very likely be second or third in command on a comparably sized merchant ship and routinely stand the deck watch. Within the navy hierarchy, a successful cruise on a merchant ship was deemed a valuable experience for an ambitious young naval officer, and furloughs for such purposes were not only approved but encouraged. Buchanan took two: once in 1821–22 for a cruise to China, and once in 1826 for a chance to experience firsthand the perils and rewards of command at sea.[1]

During these same years the navy was trying to define and institutionalize its own role more clearly. In the aftermath of the peace with Britain in 1815, Congress had authorized the expenditure of a million dollars a year to build a fleet of a dozen ships of the line, including at least one first-rate battleship, the 120-gun *Pennsylvania,* the largest warship of its type in the world. But as the euphoria of remembered victory faded in the peaceful 1820s, such vessels proved not only expensive but also impractical. Impressive flagships for the Mediterranean Squadron they may have been, but they were all but worthless when assigned many of the navy's other peacetime jobs: convoying trade, guarding the American whaling fleet in the Pacific, or chasing pirates in the Caribbean. As early as 1821, therefore, budget-conscious congressmen began to pare back the funds committed to battleships and to invest instead in smaller, handier, and more practical sloops. Much of Buchanan's naval service in this era, therefore, was in smaller warships. In one respect, at least, this was a professional blessing. Small ships meant small wardrooms, giving ambitious junior officers like Buchanan more opportunity to hold meaningful jobs—certainly more meaningful than any job he had had on the *Franklin* or was likely to have on the gigantic *Pennsylvania.*

Twenty years old when he returned from the Med for the second time, Buchanan was eager for continued active service. Six years before, as a brand-new midshipman, he had been unwilling to cool his heels during the two months it took to complete the refit of the *Java* and had found employment on a merchant vessel bound for Cuba. Five years of active duty in the Mediterranean had not endowed him with the gift of patience. Unwilling to wait idly for new orders in 1821, he requested a furlough in order to serve as third officer on the *Dorothea,* a merchant ship bound for the China coast. As fourth in command of a ship with a crew of twenty-seven, Buchanan was in effect an acting lieutenant. Besides, a cruise to an exotic location more than halfway around the world promised adventure and profit as well as experience.[2]

The *Dorothea* departed Philadelphia in April 1821, and Buchanan took his regular turn as officer of the deck as the ship ran southeast before the wind. Crossing the equator on 23 May, the *Dorothea* continued southward, rounded the Cape of Good Hope without stopping, and entered the Indian Ocean. Day after day of steady winds pushed the ship eastward until it reached the Sunda Straits. Then it sailed northward across the South China Sea and arrived finally off Portuguese Macao on 17 August after 125 days at sea without touching land. It was a noteworthy but not remarkable maritime feat. The China trade was sufficiently lucrative that the promise of a substantial bottom line at the end of the cruise provided many a ship's captain with adequate motivation for a swift passage.

Buchanan spent six months in China. It is not clear why it took Jacob Harman, the *Dorothea*'s captain, so long to negotiate a satisfactory return cargo. But during such a lengthy stay Buchanan would have had many opportunities to explore: to visit crowded, bustling, and exotic Canton; to coast downriver to Macao and Hong Kong; and even to journey up the Pearl River to catch a glimpse of China's hinterland. Whatever impressions of the country he may have accumulated are not recorded in his journal, which he kept only while at sea. The *Dorothea* finally left Canton in February 1822, and a favorable and steady trade wind carried the ship south across the South China Sea and then west across the Indian Ocean. The *Dorothea* kept company with an English ship during most of the Indian Ocean crossing until sighting the coast of Africa on 15 April, then tacked southward. The ship rounded the Cape of Good Hope on 19 April, and after an uneventful crossing of the Atlantic arrived back in Philadelphia on 9 June 1822, having been gone fourteen months.[3]

Buchanan's sojourn to the Far East had taken him to a part of the world he would not otherwise have seen for many years. The experience gave him a valuable insight into maritime commerce and was a useful introduction to Asian culture, a perspective that he would draw on thirty years later when he commanded a vessel in the naval expedition to Japan led by Matthew Perry. In addition, his relatively exalted responsibilities (for a midshipman) gave him the chance to hone his skills as a navigator and to become comfortable with the duties and responsibilities of an officer. Very likely it was while crossing the Atlantic Ocean in the pitch blackness of some mid-watch that twenty-year-old Franklin Buchanan first experienced the burden and the satisfaction of being the officer of the watch on a ship at sea.

Now a seven-year veteran, Buchanan's varied experiences had positioned him well for promotion to lieutenant, but two important steps were required to fulfill such an ambition. First, he had to pass an exam, and then he had to await an opening on the lieutenant's list. The exam was a daunting obstacle for many of the "young gentlemen," for the lieutenant's exam inevitably involved complex navigational and mathematical problems, and many competent sailors failed to grasp the theoretical underpinning of their profession. But even those who passed the exam were not guaranteed promotion. They were endowed with the title of "passed midshipman," denoting an officer who was eligible for promotion, but not assured of it because more young men passed the exam than the navy could accommodate as lieutenants.

Still, nothing at all was possible without a passing grade on the lieutenant's exam, so Buchanan attended one of the navy's three shore facilities where a handful of officers and civilian "professors" offered formal instruction in the subjects likely to be covered on the exam. After a brief cram course, Buchanan took the exam near the end of the year and was subsequently listed in the new Navy Register as one of twenty-two new passed midshipmen. Of course, that same document noted that with these twenty-two added to the holdovers from previous exams, there were now seventy-five passed midshipmen awaiting promotion. Having achieved this not-so-exalted status, Buchanan received orders in the new year to report aboard the armed schooner *Weasel,* one of eight such vessels purchased in Baltimore in response to the rampant piracy in the Caribbean Sea.[4]

There had been freebooters in the Caribbean Sea since the early eighteenth century, when rogues such as Robert Teach, known as Blackbeard, built terrible reputations for avarice and cruelty. But this new crisis was the indirect and unanticipated result of the several independence movements taking place within the crumbling Spanish Empire in Central and South America. Like the American insurrectionists of 1776, the Latin American rebels of the 1820s lacked the resources to construct or purchase a conventional naval force, and therefore resorted to the traditional naval strategy of underdog powers. They conducted raids on enemy commerce (*guerre de course*) by means of privately owned armed vessels known as privateers. The revolutionary governments licensed privateers to seize or destroy any vessel of Spanish registry, and as an incentive to perform this unpaid service allowed them to keep whatever booty they could plunder. Alas, Spain's merchant fleet (like its empire) was waning, and there were simply not enough targets of opportunity to satisfy all of those who applied for letters of marque from Columbia, Venezuela, or the short-lived Confederation of Central America. As a result, many ships that began as privateers ended up as pirates, attacking neutral shipping indiscriminately to satisfy the expectations of the opportunists who had signed on anticipating instant wealth. Many American ships fell victim to this new generation of corsairs.

Most Americans sympathized with the principle of national liberation from European colonial powers, and they sympathized as well with the use of privateers to achieve it. Privateering, after all, had been a mainstay in both of America's wars against Britain. But they would not suffer their own shipping to be raided, for this or any other reason. When Lt. William H. Allen, commander of the U.S. schooner *Alligator,* was killed in a battle with a band of pirates on Cuba's northern coast in November 1822, America was outraged. Newspapers insisted that "Allen must be avenged!" In December, Congress authorized funds for a squadron of small vessels "for the purpose of suppressing piracy and of affording effectual protection to the citizens and commerce of the United States."[5] Capt. David Porter, a hero of the late war with Britain, received command of the squadron. Porter purchased eight small schooners (known locally as Chesapeake bay boats) that displaced only about fifty to sixty tons, and refitted them to carry three guns each. Porter envisioned his ships as a pack of hunters pursuing the pirates into their lairs in the same way a weasel or a ferret might chase a rabbit down its own hole, hence the names he gave to his eight small schooners: *Fox, Greyhound, Jackal, Beagle, Terrier, Wild Cat, Ferret,* and, of course, *Weasel,* the ship to which Buchanan was assigned.

Such vessels were ideal platforms to combat piracy in the West Indies, for (Hollywood notwithstanding) Caribbean pirates did not fly the Jolly Roger from three-masted sailing warships. They operated almost exclusively in small, single-masted schooners with only one or two guns—indeed, in vessels very much like those of Porter's little squadron—and they targeted unarmed merchantmen, especially those becalmed by light air. On such occasions the pirates would row out of a small bay or river mouth and clamber over the side of the hapless merchantman to pillage and kill. While a war against such foes was not quite like a war against Britain or France, it was the only war available for an eager and ambitious midshipman, and Buchanan didn't hesitate.[6]

Buchanan reported aboard the *Weasel* in the first week of February

1823 and found himself endowed with a de facto promotion. The ship's captain, Lt. Beverly Kennon, had only two other lieutenants onboard, and he designated Buchanan an acting master's mate. His goal may have been simply to add another officer to the watch bill (standing one out of three watches was far superior to serving watch-and-watch), but regardless of Kennon's motive, Buchanan's new title put him in an excellent position to secure a permanent appointment as a lieutenant.

Buchanan had been aboard the *Weasel* only a week when the squadron got under way. The eight schooners were joined by five small barges (which everyone called the "mosquito squadron") and three other vessels: the sloop *Peacock,* which Porter claimed as his flagship; the storeship *Decoy* (which carried six guns as well the squadron's supplies); and a former Hudson River ferryboat, the paddle steamer *Sea Gull.* The latter was particularly noteworthy, for it was the first steam-powered warship to be deployed by the U.S. Navy. The *Sea Gull* was a decidedly odd little vessel, but it did have the advantage of being able to operate independent of the wind. Since the Caribbean pirates often attempted to attack becalmed merchant ships, sometimes under the very eye of their equally becalmed escorts, the *Sea Gull* might well prove its worth in the campaign.

The different speeds of the various vessels soon separated the squadron into twos and threes as the ships proceeded southward; the *Sea Gull* couldn't keep up and had to be towed. Buchanan's *Weasel* sailed in company with the *Terrier.* Nine days out, near the Florida Straits, the lookout on the *Weasel* spotted a strange sail that abruptly changed course after sighting the Americans. The *Weasel* set out in pursuit, and its superior speed soon brought the strange sail within range. Resignedly the chase hove to, awaiting its fate, and Kennon ordered Buchanan to investigate. A boat's crew rowed him across the open water between the two ships. Bumping alongside, Buchanan grabbed hold of the lines and warily pulled himself up onto the deck. If this vessel were indeed a pirate ship, he might soon find himself confronting a gang of cutthroats. What he found instead was a terrified ship's captain who apparently believed that Buchanan was himself a pirate. "The Captain of the Schooner was very much alarmed when I boarded her," Buchanan wrote in his journal that night. "He felt confident from our appearance that we were pirates, our vessel resembling those of pirates very much. . . . He was soon convinced, however, that he was in the hands of Friends and not Enemies."[7]

Real pirates were not far away. Three days later, the *Weasel* was cruis-ing near the passage between Puerto Rico and St. Thomas when the lookout called down that a sail was in sight to windward. Immediately Kennon ordered the ship cleared for action and made sail in chase. The unidentified vessel was a schooner much like the *Weasel*, and its captain appeared desperate to escape, tacking several times. Whether this was because it was a pirate ship or because it feared that the *Weasel* was itself a pirate was as yet unclear. Buchanan had his own opinion. "She was a long, low schooner," he wrote in his journal, "and from her appearance [I] took her to be a pirate." Kennon ordered the national colors dis-played, and he set the crew to work manning the long sweeps in the hope of closing the distance. Soon the forward bow chaser was in range, and Kennon ordered a shot fired across the bow of the chase. But rather than heave to, the schooner instead turned sharply toward the land. Growing darkness and shoal water forced Kennon to give up the pursuit, and the pirate, if indeed it was such, escaped.[8]

Such encounters were typical of America's "war" against the Carib-bean pirates in the 1820s. The enemy vessels proved to be elusive and slip-pery, and actual captures were few. Although vessels from the U.S. squadron did capture one schooner and one felucca, their primary achievement was to deter many pirates from cruising at all. Ironically, this resulted in a sharp increase in brigandage ashore as the former pirates turned to simple thievery. The *Weasel* made no captures that season, and when warmer weather arrived with the onset of summer, it and the other vessels of the squadron returned north to avoid the pestilence that was believed to infect the very air of the Tropics at that time of the year.

Back in the States, Buchanan received welcome news of his promo-tion to lieutenant, which arrived simultaneously with orders to report to the sloop-of-war *Hornet*, a much larger vessel boasting twenty guns and a crew of 140, under the command of Edmund P. Kennedy. As the sixth lieutenant on the *Hornet*, Buchanan would be the most junior officer onboard save for the midshipmen, but he had grasped the bottom rung of the promotion ladder. As long as he avoided making any disastrous errors, seniority would enable him to assume increasingly responsible duties until he eventually achieved command.

Buchanan spent a year on the *Hornet* searching the Caribbean littoral for pirates (mostly in vain), returning periodically to Key West to resup-ply. He was a conscientious lieutenant. Although he no longer had to keep a daily journal for the executive officer to inspect, he continued to take careful notes about the prevailing winds and currents, the composition of the bottom, the placement of shoals and rocks, and even the location of fresh water sources and the efficiency of local pilots. Clearly he anticipated that these notes would be a valuable future reference, perhaps when he was in command of his own ship. He was, in short, an avid student of his profession. Very likely he also studied his commanding officer to learn as much as possible about the secrets of effective command. Like Oliver H. Perry, Edmund P. Kennedy was the kind of officer who inspired what one authority described as "fanatical devotion" among his junior officers. But he was not loved by his sailors. Kennedy had begun his naval career as a petty officer, and the habit of management by threat had never left him. As a commanding officer, he had a short temper and was free with the cat-o'-nine-tails.[9]

When the *Hornet* returned to the Chesapeake Bay in 1825, Buchanan was once again detached. The war against Caribbean piracy was winding down. Most of the small schooners Porter had purchased for the war against the pirates were sold, and Buchanan returned to Philadelphia to await new orders. As before when orders were not swift in finding him, he sought, and found, an opportunity to expand his professional experience outside the navy. This time he would have an opportunity to command—and not a merchant ship, but a full-sized frigate.

Like Caribbean piracy, the circumstances that brought Buchanan this unusual opportunity arose out of Latin American politics. Brazil, which had recently won its independence from Portugal, was embroiled in a war with neighboring Argentina and had contracted to buy a frigate from an American shipyard to reinforce its blockade of the Río de la Plata. The U.S. builders wanted someone to deliver the ship safely to Rio de Janeiro. Command of a frigate—even if only to deliver it to others—was a role far beyond even the most ambitious dreams of a junior lieutenant, and Buchanan immediately applied. For the second time in five years he requested and was granted an extended furlough. It would not affect his relative seniority in the navy, and the time lost from active service would be more than compensated by the experience of commanding a large man-of-war.

Thus it was that in October 1826, having just turned twenty-six, Buchanan found himself in command of the newly built frigate *Baltimore* anchored in the Chesapeake Bay a dozen miles north of Annapolis. On Monday, 30 October 1826, he gave his first orders as a ship's commanding officer and watched with suppressed excitement and some satisfaction as the big vessel slowly worked down the bay to its anchorage off the Virginia capes. On 3 November, the pilot came onboard and the ship stood out to sea. Once the pilot had been dropped off near Cape Henry, the *Baltimore* and the final responsibility for its safety would be Buchanan's, and his alone.[10]

Buchanan had always appreciated the huge gulf between a ship's captain and the rest of the wardroom, but now he experienced the difference in a visceral way. The first thing to change was his sleeping habits. As captain, he did not stand watch; but in one sense he was on watch all the time, for he was ultimately responsible for everything that happened on the ship. As meticulous as he was with the smallest detail of his professional assignments, it is hard to imagine that he did not now pay scrupulous attention to every aspect of the ship's passage. And it was not just his acute awareness of possible dangers that made the voyage seem more perilous than usual—it was.

Only a few days out, off the Carolina capes, the *Baltimore* ran into heavy squalls and Buchanan ordered the crew into the rigging to double-reef the topsails. He noted that the *Baltimore* rode deep in the water, "plunging very heavy, taking in much water forward." The storm lasted all night. Finally, at dawn, Buchanan noted with some relief that the clouds were breaking up and the wind moderating. After first light he ordered the crew aloft again to shake the reefs out of the topsails, and he even ordered the steering sails set on the larboard side. Then, at 9:00 A.M., a sudden gust carried away the mizzen topgallant mast. At once he called to the crew to take in the steering sails, and he sent others aloft to strike the royal yards, removing as well the wreck of what was left of the mizzen topmast. Again the ship stabilized on its course.[11]

Regardless of these difficulties, or perhaps pleased that he had managed despite them, Buchanan's confidence grew, and he felt satisfied with his first command, especially with the *Baltimore*'s performance in bad weather. "Ship proved to be a fine boat," he confided to his journal that night. It was just as well that it was, for three days later, a few hours past midnight on 12 November, the winds again strengthened and continued strengthening. Heavy seas crashed over the deck, and the wind threatened to tear the sails away altogether. Again Buchanan called on the crew to shorten sail. They clambered aloft in the dark of night under the urgings of the petty officers, but even as they climbed, the winds rose another octave, and soon it was evident that the ship was in the middle of a full hurricane. Buchanan sent fifty men aloft, practically the whole crew, but they fought mostly in vain to gain control of the wet canvas. This time dawn brought no respite: the weak morning light was barely perceptible in the dark of the storm. Several of the men attempting to gather in the sails were badly injured, crushed between the yard and the mast as the ship tossed violently in the heavy seas and howling wind.[12]

On deck, where waves were still crashing over the bulwark at each roll of the ship, Buchanan ordered all the hatches battened down to prevent water from collecting belowdecks. Even so, the ship took on water at an alarming rate. Buchanan later attributed this to the fact that the carpenters in the yard had not properly sealed the gun ports. Whatever the cause, he had to detail more men to keep the pumps going constantly, though the combination of heavy rain mixed with equally heavy sea spray made it a losing game. The decks, the storerooms, the staterooms, cabin, wardroom, and steerage were all afloat.

Worse than that—far worse—the mainmast appeared to be in danger of going over the side. The *Baltimore* was on what amounted to its shakedown cruise, and some settling was to be expected. But Buchanan was astonished and alarmed to note that the high seas seemed to be working the main mast loose in its step. It swayed alarmingly from side to side with each roll of the ship. As it rolled one way, the mast canted over, stretching the rigging until it was as taut as so many piano wires, keening a high-pitched wail of imminent disaster, while on the leeward side the lines hung limp in loose falls. Then the ship would heel over, the mast would shift again, and the loose ropes would twang taut. At each roll Buchanan wondered if they would hold. He knew that if they failed, the ship was lost.[13]

After five hours, the crew finally managed to secure the sails, and with the coming of another dawn the weather finally moderated. Buchanan was able to draw his first calm breath in thirty-six hours. With a semblance of order restored, he noted laconically that during the night, the officer of the deck had neglected to remember to wind the ship's clock.[14]

The rest of the voyage south was almost anticlimactic, although hardly uneventful. On the nineteenth, Seaman Francis C. Doane fell from the mizzen topgallant rigging and was instantly killed, the first man to die under Buchanan's command. The next day at noon, Buchanan performed the funeral service as Doane's body was committed to the deep. Although there were no more hurricanes, the ship continued to encounter "thick, cloudy, rainy weather" with frequent squalls. Buchanan was on the deck most of the time supervising the crew as the men made and shortened sail at need. Another squall hit on 6 December, and another, even stronger, struck with great suddenness two days later just before midnight. It carried away the jib boom, the fore topgallant mast, and the main royal mast, and Buchanan again had to order the crew into the wrecked rigging in the full dark on a tossing sea to clear away the jumbled mess aloft.[15]

These perils did not prevent the appearance of King Neptune and his court when the Baltimore crossed the equator on 14 December. Fifty-eight members of the crew, all but a few old salts, had never crossed the equator before, and each of the "pollywogs" was subjected to initiation by their more experienced "shellback" shipmates.[16] Two days later the weather was sufficiently passive to allow Buchanan to call the crew to quarters and observe the exercise of the great guns. Perhaps with the ship's arrival at Rio de Janeiro only days away, he wanted to ensure that his crew did not disgrace him when called on to fire a salute to the Brazilians.[17]

The Baltimore arrived in Rio on Christmas Day, 1826. At 8:00 A.M. Buchanan espied the characteristic hump of Sugarloaf, and at 11:00 the Baltimore passed through the anchored Brazilian navy and some of its prizes. By 4:00 P.M. the ship was safely anchored inside the harbor. Without mishap, his crew fired a twenty-one-gun salute, which was, to Buchanan's great satisfaction, immediately returned by the fort ashore. The voyage from Cape Henry had occupied fifty-two days, and Buchanan had completed his first assignment as a ship's commanding officer. On 5 January, he turned the Baltimore over to Capt. Charles Thompson of the Brazilian navy, and his assignment was complete.[18]

Four days later, Buchanan boarded the brig Ruth for the return trip. Although he traveled as a passenger, he nevertheless interested himself deeply in the workings of the ship, maintaining his sea log as if he were aboard a man-of-war. Now that he was no longer responsible for the safety of the ship, he occasionally lapsed into contemplation of the beauty of the sea. Inspired, apparently, by a particularly lovely sunrise, he penned in his journal a maudlin poem:

The sun when arising bespangles the dew
And tints with its glory the skies,
All nature's in motion, how charming the view,
When day is beginning to rise.[19]

After a largely uneventful journey, the *Ruth* took on a pilot off Cape Henlopen, Delaware, on 30 March and worked its way up to Philadelphia, where it anchored at 8:00 P.M. on 2 April 1827.

Buchanan had one more tour of duty in the Caribbean as part of the navy's war against piracy. In the summer of 1827 he served as the fifth lieutenant on the new eighteen-gun sloop-rigged corvette *Natchez*, under the command of George Budd. With his discerning seaman's eye, Buchanan noted critically that the *Natchez* was "a good sea boat, but [its] lower masts [were] too taut." After an uneventful voyage south, the ship arrived off Santiago (which Buchanan rendered in his journal as "St. Iago"), Cuba, in late July. The *Natchez* cruised through Cuban waters in defiance of the presumed miasmas of the tropical summer, circumnavigating the island of Cuba and exploring the Bahama Islands as well. If its search for pirates was mostly in vain, at least the *Natchez* showed the flag and made the pirates wary.[20]

As it turned out, the hurricane season was a more dangerous foe than any pirate. On 17 August, as the *Natchez* cruised near Grand Cayman Island, a sudden squall blew up quickly into a hurricane that ripped the double-reefed sails from the yards and blew away the fore and main royal masts. That loss so weakened the rigging that the mainmast threatened to go over the side. The ship heeled over alarmingly, and the lee rail went underwater. Although the hands manned the pumps with a will, the waist of the ship began to fill, and the *Natchez* wallowed heavily in the troughs of the waves. For four days the *Natchez* battled the storm. The starboard quarter boat was smashed, but the ship survived and limped back to Havana to refit.[21]

After executing temporary repairs in Havana, the *Natchez* shaped a course for Pensacola, Florida. It was en route there that Buchanan first sighted the entrance to Mobile Bay, which he would defend unsuccessfully from an invader thirty-seven years later. The *Natchez* anchored in Pensacola Harbor and fired a twelve-gun salute to Commo. Charles

Ridgely onboard the *John Adams*. Two days later, Ridgely transferred his flag to the *Natchez*. Presumably this affected Buchanan's berthing: the commodore bumped the captain from his cabin, the captain took the first lieutenant's berth, and the first lieutenant joined the crowded wardroom.

It is an insight into Buchanan's notion of his professional duties that he made very careful notes at both Havana and Pensacola about how to enter the harbor, another example of his detailed preparations for what he clearly expected to be his life's profession. Whole pages of his journal were devoted to entries such as "Directions for going into Pensacola," "Directions for standing into Matanzas," and "Directions for standing into Key West."[22]

Ridgely was still onboard when the *Natchez* returned to its cruising ground in October, in company with the *Erie* and the *Hornet*. Lt. William B. Nicholson, the officer immediately senior to Buchanan in the wardroom, was confined to his bunk suffering from fever, but he chose to remain onboard nonetheless. Within hours, however, the fever completely consumed him and he died. Nicholson's death did not interrupt the cruise. He was buried at sea as the ship continued southward for Havana. The *Hornet* and the *Erie* headed off on independent patrols, and the *Natchez* arrived at Havana alone. For a week, it stood off the entrance to the harbor inspecting the traffic in and out, boarding vessels that looked suspicious. Ridgely suspected that the Spanish authorities were less than fully committed to the war against piracy, but his activities cannot have won him many friends in the Spanish colonial government.[23]

After a cruise along the Mexican coast, the *Natchez* returned to the piratical haunts of southern Cuba in March 1828. The ship cruised leisurely along the coast, looking into the river mouths and inlets, but since the pirates operated with small boats well up the rivers, there was no way the *Natchez* could ferret them out. Budd therefore determined to send in an armed boat's crew: the ferret down the rat hole. Off the Isle of Pines, he ordered Buchanan to take command of the ship's first cutter with a crew armed with pistols and cutlasses, and to search the small bays and river mouths along the coast. It was Buchanan's first independent command as a U.S. Navy officer. For four days he and his crew sailed and rowed along the coast, looking into likely inlets and rowing carefully up narrowing rivers until the green foliage brushed the thwarts of the cutter, but they found nothing suspicious. Disappointed and sun-burned, Buchanan returned to the *Natchez,* which then made sail once again for Pensacola.[24]

On the last day of the month, as the *Natchez* approached Pensacola, Captain Budd gave Buchanan the deck and ordered him to take the ship into port. Conditions were far from ideal: the wind was blowing "very fresh" from the north into Buchanan's face, and he had to contend as well with a tide of three knots that was running out of the harbor. Buchanan managed to get the *Natchez* safely across the bar, but the ship made almost no headway against the contrary wind and tide. For an hour he beat back and forth, making virtually no progress, until, just at noon, the *Natchez* struck hard on the northeast tip of Cancuz Shoal in two and a half fathoms of water. Budd sent into the shipyard for two schooners and set the crew to work offloading the ship's guns and stores into the schooners in order to lighten the ship. Afterward, the ship's anchor was lowered gingerly into a cutter and rowed out beyond the starboard quarter and dropped. Then the crew wound in on the capstan and kedged the *Natchez* off the bar.

Buchanan was chagrined by the whole experience, but he felt no shame. He blamed Budd for even attempting to enter port under such conditions. His private notation that "it is imprudent to attempt to beat a Ship in against an ebb tide" was written less as a reminder to himself than as an unspoken accusation aimed at his commanding officer. At least he was able to record that the ship "sustained no damage."[25]

Buchanan soon had another chance to prove his mettle as an inshore pilot. When two days later the *Erie* appeared off the harbor entrance and signaled for a pilot, Budd sent Buchanan. And three weeks after that, when the *Shark* struck the middle ground shoal while standing out to sea, Ridgely sent Buchanan to pilot it out of the harbor.[26]

In July, news reached Pensacola that a pirate schooner was operating along the Cuban coast near the Isle of Pines. Aware that the ship-rigged *Natchez* had little chance of catching a fore-and-aft-rigged schooner, Budd chartered three small vessels at Key West and placed each in the care of a lieutenant. Buchanan got the schooner *Lily.*

Twenty-seven-year-old Lieutenant Buchanan departed on an independent cruise with two midshipmen and a crew of thirty-five under his command. Off Cape Antonio he sighted a suspicious vessel—a hermaphrodite brig crammed with men. It did not meet the description of the pirate, but Buchanan suspected at once that if it was not a pirate, it was very likely a slaver. Buchanan did not view the slave trade as morally offensive, but it *was* against the law, and the capture of a slave ship would be a feather in his cap professionally. He gave chase at once. He pressed on as much sail as the *Lily* would carry—indeed, a bit more than it could carry, for after a pursuit of some sixteen hours, the foretop mast carried away and the slaver, if such it was, escaped in the darkness. A disappointed Buchanan continued his cruise off the Colorados Reef near the west end of Cuba, but he saw no other suspicious vessels, and he returned empty-handed to Pensacola on 25 July.[27]

There, yellow fever struck the squadron. In those years, and throughout the nineteenth century, disease was a far greater threat to life than combat, even in wartime. So many infected sailors were sent ashore that only a skeleton crew was left onboard the *Natchez*. Tents had to be erected to house the sick, which eventually numbered some 150 men. Buchanan was placed in charge of the camp, and he stayed there two and a half months. Nine men died before the arrival of cooler weather in November signaled the end of the fever season. When the fever moderated and the *Natchez* left Pensacola to carry the survivors north to New York, Buchanan went with them. He sighted New York Harbor on 22 November 1828, and the *Natchez* anchored two days later off the navy yard.[28]

Altogether, Buchanan served most of five years cruising the Caribbean in search of pirates. Only twice had he actually seen a pirate ship—or what he thought was one—and in neither case did he effect its capture. Indeed, after thirteen years in uniform he had yet to fire a shot in a battle with an enemy. But he had experienced a wide variety of adventures, he had learned a great deal, and he returned from the Caribbean, at age twenty-seven, a confident and experienced officer.

❧ 3 ❧

NANNIE LLOYD

One who will have a claim to control me
in all my operations through life.

Ohne of the "young gentlemen" with whom Buchanan sweated out the lieutenant's exam in 1822 was fellow Marylander Charles Lowndes. That shared experience was enough of a bond to induce Lowndes to invite Buchanan to his wedding, which was to take place in May 1826. Just before departing for South America in the *Baltimore,* therefore, Buchanan traveled to St. Michael's Parish in Talbot County on Maryland's Eastern Shore to witness Lowndes's marriage to Sarah Scott Lloyd. His presence at that event was fateful, for among the bride's attendants was her younger sister, dark-haired eighteen-year-old Ann Catherine Lloyd, whom everyone called Nan or Nannie, and who was destined to become Buchanan's wife. Buchanan's visit to the Eastern Shore was a turning point in his life in more ways than one, for in marrying Nannie Lloyd, Buchanan linked himself as well to the extended Lloyd clan, which became for him a second family. In time, the culture of the Lloyd family of Talbot County would define both his politics and his social values and would have far-reaching personal and professional consequences.[1]

Buchanan's courtship of Nannie Lloyd was no whirlwind romance. They met in May 1826 and married in February 1835, nearly nine years later. Of course, much of that time Buchanan was away at sea. After attending Lowndes's wedding, he left almost at once to ferry the *Baltimore* to Rio; then he spent eighteen difficult months in the Caribbean on the *Natchez*. After that he spent another year and a half as the first lieutenant on the frigate *Constellation*. Not until he returned from that third tour of the Mediterranean, late in 1831, did he have an opportunity to renew his acquaintance with Nannie Lloyd.

Buchanan's cruise on the *Constellation* was largely uneventful, although it did have two important consequences. First, it provided him with several opportunities to visit not only the periphery of the Mediterranean basin but also several inland cities of historical or cultural significance. Now that the difficulties with the North African pirates had been resolved, Mediterranean service resembled what one old salt called a perpetual yachting party. The ships of the U.S. squadron showed themselves twice a year off the Barbary Coast, but the rest of the time they cruised to friendly and picturesque ports of call where dinner invitations and other social opportunities awaited them. On this cruise, Buchanan and several other officers, including his friend Frank Du Pont who was serving on the *Ontario,* decided to strike off inland to visit some of the great cites of Europe. In Italy they toured Milan, Turin, Pisa, and Florence; in Greece they traveled through the Peloponnesus, stopping at Argos, Mycenae, and Corinth. Near Tunis, Buchanan traveled to the ruins of ancient Carthage, where he may have contemplated the feats and the fate of Hannibal.[2]

A second noteworthy aspect of this cruise illuminates an important element of Buchanan's emerging command personality. It was during his tenure as first lieutenant on the *Constellation* that he first demonstrated his commitment to the kind of rigid discipline that was to be his signature as a naval officer. It was the primary duty of the first lieutenant on a ship of war not only to oversee the day-to-day routine of the vessel, but also to enforce discipline aboard ship. For the most part, captains were content to give their first lieutenants broad latitude in deciding how to maintain that discipline. Some first lieutenants relied on developing a sense of camaraderie with the men; others viewed obedience as a simple duty and enforced it with corporal punishment. From the beginning of the cruise it was evident that Buchanan fell into the latter group.

Buchanan was a great believer in rules. And the consequences for violating one were clearly spelled out in the navy regulations. Explanations or extenuating circumstances were, to him, merely excuses. He routinely viewed unsatisfactory performance as a failure of will. He had, in particular, a very low tolerance for any manifestation of self-indulgence—especially laziness or drunkenness—sins best discouraged, he believed, by the application of physical punishment. In the U.S. Navy of the 1830s, the cat-o'-nine-tails was the standard form of punishment for a long list of transgressions, and Buchanan had no qualms about ordering its use. On this cruise, his literal application of the regulations and liberal use of the cat earned him the fear and enmity of most of the crew.

It was a resentment that did not fade. After the *Constellation* returned to the United States in November 1831, dropping anchor in Hampton Roads, Buchanan became the target of threats shouted at him in the streets of Norfolk by sailors who vowed revenge. After being discharged from the *Constellation* that same month, Buchanan bought a ticket on a bay boat bound for Baltimore on the first leg of a trip to his mother's home in Philadelphia. On boarding, he discovered that several dozen crewmen from the *Constellation* had booked passage on the same vessel. A few of Buchanan's friends implored him to secure another conveyance lest he be set upon and tossed over the side. Characteristically, Buchanan sniffed at such advice and took his reserved place in his private cabin, though he kept his sword cane handy.

Early in the voyage, small groups of sailors came to his cabin to complain to him of the harsh treatment he had meted out on the late cruise. When, toward evening, he went up on deck, a crowd of angry sailors quickly gathered. A witness later described the confrontation: "The seamen gathered around him, and gave vent to their feeling in blasphemous oaths. One man remarked that he had been more than twenty years in the service; that he had fought at Tripoli, and had never been punished until ordered by Lieutenant Franklin Buchanan." Others shouted that Buchanan was a tyrant, a poor seaman, and that he should be driven from the service. Buchanan made no reply. Coolly he bore their insults for several minutes, then, still silent, he faced about and returned to his cabin. The witness who recorded the event fifty years later made Buchanan the hero of the piece: "There he stood in statue-like repose, not a word escaping his lips. He seemed rooted to the deck. For a full five minutes or more he braved the tempest, but not a man dared lay the weight of his finger upon him. Quietly and gracefully, he turned upon his heel, and passed down the stairway into the after cabin and went to bed." But the most revealing aspect of this vignette is not Buchanan's courage or dignity in facing down an angry mob; it is the extent of the anger of this group of veteran sailors. Such a scene could hardly be imagined involving almost any other officer of the service.[3]

Buchanan arrived safely at Philadelphia in time for Christmas, then remained ashore for the next year and a half awaiting orders. During that eighteen months his relationship with Nannie Lloyd flourished. They may have renewed their acquaintance earlier in Annapolis, but sometime in the spring or summer of 1832 Buchanan returned to Talbot County to advance his suit. Such a trip involved taking the steam ferry from Annapolis to Easton, then a carriage ride northward across the Miles River ferry and past mile after mile of Lloyd fields to an entryway marked by a half-mile-long avenue of massive oak and chestnut trees. That boulevard led to an elliptical greensward beyond which rose the sprawling two-story Georgian mansion that had been the Lloyd home since 1790, replacing an even older home that dated back to the mid-seventeenth century. Behind the house was an elaborate boxwood garden that led to a glass-fronted orangery filled with lemon and orange trees and topped by a billiard room overlooking the Wye River.

   Buchanan was no country bumpkin; he was at ease in the finest homes of Baltimore and Philadelphia. But he could hardly avoid being impressed by the grandeur of Wye House. This estate—and indeed most of Talbot County—was the private domain of Edward Lloyd, Nannie's father, who was not only a former state governor and U.S. senator, but also one of the richest men in Maryland. His wealth had been handed down undivided through five generations of Edward Lloyds, and it was measured in thousands of acres and hundreds of slaves on dozens of plantations. The Lloyd family lived in comfort and luxury that was impressive even by the standards of the landed gentry. A contemporary recalled that Wye House "was almost constantly filled with company who were entertained with an ease and an elegance to be met with in few houses in Maryland." In describing a visit by several of her children's friends, Nannie's mother reported that "they have amused themselves in riding, walking, sailing, & rowing. . . . Their hours are dreadful, breakfast from 10 to 12 o'clock, & dine at candlelight. The gentlemen up at about 11, retire about one in the morning. The ladies take their pickled oysters and eels in their chambers & keep up a lively time for a long while after they go to their rooms."[4]

But this life of gaiety and dissipation had a darker side as well. In addition to his wealth and fame, Edward Lloyd was unique in Maryland in his commitment to a form of plantation slavery more commonly associated with the Deep South Cotton Belt than with border-state Maryland, where slavery often took on the aspect of tenantry. The extensive Lloyd lands on the Eastern Shore were organized as a series of plantations, where the slaves (more than seven hundred in all) lived in barracks-like quarters and were managed by hired overseers whose performance was measured by how much profit they returned each year. This sprawling private empire of wheat and slaves was under the overall supervision of a bailiff, or steward, who reported directly to Lloyd.[5]

Colonel Lloyd, or "Edward the Governor" as he was sometimes known to distinguish him from his ancestors and descendants of the same name, was an old-fashioned farmer distrustful of gadgets or so-called scientific farming; he put his faith in the efficient management of human labor organized under strict discipline. He harbored no internal doubts about the wisdom or morality of the peculiar institution. Applauding the arguments of John C. Calhoun, he held slavery to be a social blessing that defined a labor system in which every creature knew and understood his proper role. As a congressman in 1807, Lloyd had been one of the few to vote against the termination of the international slave trade. Similarly, he had voted against the Missouri Compromise in 1820, objecting to the prohibition of slavery in any part of the Louisiana Purchase. As a result of this commitment to slavery in a geographically isolated portion of Maryland, Talbot County in general, and Wye House in particular, was a kind of living anachronism within the state: an insulated private kingdom. Young Frederick Douglass, who was a slave at Wye House during the time that Buchanan courted Nannie Lloyd, later recalled the place with chilling precision: "There were certain secluded and out-of-the-way places . . . , seldom visited by a single ray of healthy public sentiment, where slavery, wrapt in its own congenial darkness, could and did develop all its malign and shocking characteristics. . . . Just such a secluded, dark, out-of-the-way place was the home plantation of Colonel Edward Lloyd in Talbot County, Eastern Shore of Maryland."[6]

A vignette from Douglass's *Narrative of Slave Life* helps to illuminate the underside of the world in which Nannie Lloyd grew up. It concerns her father's relationship with an elderly slave called Old Barney, who was in charge of the stables at Wye House and who was thus one of the few slaves with whom Lloyd had a personal relationship. When Colonel Lloyd arrived at the stable one morning and found that the horse he had planned to ride had not been groomed to his expectations, he ordered Old Barney to remove his coat and shirt and to get on his knees. He then personally applied thirty strokes with his riding whip to Barney's bare back. Frederick Douglass was only a boy at the time, but he remembered the incident vividly many years later. It was not so much the brutality of it that affected him—Douglass admitted that Barney's "physical suffering" was probably not severe—and there appeared to be no particular animosity on either side. It was the matter-of-factness of it that made it so memorable. These two old men each accepted as a matter of course that whipping was a proper part of their relationship. Each was simply doing his part within the system: one had an obligation to whip; the other, an obligation to be whipped. It is not stretching the comparison too far to suggest that just as Buchanan applied the prescribed punishment to violators of the navy regulations, so too did Edward Lloyd apply the prescribed solution to problems of slave management. Each man simply accepted his role in the natural order of things.[7]

In Lloyd's view, and ultimately Buchanan's as well, the threat to a stable society did not come from plantation masters who fulfilled their patriarchal responsibilities by enforcing discipline in their homes and fields (or from naval officers who enforced discipline aboard ship). It came from those outside the system who attempted to discredit or destroy a time-proven method of social order. As far as Lloyd was concerned, it was men like the execrable William Lloyd Garrison, whose abolitionist newspaper the *Liberator* first appeared that January, who constituted the greatest threat to society.

Buchanan left no contemporary evidence of his initial impression of plantation life at Wye House. His subsequent letters make it clear that he was more impressed than offended. Certainly his introduction to life at Wye House did nothing to cool his ardor for a match with Nannie. It is not clear when he asked for her hand, but by June 1833 the two young people had reached an agreement between themselves and had become secretly engaged. That month Buchanan wrote his friend Frank Du Pont to congratulate him on his forthcoming nuptials and to confide that he, too, was about to take such a step. In veiled language, he reported that he had committed himself to "one who will have a claim to control me in all my operations through life."[8]

Although it was now time for him to return to sea, for once he was not anxious to go. Du Pont advised him to stake a claim for the first lieutenancy on the frigate *United States*, but Buchanan decided that he would instead accept the orders he had received to join the wardroom of the ship of the line *Delaware*. He was not particularly excited about the assignment, but the cruise on the *Delaware* was scheduled to last only a year, whereas the *United States* would most likely be gone for three. He confessed to Du Pont that it was Nannie's desire that he take the shorter cruise. "She feels the separation," Buchanan wrote his friend, "but says it is better now for one year, than for three hereafter." Buchanan, too, would suffer from the separation. He wrote Du Pont that "this one year will be the longest I ever experienced."[9]

Buchanan reported aboard the *Delaware* in Norfolk as its first lieutenant in June 1833. He wrote Du Pont that the officers onboard made up "a pleasant mess," and he was pleased as well that the captain, Henry Ballard, allowed him to ship his personal servant as part of the crew. President Andrew Jackson made a formal visit to the ship on 29 July, and the next day the *Delaware* got under way en route to Cherbourg to deliver the new American minister, Edward Livingston, to Paris. As had been the case on the *Constellation*, Buchanan's regime as first lieutenant on the *Delaware* was punctuated by the almost routine call for "all hands to witness punishment!" On such occasions, the crew would dutifully line up in the waist of the ship and watch as the boatswain applied one or two dozen lashes to the naked back of some sailor who had run afoul of the ship's punctilious first lieutenant. Buchanan was not sadistic; he took no pleasure in such events. They were simply the price of efficiency and the natural consequence of delinquency.[10]

After a stop in Cherbourg to deliver Livingston—a stop that included an overland trip to Paris for many of the ship's officers, among them Buchanan, who attended a formal dinner hosted by King Louis Philippe himself—the *Delaware* sailed on to the Mediterranean for the customary round of port visits. The American squadron wintered in Port

Mahon, but Buchanan's plans to be back in Maryland after a single year were wrecked in the spring when Commo. Daniel T. Patterson transferred his flag from the *United States* to the much larger *Delaware* and brought along his own suite of officers. In consequence, Ballard, Buchanan, and most of the officers on the *Delaware* were transferred to the *United States*. Thus it was that Buchanan ended up on the *United States* after all, and his stay in the Med was prolonged another year.[11]

With Buchanan as its first lieutenant, the *United States* made the usual round of friendly ports in the summer of 1834. This time, however, Buchanan stayed aboard ship when Ballard and the rest of the wardroom officers toured Pisa and Florence. The only untoward event of the cruise occurred in Marseilles. While Ballard and several other officers were off touring Toulon, and Buchanan was ashore, Lt. Andrew K. Long supervised the firing of a salute in honor of the birthday of Louis Philippe. Alas, the gunner failed to ensure that the shot had been drawn from the guns, and the first three shots of the salute sent twenty-four-pound cannonballs flying into the hull of the nearby French ship of the line *Suffern,* killing three men and seriously wounding three others. Captain Ballard and his party returned to the ship that afternoon and spent the next several days explaining and apologizing. Three days later, the French prefect of marine visited the *United States* and the gunner successfully fired a fifteen-gun salute "without incident."[12]

Cruising eastward, the *United States* entered the Aegean in late summer and anchored among the ships of a large British fleet under Admiral Sir Josias Rowley, which was there to make a statement in support of the Greeks in their struggle for independence from the Turks. The British acknowledged the arrival of the *United States* with a fifteen-gun salute, which the *United States* safely returned with a twenty-four-gun salute in honor of Rowley's exalted station. During the customary reciprocal visits, Ballard accepted Rowley's invitation for the American frigate to participate in a sailing trial against vessels of the British squadron. Both commanders were eager to see how the American frigate matched up to its British counterparts. The next night, Buchanan smugly recorded the results of the race in his journal: "Beat out of the bay of Smyrna with a fresh breeze, and when the signal of recall was at sunset made, the U. States was several miles ahead and to windward of all the fleet."[13]

* * *

The *United States* returned from the Mediterranean in the fall of 1834. After arriving at New York in December, Buchanan made his way south, first to Philadelphia for a visit with his mother, and then on to Talbot County for a reunion with Nannie. He found her mourning her father, who had died the previous June. Her father's death had hit Nannie hard. She grew "weak and debilitated," in the words of one family member, and one morning in August she actually fainted at the breakfast table. Her weakened condition did not cool Buchanan's affection, and he resolved to solemnize their relationship. Nannie's brother (inevitably named Edward) was now the head of the family. In that role, "Edward the Farmer," as he came to be known, blessed Nannie's match with Buchanan, and on 19 February 1835 the thirty-four-year-old navy lieutenant and the twenty-seven-year-old Eastern Shore aristocrat were married by the Reverend George McElhiney at St. Anne's Episcopal Church in Annapolis.[14]

The newlyweds lived for several months at Wye House before moving across the bay to Annapolis, where Buchanan paid $2,650 for a six-room, two-story house on Scott Street immediately adjacent to the army post at Fort Severn. It had a smokehouse, wash house, water pump, and poultry yard in the back, and a stable and wood house to the side. The purchase was a bit of a stretch for Lieutenant Buchanan, and indeed, money worries were a constant theme in the lives of the newlyweds. Buchanan was not a rich man, and living on a lieutenant's salary proved to be difficult for the daughter of the state's wealthiest planter. Nannie was not the sole culprit, however. Her husband was also to blame. He gave his wife extravagant presents that he could not afford, and invariably by the end of the month (and usually long before) the young couple had run out of funds and had to borrow to make ends meet. Nannie's weekly letters to her mother were filled with concerns about money. The growing debts eventually involved Buchanan in litigation: he sued others to obtain monies that he believed were due him, and he regularly had to fend off creditors himself. Nannie begged loans from her mother and her brother, loans that eventually ran into the thousands of dollars and must have been something of an embarrassment for her husband.[15]

The couple's worries about money were magnified by their growing family. Their first child was born in December 1835, ten months after their marriage, and was named Sallie for Nannie's mother. She was a sickly baby who battled the usual childhood ailments, and for a time her parents feared that she would not survive. But by the next fall she had recovered sufficiently to allow a visit across the bay to Wye House. Edward had by then removed to Mississippi in the hope of developing a new plantation in the Cotton Belt, and his mother wrote to him: "Nannie and her husband are with us, their child more improved than any I ever saw. She appears to be perfectly well and is getting quite robust."[16]

Other children came in time. Letitia McKean, named for Franklin's mother, was born two years after Sallie, and Alice Lloyd came two years after that. Buchanan may have been hoping for a son to follow these three girls, but in 1841 his wife presented him instead with twin daughters, whom they named Nannie and Ellen. Elizabeth was born in 1845, and then finally a son, Franklin Buchanan Junior, was born on 16 January 1847. Altogether the Buchanans had ten children, although only nine survived infancy.

Buchanan was a doting father. When he was home from the sea he played card games with the children and went on walks with them, and he always brought them presents from abroad. He wanted them always to wear bright colors. On one occasion, as he and Nannie were returning home from a church meeting, Sallie, the eldest, ran to them with tears in her eyes to beg her father to rescue the family cat. It had jumped down the well to escape the family dog and had become trapped. Still in his Sunday best, Buchanan undertook a rescue and "after many efforts" succeeded in presenting Sallie with her cat.[17]

The children's health was a constant concern. One February night, seven-year-old Letitia awoke with a wracking cough, whooping alarmingly and unable to catch her breath. Nannie was in a panic and later wrote her mother, "I felt so thankful I have Mr. B. with me." Buchanan immediately dispatched a servant to bring the doctor, ordering him to find the younger and closer Dr. White for fear that the children's usual doctor, the elderly Dr. Thomas, might not be willing to travel at night in winter. As it turned out, Letitia had recovered and was breathing normally by the time the doctor arrived. Nannie was relieved when Dr. White told her that she had done all the right things. Even so, she confessed to her mother that "we did not go to bed till daylight, as all the servants and all the household seemed so anxious and distressed for poor Let[itia]."[18]

Through all these major and minor family crises, Buchanan remained a considerate and attentive husband. He returned from his cruises bear-

ing scarfs, boxes, pretty cloth, and new inventions for his wife's delight.
"C_n you read my steel pen writing?" Nannie wrote her mother in 1845.
"Mr. B. brought me a supply and I am trying to learn." He had also
brought her jars of pickles and olives. "He recollected my fondness for
them & brought me a supply. . . . He never forgets my fancies."[19]

During these years Buchanan had a variety of assignments that allowed
him to remain close to home. After eight months as a member of an ordnance and survey board charged with testing light and medium guns in
Annapolis and Norfolk, he spent the years 1836–39 as commanding officer of the navy's receiving ship in Baltimore. Although this was technically a sea command, Buchanan spent nearly all his time supervising relatively minor supply and manpower questions within Baltimore Harbor.
He was therefore able to go home in the evenings to the small house he
had rented for his family in Baltimore. Then, in 1839, anticipating war
with America's old enemy England over the location of the Maine border, he requested active service and received orders to the frigate *Constitution* as flag lieutenant to Commo. Alexander Claxton.[20]

When diplomats resolved the border dispute and the war fizzled out,
Buchanan found himself instead embarked on a cruise into the Pacific.
It was his first naval service in that ocean, and the trip was notable as
well because his older brother was also onboard, McKean Buchanan
having obtained a warrant as a navy paymaster in 1823. The two brothers
had seen very little of one another during the preceding quarter of a century. McKean, who was two years older, had left for the University of
Pennsylvania when Franklin was only twelve, and had returned just as
Franklin was going off to sea. Although each man served a lengthy career
in the navy, this was the only service the two brothers had together. At
least there was no problem of rank between them. As Claxton's flag lieutenant, Franklin was not in the direct chain of command, and neither
was McKean, whose position as paymaster made him a kind of elevated
clerk responsible for keeping the account books in order. It was a point
of some pride to McKean that he knew every sailor by sight. Each Sunday when the crew was mustered at quarters, McKean would accompany
the captain as he made his way around the ship and would call off the
name of every man onboard from memory.[21]

The *Constitution* sailed south in April, touching at Vera Cruz and
Havana en route to Cape Horn. The flag lieutenant had little to do with

the day-to-day running of the ship, including shipboard discipline. Perhaps because of that, Buchanan was relatively popular with the crew. When the cry "man overboard" sounded on the first day of June with the ship near the Cayman Islands, it was Buchanan who supervised the launching of the ship's boat and successfully rescued the victim. His action won the enthusiastic approval of the crew, including one sailor who later wrote that Buchanan "in this as well as similar instances during our cruise has always been one of the first individuals to jump into a boat when a shipmate was about to meet his watery grave."[22]

From Havana, the *Constitution* continued south across the equator to Rio, then south again to the Falkland Islands, all under blue skies and moderate winds. With the weather so good and the winds so favorable, many onboard began to hope that the much-feared passage of Cape Horn would be uneventful. The snowcapped peak of the cape came into sight on 29 September, and the crew crowded the rail for a glimpse of this feared landmark. But even as they watched, a dark mist enshrouded the peak and heavy clouds billowed up from the south. A "sudden and fierce" storm heeled the *Constitution* onto its beam-ends and marked the onset of seventeen days of terrible weather as the ship scudded along under bare poles. Save for those on duty, the crew remained below with the gun ports sealed. The entire passage was more inconvenient than perilous, especially at meal times. When hot food could be served at all, the sailors had difficulty transferring the food from plate to mouth, and as each successive quartering wave approached the ship, the cry rang out: "Look out for your beans!"[23]

The *Constitution* finally reached Callao, Peru, in late November. The three months Buchanan spent there proved to be a tedious anticlimax. The *Constitution* lay at anchor in what one sailor described as "our usual dull way—nothing to do throughout the day but wash the decks, clean the bright-work, and spread the awnings." Despite the opportunity to serve with his brother, Franklin Buchanan chafed at his dull round of duties. He had requested orders to the *Constitution* because he had expected a chance to win glory in a war against the Royal Navy. Instead he found himself confined to mostly administrative duties in a distant foreign port where the cultural attractions were, to his mind at least, much less inviting than those of Pisa, Florence, or Milan. In February 1840, after only nine months on the *Constitution,* he asked Claxton for orders to return to the United States on the grounds that his health was deteriorating. Claxton, whose own health was at least as precarious as Buchanan's, nevertheless acceded, and Buchanan transferred to the *Falmouth*, which carried him back to New York, arriving on 20 June.[24]

Neither his professed poor health nor his interrupted tour of service on the *Constitution* affected Buchanan's standing in the navy. In September 1841 he received the welcome news that he had been promoted to the rank of commander. But an equally important milestone that year was the Buchanan household's move across the Chesapeake Bay from Annapolis to Maryland's Eastern Shore. Very likely, Nannie reminded her husband that during his long absences at sea she found it very difficult to visit with her mother, and she probably conspired with her brother to make a permanent move from Annapolis to Talbot County financially possible. In any event, it is a matter of record that Edward Lloyd purchased for his sister an estate known as the Ferry Farm a few miles west of Easton and only half a dozen miles south of Wye House. There the Buchanans occupied the Rest, a sprawling plantation-style house that became their permanent home.

Directly across the Miles River from the Rest, and within a long stone's throw, was the Anchorage, the home of Charles and Sarah (Lloyd) Lowndes, at whose wedding Franklin and Nannie had met. The network of Lloyd in-laws throughout Talbot County also included Edward S. Winder, who had married Elizabeth Lloyd in 1820. (Their son, Charles Sidney Winder, became a Confederate general and eventually died of wounds received at Cedar Mountain.) And within two years, Nannie's youngest sister, Mary Eleanor, would marry navy officer William T. Goldsborough and move into a home nearby.

Buchanan's entry into this close circle of Lloyd relatives and in-laws symbolized not only their acceptance of him, but also his acceptance of them. He had been only seven when his father died, and he had left his mother's home at fourteen to become a midshipman. He had grown up, almost literally, in the navy. Now an adult, he discovered that the genteel and well-ordered life of Talbot County was not only pleasing to his wife but a comfortable fit for him as well. Buchanan embraced the Lloyd family's culture of gentility and comfort, a culture that was based on unchallenged assumptions about social order and hierarchy, and inevitably about slavery as well. He became a slaveholder himself and a vocal defender of the "peculiar institution." Even though his father had belonged to an abolitionist society in Baltimore, Franklin Buchanan, like his Lloyd in-laws, became a spirited and unwavering champion of the virtues of chattel slavery. In effect, while Franklin Buchanan's marriage to Nannie Lloyd in 1835 made her a Buchanan in name, it is also accurate to say that it made him a Lloyd in spirit.

~4~

COMMAND

The USS *Vincennes*

The high toned man of honor.

I n November 1842, Buchanan received orders to report to the eighteen-gun sloop-of-war *Vincennes* as its commanding officer. It was a plum job in the U.S. Navy of the 1840s, and particularly so for a newly promoted officer who ranked eighty-first among active-duty commanders on the Navy List, below thirty-seven other commanders who had never held a command at sea. Buchanan's record of service was sufficiently distinguished to justify a command, but his selection was largely the result of circumstance: the *Vincennes*'s crew was composed almost exclusively of sailors transferred from the USS *Mississippi*, aboard which Buchanan was then serving as the first lieutenant. He was therefore ideally positioned for the command.

Nevertheless, the appointment raised a few eyebrows, and more than one disappointed senior officer charged that Buchanan's selection was the product of "partiality." The unusual public controversy over Buchanan's new command was the manifestation of a larger issue within the navy that pitted junior officers against their seniors. Rising younger officers like Buchanan felt frustrated by a Navy List that was crowded with very senior but (in his opinion) marginally competent officers. Senior officers, on the other hand, who had paid their dues through long service, sought the perquisites they believed were due them. The issue was fought out in both private letters and public newspapers. Critics of Buchanan's appointment noted that many senior men with exemplary careers had been passed over; his defenders argued that "merit and acknowledged talent" and not "mere claims of years standing on the Navy Register" should be the determining criteria for selection to command. One, who signed his letter "Blue Jacket," went so far as to claim that "if all that constitutes the officer and gentleman, the high toned man of honor with twenty eight years of service in acquiring what all accord to him, the 'finished sailorman,' was ever concentrated in one person, that one is 'Franklin Buchanan.'" Buchanan may have deserved the accolade, but his appointment to command, and the ensuing public debate, made him a symbol for the advocates of reform in the U.S. Navy—at least on the issue of promotion by merit rather than seniority. It suggests as well that he was becoming adept at managing the internal politics of a navy career.[1]

The chain of events that made Buchanan's elevation to command possible began in the summer of 1842, when he left the comforts of the Rest to assume the job of first lieutenant on the newly commissioned steam frigate *Mississippi,* one of two paddle-wheel steamers that marked a milestone in the U.S. Navy's halting transition from sail to steam. He served only seven months on the *Mississippi,* and during most of that time the paddle wheeler rested quietly at anchor off Pensacola while the engineers tinkered with the engines. The experience left Buchanan with mixed feelings about the benefits of steam propulsion. He could see that under most circumstances steam warships had obvious advantages over sailing vessels in terms of speed, maneuverability, and tactical flexibility. Alas, the *Mississippi* was something of a transitional vessel in that it carried a full suite of masts and spars as well as a steam plant. While this rigging was useful when the wind was favorable, under steam the *Mississippi*'s top hamper constituted such a powerful drag on forward motion that it could barely make headway. While rounding Cape Hatteras en route to Pensacola, it had required a full twenty-four hours to make seven miles. Buchanan believed that, as configured, the *Mississippi* would very likely be unable to claw its way off a lee shore.[2]

Then, too, as the ship's first lieutenant Buchanan had not only to oversee the day-to-day management of shipboard routine, but also to maintain a high standard of cleanliness, a goal that was all but impossible on the coal-burning *Mississippi.* He had to battle constantly with the smoke and the coal dust, which seemed to permeate everything, even the food and water. He complained that "the limbers become choked with the small coal," and that cinders and ashes fouled the water supply, making it "offensive."[3] But Buchanan was no Luddite. Rather than invoke the good old days before steam engines ruined the navy, he put his mind to work contriving ventilators that could be used to clean the air and the water. Before he could bring these plans to fruition, however, the *Mississippi* was ordered into the dockyard at Boston for a thorough overhaul, and the crew was transferred: either to the ship of the line *Ohio*, or, like Buchanan, to the *Vincennes* in New York.

Buchanan assumed command of the *Vincennes* from Comdr. Joshua R. Sands in a formal ceremony aboard ship on 17 December 1842. As he cast his eye about the ship, Buchanan must have been pleased with his first command. Laid down seventeen years earlier as a second-class sloop-of-war, the *Vincennes* was 127 feet long at the waterline and carried a crew of 150. Despite a generous beam of 34 feet, it had a reputation as a fast ship, and had performed superbly during a recent round-the-world cruise as the flagship of the Great United States Exploring Expedition (1838–40). The *Vincennes* was, in short, a particularly desirable command. Of course, that did not prevent Buchanan from seeking ways to improve it. He was a bit disappointed, for example, that the ship's launch—kept on chocks amidships—was significantly oversized, a legacy of the *Vincennes*'s recent role as an exploring ship. The launch dominated the deck and made even routine activities aboard ship more challenging. Buchanan applied to the Navy Department to swap it for a smaller version, but to no avail.[4]

He also supervised the provisioning of the ship. The ship's purser, Joseph Bryan, had transferred to the *Vincennes* from the *Mississippi* along with his skipper, and Buchanan immediately put him to work accumulating ship's stores for the coming voyage. The barrels of flour and salt pork for the crew could be purchased with public monies, but food for the wardroom had to be paid for by the officers themselves. Because a recent act of Congress prohibited the traditional practice of granting advance pay, Bryan was cash poor; and merchants in New York were reluctant to grant credit to outbound vessels. Certainly Buchanan's own distressed financial circumstances prevented him from picking up the slack. Then, too, Bryan was handicapped in his efforts to provision the wardroom of the *Vincennes* by his need to close out the books on the *Mississippi*. Buchanan sought to cut through the difficulties, writing to Secretary of the Navy Abel Upshur to ask for "2 or 3 months" advance pay, and ordering Bryan to stop working on the *Mississippi*'s accounts until the *Vincennes*'s needs had been met.[5]

Buchanan was in a hurry; he wanted to be able to report the *Vincennes* ready for sea as soon as possible. It would demonstrate his efficiency and enthusiasm, and validate the Navy Department's good judgment in selecting him for command. Two days after Christmas, and only ten days after assuming command, he wrote Upshur to report that the *Vincennes* was indeed ready for sea—ready, that is, except for the absence of a marine guard. Ten days later he again reported the *Vincennes* ready for sea—except for the cash Bryan would need to pay the sailors during the cruise. This correspondence established a pattern. A week later Buchanan again reported the ship ready—except that he was short two seamen, five ordinary seamen, and two ship's boys; and a week after that he was waiting only for the return of Acting Master Barney, who was serving on a court martial in Philadelphia. His regular letters reminded the Navy Department that he was pressing ahead with all dispatch and that any delays were beyond his control, and at the same time they acted as gentle reminders of his continuing needs.

On the whole, Buchanan was pleased with the ship and its crew. "The crew generally are stout active men and in good health," he reported to the Home Squadron commander, Charles Stewart. "The Magazine and Battery, the powder, shells, shot &c. are in good condition [and] the equipment and outfits are complete." Indeed, his only complaint was that he was required to carry more supplies and equipment than he believed to be necessary. "The *Vincennes* is as full as an egg," he complained privately to Du Pont. "Her sailing trim is injured by it as well as her appearance."[6]

In addition to overseeing the accumulation of the material goods necessary to put to sea, Buchanan also began to put his personal stamp on the management of the officers and crew. He knew precisely how to assure himself of a docile crew: as before, he established a strict regimen of discipline and enforced it with physical punishment. There was already some discussion in Congress and elsewhere about abolishing the cat-o'-nine-tails in the navy, but Buchanan thought all such talk was pure nonsense. He believed that commanding officers who declined to apply the whip reaped the consequences of an inefficient ship. Privately, he ridiculed Robert F. Stockton, the commander of the *Congress,* as "no disciplinarian," claiming that Stockton was "opposed to any punishment," and that as a result, Stockton's ship was "a perfect hell."[7]

At his core Buchanan was a confident authoritarian whose worldview was of an ordered universe in which each individual knew and understood his place, and where authority and command carried obligations as well as privileges. His notion of discipline did not include spit and polish; it mattered little to him if pipe clay was applied to belts, or coal black to boots. But he had a very low tolerance for individuals of any rank who failed to meet the obligations of personal responsibility or exhibited evidence of moral weakness. In that respect, he was a curious combination of southern autocrat and Yankee Puritan. Buchanan had a clear idea of the public responsibility of every naval officer. He could understand how sailors serving before the mast might fall victim to human weaknesses such as licentiousness and drunkenness. (He once wrote, "Sailors are generally reckless, thoughtless beings.") But he expected officers to be, as he would say, "high toned," and he would not tolerate any evidence of moral weakness in his own officers. The worst crime an officer could commit, in Buchanan's view, was drunkenness: it demonstrated weakness, it undermined discipline, and when it became a public spectacle it brought discredit to the navy. "The crime of drunkenness," he wrote to the secretary of the navy early in his command, "causes all the insubordination and consequent punishment to officers and men. My experience has convinced me of that fact, and hence my determination never to overlook such an offence when committed under my command."[8]

His first opportunity to demonstrate his intolerance for public drunkenness came even before he took formal command of the *Vincennes.* In mid-December, he learned that two of the ship's junior officers, Acting Master Thomas Mahon and Passed Midn. Charles R. Smith, while dining together at the American Hotel had become so drunk as to make a public nuisance of themselves. They had become loud and offensive, and when asked to restrain themselves, they had become abusive as well. The ensuing fracas had attracted the attention of all those in the dining room, and among the witnesses was navy lieutenant John H. Marshall, who happened to be dining with a member of Congress. It was Marshall who reported the incident to Buchanan.

Rather than summon the two men to talk to them informally, Buchanan instead wrote each an official letter demanding an explanation. Finding their replies unsatisfactory, he reported the incident to Secretary of the Navy Abel Upshur and requested their immediate transfer from his command on the grounds that "their example to the other Midshipmen . . . is very injurious." Before Buchanan got a reply to this request, Mahon made things much worse for himself by a second display of public drunkenness, again in the American Hotel bar, where his behavior was again witnessed by Lieutenant Marshall. Worse yet, Mahon was on this occasion accompanied two other "young gentlemen" from the *Vincennes* midshipmen's mess, and while returning to the navy yard on the public ferry, one of the midshipmen relieved himself over the side in full view of the astonished passengers. Previously indignant, Buchanan was now coldly furious. He wrote to the midshipmen that they should expect no clemency, and, in a curious choice of words, wrote to Upshur that exposing oneself in public was "an offence I never overlook."[9]

Upshur's initial response to Buchanan's complaint—a formal letter of reprimand for both Mahon and Smith—was still en route to Norfolk when Buchanan's new charges arrived. With this new information at hand, the secretary acceded to Buchanan's request that Mahon be stricken from the ship's roster.

Smith, who had not been involved in the second fracas, survived. But not for long. Four months later, Smith was in trouble again. This time, Lieutenant Mitchell found Smith drunk on duty. It was bad enough that Smith was apparently addicted to drink, but what Buchanan found intolerable was that he was also apparently uncontrite. Mitchell reported to Buchanan that when he had confronted Smith, the midshipman had replied in a surly tone. Buchanan reported the incident to Upshur, again requesting the officer's dismissal, and this time the secretary agreed.

Contrition was important to Buchanan. The same week that Mitchell found Smith inebriated aboard ship, Buchanan learned that another of his officers, Lt. Robert E. Hooe, had embarked on a four-day drunk ashore and had so thoroughly ruined himself that he had to be hospitalized. Initially, Buchanan responded with a cool letter of reprimand expressing regret that Hooe had acted so disgracefully and advising him not to rejoin the ship. But when Hooe sent him an abject apology in which he promised, at the risk of his commission, never to be found again in such a state, Buchanan relented and agreed to let him rejoin the ship. "Your frank acknowledgement of your error and determination of amendment, I am rejoiced to hear," he wrote, "and believing [that] you are sincere, it will afford me pleasure to receive you again on board."[10]

Sadly for Buchanan's already weak faith in human nature, Hooe did not live up to his promise. Barely three months after returning to the *Vincennes*, he came aboard one evening "in a state of intoxication." Feeling betrayed, Buchanan reminded Hooe of his pledge and suggested that it would be honorable and appropriate for him now to resign his commission. Hooe refused, insisting that his drunkenness ashore did not interfere with his duty aboard ship, and that he had therefore not violated his pledge. Buchanan was not inclined to quibble. "You have but to ask your own conscience and your messmates whether you have not violated your pledge," he wrote. Having given Hooe the chance to resign and thereby save himself from humiliation, he saw no option now but to proceed with formal charges. "I have this day preferred charges against you," he informed Hooe, "and requested your trial." As evidence, Buchanan forwarded Hooe's previous pledge of good behavior to the squadron commander along with his own letter demanding Hooe's dismissal from the service.[11]

Buchanan's Puritan instinct was offended as well by the news that two of his senior petty officers—the boatswain and the carpenter's mate—were guilty of "illicit connexion" with several of the ship's boys. Lacking evidence, he ordered the ship's three lieutenants and the purser to form a committee and quietly investigate. Apparently nothing came of their investigation, though ten weeks later Buchanan did discharge Seaman John Baker as "untrustworthy of being retained in the service" because he had been "detected with a Boy in his hammock."[12]

The management of humanly imperfect officers and seamen was a constant undercurrent in Buchanan's daily responsibilities, but as the commanding officer of a ship of war on a foreign station, he also had more elevated, if equally troublesome, problems. Although the threat of piracy was now much reduced in the Caribbean and the Gulf of Mexico, Buchanan would discover that a commanding officer in the U.S. Navy encountered other perils: wily foreign diplomats, politically ambitious American ministers, and avaricious entrepreneurs. In charting a course among these political rocks and shoals, Buchanan often found himself thwarted and frustrated.

The *Vincennes* left New York in late January 1843 and arrived at Santiago, Cuba, without incident in early February. Buchanan sent word of his arrival to the American consul, dutifully informing him that he would "be pleased to receive from you such information and advice as may be deemed necessary to enable me to carry out the object of my cruise and the wishes of our government." The usual visitors came aboard: the Belgian minister arrived on 8 February, the Spanish minister of marine the next day, and the American consul (accompanied by the local governor and a party of ladies) the day after that; all received the appropriate salutes.[13]

From Santiago, the *Vincennes* cruised westward along Cuba's south coast, already familiar to Buchanan from many earlier visits, and the locus of much piratical activity. After arriving off the Isle of Pines, he dispatched the largest three ship's boats, including the oversized launch, along with eight officers and forty men with orders to explore "the Isle of Pines, Indian and St. Philip Keys, and running down the south coast of Cuba" to Trinidad, where the *Vincennes* would join them in twenty days. Buchanan enjoined his officers to "inquire strictly into the character of any suspicious vessels you may meet with, particularly those under the American flag who have the appearance of being concerned in the Slave Trade. The Law on that subject give[s] you the right, and power, to capture them if so engaged, and to send them to the U. States for trial." Having thus sent off three of his five boats and a third of his crew, Buchanan set sail for the rendezvous at Trinidad on Cuba's south coast.[14]

The *Vincennes* stood in toward the harbor at Trinidad late in the afternoon of 21 February and took on a local pilot. Under topsails and jib, the vessel glided slowly past Key Blanco. Even at the twentieth parallel the sun was already dipping below the horizon when at 6:40 the *Vincennes* struck a reef. Buchanan took soundings and found deeper water to starboard. He therefore put the helm over and braced up on the port tack, bringing the ship's head around. But though the stern moved slightly, the bow remained firmly wedged. Hard aground now, he ordered the sails furled and dispatched Lieutenant Schenck in one of the ship's two remaining boats to obtain help from town. Meanwhile, he set the only other ship's boat to rowing all around the *Vincennes* searching for the deepest water. There was only three and a half fathoms under the bow, but the bottom plunged to five fathoms astern and then deepened rapidly to nineteen fathoms. He therefore prepared to drop a kedge anchor astern.

Because the ship's oversized launch was off circumnavigating the Isle of Pines, the kedge anchor had to be hoisted over the side and settled gently into the much smaller gig. The men pulled at their oars and carried it out astern, dropping it in seventeen fathoms. Aboard the *Vincennes,* men spit on their hands and prepared to wind home the capstan. The slack came out of the line as it rose from the sea, dripping water as it grew taut and squeezed the moisture from the hemp. The men working 'round the capstan slowed as the anchor flukes dug in, then they gained momentum again. But the *Vincennes* did not move. Instead, the kedge anchor scoured the bottom and returned to the ship.

By now it was nine o'clock and fully dark. Aground near the shipping channel, Buchanan began to worry that other vessels might plow into his ship while he struggled to get it off the unmarked reef. He ordered that a gun be fired every few minutes, sent up rockets, and burned a blue light at the masthead to show his position. The wind began to freshen and created a swell running into the harbor. Instead of lifting the *Vincennes* over the reef, however, it raised the ship off the bottom just enough to slam it back again with each successive wave. Desperate to lighten ship, Buchanan ordered the men to empty the water casks in the hold and set others to work pumping the water over the side. Others he set to work carrying cannonballs and barrels of salt pork up from the hold and tossing them over the side. He ordered the construction of a large raft of empty barrels and extra spars and used it to float the stream anchor out astern. Alas, it too came home without freeing the vessel.

Genuinely anxious now, Buchanan ordered that tackle be rigged to hoist the guns of the main battery preparatory to throwing them over the side. While this was going on, a Spanish schooner came alongside with Lieutenant Schenck onboard. It had come out from Puerto Casilda at Schenck's earnest entreaty, but after looking over at the stranded *Vincennes,* its skipper was unwilling to take the guns onboard, or even to carry out an anchor for Buchanan. The Spaniard had come out for a rescue mission, not a salvage job. Resigned, Buchanan prepared to toss the ship's guns over the side. But even as he made the final preparations, the wind shifted and hauled to the west, and began blowing up into a squall. The loss of the ship's water and provisions had raised the draft of the *Vincennes* about a foot, and with this fresh breeze behind him, Buchanan resolved to bend on as much canvas as he could and force the *Vincennes* over the bar. At first the new approach resulted only in much heavier thumping, but then the vessel began to move, almost bouncing over the reef, and it gradually forged ahead into four fathoms, and then five; finally the ship floated free, with all its guns still onboard.[15]

Buchanan spent the next day refitting and attempting to salvage much of what he had ordered thrown overboard. Still lacking his small boats (the oversized launch would have been particularly useful here), he had to lease lighters from townspeople, who, seeing an opportunity for profit, charged what Buchanan considered exorbitant rates. At least he managed to recover most of the anchors, cables, salted meat, and other articles that had been thrown overboard in the crisis of the previous night. The work was halted at midday in order to fire a twenty-one-gun salute in honor of George Washington's birthday. That afternoon the American consul, H. P. Hastings, arrived to offer his help. Buchanan was delighted to be able to tell him that he had things well in hand.

He did, of course, have to report the incident to the squadron commander, and he wasted no time in doing so. Even as the men scrambled over the ship putting things back in order, Buchanan sat down to write to Stewart. He was no doubt profoundly relieved to report that the ship had sustained no permanent damage, but he did have to inform Stewart that he had been compelled to pay out some four hundred dollars as rental fees for the lighters used to conduct the salvage operations.[16]

With repairs completed, Buchanan sailed the *Vincennes* to the prearranged rendezvous with his three boats. He was standing off and on near Cape Antonio on 4 March when the lookout at the masthead reported three small boats putting out from shore. They came alongside, and Buchanan was probably as relieved to learn that none had met with disaster as he was disappointed to hear that they had failed to make any captures.

In addition to his largely profitless encounters with pirates and slavers, Buchanan's command of the *Vincennes* also involved him in political events in Mexico. Relations between the U.S. government and Generalissimo Antonio López de Santa Anna of Mexico were very precarious, and rapidly becoming more so. Santa Anna had never acknowledged the loss of Texas in 1836, and talk of possible American annexation of Texas made an open confrontation between the two countries appear increasingly likely. Buchanan was ready for war if it came to that. But his role in

1843 was more that of a diplomat than a warrior, and diplomacy had never been one of his strengths.

Buchanan's partner in guarding American interests along the Mexican Gulf coast was the American minister to Mexico, Waddy Thompson, a former congressman who affected the title "General" by virtue of his rank in the South Carolina militia. Thompson had two major goals: while seeking to avoid an open rupture between the United States and Mexico, he continued to press Santa Anna to release the several hundred prisoners still being held from the Texas War of Independence. As far as Thompson was concerned, it was Buchanan's job to aid him in these efforts in any way possible. Their conflict emerged from the fact that Buchanan did not deal well with trespasses on what he considered his personal perquisites.

After dropping anchor off Vera Cruz in April, Buchanan reported his arrival to General Thompson. He received no acknowledgment, but a few days later three men—former prisoners of war—showed up with a message from Thompson asking Buchanan if he would be good enough to carry them to America. While he was at it, the message said, he should stop at Tampico to pick up a Mr. Crittenden and ferry him back as well. Buchanan welcomed the men onboard and instructed his clerk to write Thompson an acknowledgment. But as he thought it over, he became increasingly annoyed with the presumptuousness of Thompson's request. The presence of three "guests" aboard the ship would necessarily be at his personal expense, and given the state of his finances, that was no small matter. After thinking it over, Buchanan recalled his clerk and dictated a new reply. Although he masked his comments in the guise of an apology for the spartan conditions his "guests" must accept, what Buchanan really wanted Thompson to know was how inconvenient their presence would be for him. "The *Vincennes* has her full complement of officers," he wrote, "and as the accommodations are arranged for that number of persons only, those gentlemen together with Mr. Crittenden, must of necessity occupy my cabin, which is very small, and of course subjects me to great inconvenience. Under these circumstances they must be satisfied with such comforts as I can bestow upon them during the three weeks passage we are likely to have at this Season of the year."[17]

Buchanan couldn't quite bring himself to complain openly to Thompson, but he did express his discontent to Louis S. Hargous, an American merchant who held a near monopoly on local trade out of Vera Cruz. To him Buchanan complained of "the practice of our Ministers directing officers Commanding ships of War, to receive on board Foreigners as passengers." One or two gentlemen he would not object to, Buchanan wrote, but he did not even know who these people were, or for what purpose he was to carry them. "The general [Thompson] does not even condescend to mention who or what the gentlemen are." It is not clear what Buchanan expected Hargous to do about it, but his compulsion to vent his anger to someone led him to make indiscreet comments to a private citizen about a public official.[18]

In the end, Buchanan did carry the three men to Pensacola, but he did not have to take Crittenden, and the trip took only twelve days, not three weeks. Even so, when he arrived at Pensacola, he wrote to Secretary Upshur to complain about Thompson's presumptuousness. "I respectfully request to be informed whether the services of this ship are placed at the disposal of the American Minister at Mexico, to convey passengers to the United States at his pleasure." He noted that the passengers he had been compelled to convey had adequate means to take passage on a commercial steamer bound for New Orleans, and that by hosting them in his cabin and at his table he was not only greatly inconvenienced, but personally out of pocket. "I cannot yield the right to an American Minister to dispose of my funds," he raged, "or place at my table, any person (other than a public officer of the government) without my approbation or consent."[19]

The *Vincennes* returned to its cruising off the Mexican coast near Vera Cruz in June. Because his orders charged him with "the protection of American commerce," Buchanan reported his return not only to General Thompson, but also to Hargous and the community of American merchants. Accepting his offer at face value, a group of merchants approached him to propose that he transport a rather large amount of specie to the United States for them. Buchanan was very much aware of a long-standing tradition that allowed commanding officers of warships to convey private property for American citizens—and to charge a percentage of the value of the cargo as a commission that went directly to the ship's commanding officer. Even a small percentage of a cargo of specie was likely to be substantial.

News of Buchanan's agreement to this proposal got about, and there was an immediate protest from other local shippers, who objected to what they described as unfair competition. Their protests reached General Thompson, whose inquiry about Buchanan's plans carried an implied accusation. Buchanan was taken aback by the protest, and he denied with some heat that he was motivated by the prospect of personal profit, insisting that he had agreed to the merchants' request solely out of a sense of duty. He argued that "it is the duty of men of war to protect and assist Merchant Vessels, while engaged in their lawful pursuits, and not to throw obstacles in their way." To Hargous he wrote: "I do so as a matter of duty and favour to the Merchants in accordance with my instructions without the slightest wish to interfere with the Merchant Vessels employed in this business. No personal advantage to be derived from carrying specie as freight, can induce me to pursue any other than an honourable and correct course while engaged in this service." In the end, the local merchants decided not to use the *Vincennes*.[20]

Once again, Buchanan felt constrained to write to the secretary of the navy requesting a clarification. Whether he was motivated by frustration at missing out on a possible windfall or by his recognition of the potential damage to the navy's reputation, the public outcry inspired him to urge a change in policy. He declared that the practice of charging a percentage of freight should be outlawed, and that U.S. Navy officers who carried specie or any other commodity on behalf of American merchants overseas should be required to do so as agents for the U.S. government. "I am aware sir," he wrote to the new navy secretary, Harold Henshaw, that "this has not been the practice, and the Navy has suffered in reputation in consequence of the improper course pursued by some of its officers in receiving on board money, the freight of which was for their own personal benefit."[21]

If Buchanan proclaimed himself too pure to accept a fee from commercial agents, accepting a fee from government agents was a different matter. A treaty then existing between the United States and Mexico obligated the Mexicans to make regular indemnity payments to the United States, and on 4 June, Waddy Thompson notified Buchanan that the next payment from Mexico was due in about a month. If the *Vincennes* was still present when it was delivered, Thompson wrote, he would call on Buchanan to take charge of its delivery to the United States. Soon afterward, Buchanan sailed for Campeche and then back to Pensacola, although he planned to return to Vera Cruz in time to take charge of the specie payment. He requested Stewart's permission to accept the assignment and notified Thompson that he was coming back. "By the late treaty

between Mexico and the U. States," he wrote, "I observe that Mexico
agrees to pay $2\frac{1}{2}$ per centum to cover the additional charges of 'freight
commissions' &c. from Vera Cruz to the U. States. As this money comes
out of the Treasury of Mexico, and does not reduce the claim of our citizens, I should be pleased to receive it." Realizing how grasping this must
sound, Buchanan immediately went on to justify his request. "The bills of
lading are signed by me, and I am held responsible for the safe delivery of
the money in the U. States. An order from you appointing me agent to
receive and deliver it, will prevent difficulty hereafter."[22]

Buchanan arrived back at Vera Cruz with the *Vincennes* in the last days
of August—eight days after the date Thompson had given him for the
likely delivery of the specie payment. He immediately informed Thompson that he was ready to take charge of the money. He also noted the
presence of another American warship, the brig *Bainbridge,* at anchor off
Sacrificios. Buchanan communicated with its commanding officer,
Robert E. Johnson, to ask him his orders and intentions. Johnson replied
that he was waiting to pick up Thompson's next batch of dispatches. No
need for that, Buchanan informed him, the *Vincennes* would perform
that duty, and he encouraged Johnson to be off at once. "As I shall remain
here to receive and convey Mr. Thompson's despatches to Pensacola, you
need not be detained for that purpose." Although there was nothing
improper about Buchanan's suggestion, it sounded suspiciously like he
was getting a potential competitor out of the way.[23]

Buchanan finally heard from Thompson on 9 September. The American minister wrote that he did not recall requesting a warship to convey
the money, and he suggested that Buchanan must be mistaken. Annoyed
to be so cavalierly dismissed, Buchanan replied coolly: "As you say nothing on the subject of my remaining here to convey your despatches to the
United States, I shall sail tomorrow in the further execution of my
instructions."[24]

Buchanan no doubt was disappointed to have missed a windfall that
would have gone a long way toward allowing Nannie to escape their
creditors. He was further upset when he found out later that Thompson
had made an agreement with the owner of a private brig, the *Petersburg,*
to carry the payment, and that the shipping expense was to be paid out
of the principal—that is, at the taxpayers' expense. Buchanan now felt
not only that he had been insulted, but also that Thompson had made
an arrangement that had cost the taxpayers money. It made no sense to

pay a commercial shipper when a perfectly good U.S. warship was standing by to do the job for nothing.[25]

Back in Pensacola, he wrote another letter to the Navy Department to complain that in addition to the freight expenses charged to the Mexican government ($6,674.45), the shippers billed the U.S. claimants another $2\frac{1}{2}$ percent, or $3,286.68. When his protest found its way into the public media, the government felt constrained to respond. An article in the *New Orleans Picayune* expressed the official version. It was not true, the article maintained, that Captain Buchanan "offered to transport the money free of charge. He did offer to do so if the charge for freight was to be paid by the Government, but if that charge was to be paid by the claimants, as it certainly would have been, he expected to be paid for it." The article implied that Buchanan's pique resulted not from the fleecing of U.S. taxpayers, but from the loss of his own commission. Buchanan responded in a letter to the editor fraught with outraged honor. He admitted his willingness to accept a fee paid by the Mexican government but denied heatedly that he would have collected any money from the claimants. In high dudgeon he wrote: "In offering to convey it free of charge to the claimants, I did so under a full conviction that it was my duty, for doing which I neither claimed nor felt myself entitled to credit."[26]

Meanwhile, affairs between Mexico and the United States continued to deteriorate. Rumors were rife that Santa Anna was about to close the ports to all non-Mexicans as a preliminary step to a declaration of war. Buchanan arrived off Vera Cruz a few days after Christmas and found General Thompson desperately trying to stave off an open breach. Thompson told Buchanan that he had some dispatches for Washington, but he also suggested that Buchanan postpone sailing for a few days, as he might have to ask to take passage himself.[27]

A few days later, there was an anxious moment or two aboard the *Vincennes* when the huge guns of the fortress at Vera Cruz opened fire, but it turned out to be only a salute in celebration of Santa Anna's reelection as president. Buchanan remained at anchor waiting to see if Thompson would have to make a quick escape. Finally, assured that things were once again quiet, he left with the dispatch bag for Pensacola on 21 February. There the ship revictualed, a ship's party recruited new men from New Orleans, and Buchanan enjoyed an evening as the guest of honor at a formal ball.[28]

After a quick cruise to Havana, the *Vincennes* sailed to Galveston in May. The U.S. chargé d'affaires there told him that U.S. relations with Mexico were worse than ever. This was confirmed in June when General Thompson arrived aboard the steamer *Poinsett*. The *Poinsett*'s commander, Raphael Semmes, told Buchanan that war with Mexico was both certain and imminent. Buchanan took it upon himself to warn the squadron commander, David Conner, who was then en route to Vera Cruz. "By Lieut Comdg Semmes," he wrote, "I learned that General Santa Anna President of Mexico, will not listen to the proposition of our government relating to the annexation of Texas to the United States, but declares that such an act on the part of the U. States will be considered by Mexico a declaration of war. Under the impression that this news might be important as to your future movements, and the distribution of Ships of your squadron, I directed the commanders of the Somers Union and Poinsett to endeavor to intercept you on your passage to Vera Cruz."[29]

The American squadron rendezvoused at Pensacola on Independence Day, and set sail from there for Norfolk at the end of the month. As by far the fastest ship, the *Vincennes* continually had to take in sail to keep from running away from the rest of the squadron, but finally, on 6 August, the lookout sighted Cape Henry light, and the squadron dropped anchor off Norfolk the next day. On the fifteenth, Buchanan mustered the crew, paid off the hands, and discharged them. The *Vincennes* went into dry dock, and Commander Franklin Buchanan made his way by public conveyance back to the Rest.[30]

In his first command at sea, Buchanan had reconfirmed his reputation as a diligent disciplinarian; without doubt he ran a smart ship. And he demonstrated as well his ship-handling skills in saving the *Vincennes* from possible disaster on the reefs off Trinidad. But it also became evident that he was more than a bit "at sea" when it came to dealing with the more ambiguous problems associated with the treacherous world of diplomacy and negotiation. He allowed himself to become testy with the U.S. minister to Mexico; he was indiscreet with local businessmen; and he exposed himself to public criticism for his apparent eagerness to carry the specie payments of both private and public authorities. In the end, it did not matter. The Navy Department clearly considered his cruise a success, and in fact, had plans to hand him an even more responsible assignment, one in which his navywide reputation for discipline would be a particular asset.

~❧ 5 ❧~

THE NAVAL SCHOOL

A work which promises so much good to the country.

I n July 1845 Buchanan received orders from the new secretary of
the navy, George Bancroft, to report to him personally in Washington. He crossed the bay to Annapolis, took the train to Washington,
and presented himself at Main Navy in a nearly deserted capital. He
could not have been unaware of the reason for the summons. Buchanan
was a man who kept his ear to the ground, especially when it came to
keeping track of what he called "Navy news." He was certainly aware
that Bancroft had asked the Board of Examiners at the Philadelphia
"Asylum"—where midshipmen prepared for the lieutenant's exam—to
submit recommendations for the establishment of a permanent school
for midshipmen. Very likely, he was also aware that the board had
expressed support for Bancroft's proposal that such a school be founded
on the site of old Fort Severn in Annapolis, virtually across the street
from Buchanan's home on Scott Street. He may even have known that
the board had declined to nominate a naval officer to head the new institution. Bancroft had invited them to suggest a candidate, but the board
members (three commodores and two captains) begged off, citing the
"delicacy" of such a question but noting suggestively that any one of
them would "cheerfully contribute their best services in perfecting a
work which promises so much good to the country."[1]

The board members expressed their collective view that the person selected to head the new school should be at least a captain, and that he should be assisted by a commander (to act as executive officer) and three lieutenants, plus a surgeon, a purser, clerks, and others. The staff would total twenty altogether, not including marine guards and "a sufficient number of servants, cooks, etc." But Bancroft was politically astute enough to know that Congress would balk at establishing what might appear to be a financial sinkhole involving the employment of high-ranking officers onshore at the taxpayers' expense. Bancroft wanted to establish his school with as little fanfare as possible; in modern parlance, he wanted to keep a low profile. Rather than appoint a commodore or a senior captain to command, therefore, he looked for a relatively junior commander, a man with recent command experience at sea and a navy-wide reputation for strict enforcement of discipline. And so he sent for Franklin Buchanan.[2]

For two hundred years and more, the most fundamental assumption about education for naval officers was that the best school was the school of experience. Young men of good moral character but little formal education spent years at sea, learning by doing as Buchanan had done, until they passed an exam to become eligible for promotion to lieutenant. The "school of the sea" was a thorough taskmaster in terms of practical navigation and seamanship, but the "young gentlemen" often learned little about theoretical science or any other higher education besides what they got from the ship's officers, who instructed them in arithmetic and trigonometry. In theory they could have been instructed as well by an embarked schoolmaster, but in practice only ships of the line, of which the United States had but two in the 1840s, warranted a schoolmaster. On all other ships, the chaplain acted as schoolmaster, although knowledge of any of the subjects he was supposed to teach was not a prerequisite for the job. Most of the time the chaplains taught, as the instruction to them put it, "whatsoever [they] may contribute"; often that was very little.[3]

Of course, there were many who defended this system. Men who were products of it asserted with some defensiveness that it had served *them* well enough, and fought any suggestion that it should be changed. But things were changing nonetheless in the navy of the 1840s. It could no longer be argued that learning to shoot the sun and calculating the set and drift of a ship under sail constituted a sufficient professional education. Steam engineering and rifled guns with significantly greater ranges necessitated an understanding of fundamental chemistry and physics. Then, too, there was the quite different concern that life at sea was not necessarily the best moral environment for boys in their early teens. Sailors were still issued a daily tot of rum, and often spent their shore leave engaging in revelries that caused the mothers of young midshipmen to wonder if they had not committed their sons to a life of debauchery. In February 1842, the *Southern Literary Messenger* spoke for many when it asserted that "a naval academy is much needed; nay, the public interest, the honor and welfare of the service, absolutely require it."[4]

The issue gained even more prominence only a few months later when news of the so-called *Somers* mutiny became public. The *Somers* was a regularly commissioned U.S. Navy warship selected to serve as a training vessel for new enlisted recruits. Its command had been entrusted to Buchanan's old messmate from the *Java*, Alexander Slidell Mackenzie. Serving under him were two lieutenants, a purser, a surgeon, and seven midshipmen, four of them teenagers, including nineteen-year-old Philip Spenser, the son of the secretary of war. Collectively, Mackenzie and his wardroom were charged with the supervision of the ninety-three sailors onboard, seventy-four of whom were newly recruited "boys" under the age of sixteen. After an uneventful cruise across the Atlantic to deliver dispatches to the American squadron off West Africa, the *Somers* began its return trip in November. During the voyage, word reached Mackenzie that Midshipman Spenser was plotting a mutiny in collaboration with two of the more hard-boiled enlisted men. The plan, apparently, was to kill the officers and throw them over the side, then compel the ship's young crew to choose between signing on with the mutineers for a piratical cruise in the West Indies or joining their officers in the briny deep. After a brief investigation, Mackenzie arrested the three suspects and confined them in irons; but fear that Spenser's friends in the crew might attempt a rescue led him to act decisively— some said precipitously. He convened a summary court martial, which found the three ringleaders guilty of mutiny and recommended hanging as the punishment. Mackenzie followed the court's recommendation and had the three men hanged.

When the *Somers* docked in New York City in January 1843, news that a navy commander had summarily executed the son of the secretary

of war created a sensation. Although Mackenzie was formally exoner-
ated of wrongdoing, the incident and the subsequent public scandal led
to renewed discussion about the procedures used for training both
enlisted sailors and midshipmen. The event added a sense of urgency to
the on-again, off-again proposal to establish a shore-based school for
prospective naval officers. Charles Stewart, who presided over Mackenzie's court martial, concluded that future crises of this nature could be
prevented if a single national shore-based school for midshipmen were
established.[5]

It fell to Bancroft, who became secretary of the navy in March 1845,
to take the lead. His first few months in office were taken up with posi-
tioning the fleet to deal with the burgeoning crisis with Mexico, but in
June he charged the Board of Examiners at Philadelphia to report on the
desirability of establishing a permanent Naval School. He managed to
word his request in such a way as to suggest that the issue was not so
much whether a school should be established, but whether Fort Severn
in Annapolis was the best location for it. He was treading dangerous
ground here, for Bancroft knew that Congress, already suspicious of
enlarging the military establishment, would accede to the plan only if it
could be effected without any additional appropriation. In this, Bancroft
found an invaluable ally in the person of Passed Midn. Samuel L. Marcy.
Young Marcy was not only the assistant to Prof. William Chauvenet, who
taught mathematics at the Philadelphia Asylum, he was also the son of
the new secretary of war, William L. Marcy. Encouraged by his son, the
elder Marcy traveled with Bancroft to Annapolis in June to look over the
site at Fort Severn, and soon thereafter agreed to turn the fort over to
the navy. A month later, Buchanan reported to Bancroft in Washington
and learned that he was the secretary's choice to command the new
Naval School at Annapolis.[6]

During Buchanan's initial conversation with Bancroft about the new
school, it became evident that the navy secretary intended to entrust him
with virtually all of the details concerning the school's establishment and
organization. While Buchanan could solicit advice from his friend Du
Pont and from William W. McKean, who would join him on the three-
man board charged with suggesting rules and regulations for the Naval
School, Buchanan would be the only commissioned officer (other than
the instructors) appointed to the school on a permanent basis. In effect,

Buchanan would run the school single-handed. It was crucial, Bancroft told him, that the organization be as lean as possible, and he directed Buchanan "to incur no charge that may demand new annual appropriations." Beyond that stipulation, however, Bancroft was apparently willing to leave the management of the school almost entirely to Buchanan's discretion. Pleased as he was with this vote of confidence, Buchanan also experienced a moment or two of doubt. "He holds me responsible for the entire organization of the establishment," he wrote Du Pont. "I may perhaps have accepted a responsibility beyond my capability."[7]

At least Buchanan was pleased that Bancroft was "disposed to be liberal as far as the efficiency of the establishment" was concerned— "efficiency" in this context being a euphemism for discipline. Bancroft was surely aware of Buchanan's reputation in the navy for strict discipline—indeed, it was very likely one of the reasons he had selected him for the job—and Bancroft obviously expected Buchanan to live up to that reputation in superintending the Naval School. The secretary asserted that a midshipman's warrant was "a pledge for subordination, industry, & regularity, for sobriety and assiduous attention to duty," and he urged Buchanan to make of the young men "an exemplary body of which the Country may be proud," reminding him that "you have all the powers for discipline conferred by the laws of Congress."[8]

As he rode the train back to Annapolis, Buchanan mulled over his new assignment. The first class of midshipmen was due to arrive in October, barely two months away, and he had to make some immediate decisions. The first issue to be resolved concerned the curriculum. What exactly would the midshipmen be taught? On this point he did not lack for advice. The Board of Examiners had suggested using the Military Academy as a model, and Bancroft had dispatched Prof. Henry Lockwood to West Point to identify what could be learned of its program that might be applicable to the new Naval School. The board recommended that the course of study at Annapolis "be almost identically the same" as at West Point; "the only difference should be in omitting in the mathematical department the abstruse study of the Calculus, and occupying the time thus saved in more practical branches." Indeed, practicality was to be the hallmark of the new institution. Bancroft offered his own ideas about the curriculum, suggesting to Buchanan the inclusion of "mathematics, nautical astronomy, theory of morals, international law, gunnery, use of steam, the Spanish and French languages, and other branches essential in the present day to the accomplishment of a naval officer."[9]

In receipt of this advice, Buchanan compiled his own list of subjects, which he divided into four general topic areas: "English grammar and composition; arithmetic, geography, and history; navigation, gunnery, and the use of steam; [and] the Spanish and French languages." One factor he had to keep in mind was that the midshipmen at Annapolis could at any moment be recalled to sea. The course of study thus had to be contrived so that students could enter or leave a class in mid-course. As Bancroft put it: "you will be obliged to arrange your classes in such a manner as will leave opportunity for those who arrive to be attached to classes suited to their state of progress in their studies." Bancroft acknowledged that "it will be difficult to arrange a system of students which will meet this emergency," but he expressed confidence that "with the fixed resolve which you will bring to the work and with perseverance you will succeed."[10]

With the curriculum resolved, Buchanan turned his attention to the selection of a faculty. Once again he got valuable cooperation from Bancroft. There were twenty-two "professors" on the navy rolls in 1845, each of whom was paid $1,200 a year.[11] Bancroft planned to place half of them on furlough. Since the professors were not paid when not employed (unlike officers), that would yield a savings of some $13,000, which Bancroft planned to use to fund the new school. Of the eleven professors remaining after this purge, five would continue to serve at sea, three others would remain on duty at the Naval Observatory, one would be delegated to "special service," and the other two—the mathematician William Chauvenet and the natural scientist Henry H. Lockwood—would be ordered to join Buchanan at Annapolis. Buchanan contracted with a third civilian, Arsène Napoléon Alexandre Girault, to teach French.

In addition to these three civilians, Buchanan would have four officer instructors: two line officers and two staff officers. Line officer Lt. James H. Ward would teach both gunnery and steam and would double as Buchanan's executive officer; Passed Midn. Marcy, whose family connections had been so helpful, would assist Chauvenet in teaching math. The two staff officers were Surgeon John A. Lockwood (Henry's brother), who would teach chemistry, and Chaplain George Jones, who would teach

English, history, and geography. It was a small cadre, but Buchanan was generally pleased. "My officers go on as I should wish," he wrote to Du Pont in September, "I am making all hands comfortable."[12]

To make the faculty comfortable, as well as to prepare for the arrival of the midshipmen, Buchanan had to supervise important modifications to the facilities at Fort Severn. The brick wall around the old army post enclosed just under nine acres. In addition to the circular fort at Windmill Point where Spa Creek and the Severn River met the Chesapeake Bay, there were a number of buildings inside the post that could be converted to educational purposes. After a brief survey of the property, Buchanan chose the old Dulaney mansion, a two-story brick home that had been the army commandant's headquarters, as his own. A row of four smaller houses alongside it would provide quarters for Lieutenant Ward, Surgeon Lockwood, and Professors Chauvenet and Lockwood. Marcy would share quarters with Professor Lockwood. Professor Girault (who arrived late) and Chaplain Jones boarded together in the Buchanans' former home on Scott Street just outside the gate. Other buildings on the grounds had to be modified to serve as midshipmen's quarters and recitation rooms. Buchanan set carpenters to work making the necessary changes, and he approved the purchase of eighty iron bed frames (at eight dollars each) plus some chairs and tables to furnish the rooms.[13]

One element of Buchanan's arrangements that is especially intriguing in light of some of his later decisions concerns his efforts to secure the employment of an individual to serve as steward for the nearly three score midshipmen who would arrive in October. He arranged for Darius King, a free black man, to take the job, and, sensitive to Bancroft's concern for economy, he decided that King would be paid by contributions from the midshipmen themselves. For the twelve dollars a month paid by each midshipman, King would buy, cook, and serve three meals a day. That worked out to about thirteen cents per meal—clearly a bargain for the midshipmen. But Buchanan ran into difficulty when it was pointed out to him that an 1831 Maryland law—passed in the wake of the Nat Turner rebellion in Virginia—forbade the immigration of free blacks into the state unless they were under contract to a white employer. Buchanan resolved the issue by asking that King be carried on the Navy List "at a nominal pay of one cent per month" so that state authorities would allow him to move to Annapolis. Buchanan's solution to this problem suggests not only a determination to keep costs down, but also an eminently pragmatic attitude about the issue of free blacks, an attitude as yet unaffected by any personal or ideological agenda.[14]

Each week during the frenetic two months of preparations, Buchanan took the train from Annapolis to Washington to report personally to Bancroft. The secretary offered occasional suggestions, but for the most part he merely listened and nodded. It was a measure of Bancroft's satisfaction that after many of these chats he asked Buchanan to stay for dinner, and that at least once he escorted Buchanan back to the rail station in his personal carriage.[15]

While his faculty settled into their new quarters and prepared their lessons, Buchanan's own family—Nannie and their six children—moved into the Dulaney mansion. Nannie was not unhappy to move back across the bay to Annapolis. It had been their first home, and she had friends and family there. Then, too, the Dulaney mansion was a handsome property, and Nannie was eager to make it the social as well as the official center of the new school. She was delighted, therefore, when her husband returned from one of his regular trips to Washington to report that Bancroft had authorized new wallpaper and curtains. For the first time, Nannie and the children lived amid the regimentation of a naval command. She had to adjust, for example, to the naval clock, which chimed the bells every half hour, and she reported to her mother that she ran the household—including the children's activities—with "proper man of war discipline."[16]

The school opened on 10 October 1845. At eleven o'clock that morning, Buchanan stepped in front of more than two score midshipmen, ranging in age from eighteen to twenty-seven, who stood at attention in one of the recitation halls. Buchanan deliberately chose to stage the event as a formal change of command in order to imbue his young charges with the notion that they were to consider themselves under the same rules of discipline that would apply if they had been at sea. In that spirit, he read aloud "in the vigorous tones peculiar to him" the "Rules and Regulations" he had written for the school. For the most part it was a routine list of unexceptional rules that demanded "strict obedience" and "courteous deportment." The rules made it clear that all midshipmen were "required to obey the commands of the professors," who were in turn held "responsible for the regular and orderly conduct of their respective classes." Attendance at class, Buchanan declared, was mandatory, and during study hours midshipmen were "not permitted to lounge or promenade about the grounds"; nor were they to leave the grounds without permission. Unsurprisingly, Buchanan decreed that "no midshipman shall bring, or cause to be brought, within the limits of this institution, any wine, porter, or other intoxicating or spiritous liquors." He followed up this formal recitation with a speech in which he again stressed the importance of temperance and obedience. He warned the young gentlemen that he would dutifully punish any and all transgressions of the rules because he, too, was duty bound to fulfill his obligations.[17]

Of course, asserting the rules was one thing, ensuring their practical observation was another. The most senior of the midshipmen, those whose warrants dated 1840 or earlier, occupied a small frame house that came to be known as Apollo Row. They formed a so-called Spirit Club that met regularly at Harry Matthews's tavern on Main Street. These five-year veterans, known as the "Oldsters," had seen a lot of sea time and had grown accustomed to thinking of assignments ashore as a release from discipline; more than a few were inclined to test the boundaries of Buchanan's "Rules and Regulations." In those rules, Buchanan had taken care to assert that professors were to have authority over their charges, but many midshipmen were convinced that such authority extended only to academic matters, and that their own status as U.S. Navy midshipmen rendered their personal conduct beyond the concern of civilian instructors. A contemporary recalled that "student life at the school was for some years a downright battle between the rulers and the ruled."[18]

Classes had been in session for a little over a month when, on the afternoon of 24 November, Professor Girault, the French teacher, came to Buchanan's office and handed him a letter concerning an incident that had occurred in Girault's classroom that morning. As Girault described it, the midshipmen were sitting in their seats as he walked around the classroom, calling on students at random, when he noticed that one of them, Midn. David Ochiltree, a six-year navy veteran, had his book open. Saying nothing at the time, Girault continued walking. When the next student finished, Girault called on Mr. Ochiltree, who responded with what Girault called "unusual accuracy." Because he could not see if Ochiltree still had his book open, he asked him directly, "Mr. Ochiltree is your book still opened?" Ochiltree, thinking that

Girault had asked him if his book was closed, answered "in the affirmative." Girault let the matter go and continued with the lesson. But at the end of class, Ochiltree, instead of leaving the room, approached Girault and challenged him: "What right had you, sir, to ask me that question?"

Ochiltree's question was prompted by his belief that Girault had stepped beyond his authority as a professor into the realm of professional honor by implying, in a public place, that Ochiltree was capable of cheating. Admitting that he had had his book open before the recitation, but not during it, Ochiltree asked for a public apology from Girault for daring to express doubt about such an issue. Girault responded by saying that Ochiltree should have had his book closed even while the others were reciting. Even angrier now, Ochiltree declared, "You had no right, sir, to ask me that question!" This time it was a statement, not a question. Girault, who had another class of students filing in the door, did not want to bandy words with the young man and ordered him to leave the room. Ochiltree was no more likely to accept the idea that a civilian could order him from the room than he was to admit that a civilian could impugn his honor, and he responded belligerently: "Sir, I will go when I please." But then he did leave, and after completing his next class, Girault wrote up the incident and submitted it to Buchanan.[19]

Buchanan's first instinct was to support the professor and rebuke the midshipman, but before acting he asked Ochiltree to write up his version of the event. That young man characterized the incident as a question of personal and professional honor. "Mr. Girault asked me a question which was in a manner impeaching my honor," Ochiltree wrote. Girault, he insisted, had intended "to convey an idea that I was reciting from a book." Even to ask the question was a slur on his honor, Ochiltree insisted; if anyone should apologize, it was Girault. Ochiltree spoke for many of the Oldsters when he asserted that a professor's authority did not, and should not, extend to questions of personal honor. Imputations of dishonor, just or unjust, were simply not within the authority of any civilian. Ochiltree even challenged the authority of a professor to give an order to a midshipmen: "I am not aware, sir, that a Professor is my superior officer and has a right to give me an order."[20]

Buchanan checked with other midshipmen who had witnessed the event, inquiring particularly if Mr. Girault's manner had been accusatory or offensive. Satisfied by their responses that it had not, he concluded that Girault had acted entirely within his authority. It was essential to establish on the firmest possible footing the classroom authority of Annapolis professors. But Buchanan did feel some qualms about establishing this precedent on his own say-so. His commitment to discipline had heretofore consisted largely of applying existing rules of conduct and behavior; indeed, his great strength as a commanding officer was his dogged determination to fulfill his duty as he understood it. But on this occasion, as at other times in his professional career, he was less sure of himself when confronted with ambiguity. Aware that his decision in this case was likely to establish a precedent, he decided to refer the whole question to Secretary Bancroft.

In his letter to Bancroft, Buchanan wrote that Ochiltree's argument was evidence of "the disposition on the part of some of his grade to dispute the authority of a Professor over a Midn. . . . As this is the first act of insubordination towards a Professor, I respectfully request that an example be made of Mr. Ochiltree." Yet the example that Buchanan recommended was less than draconian. He asked Bancroft to write a reprimand, which Buchanan would read publicly before the assembled midshipmen. He also asked Bancroft to rule on the key issue: "the authority of a Professor to order a Midn to leave the recitation room for an act of insubordination."[21]

Bancroft had appointed Buchanan to the Naval School in the first place because of his reputation as a disciplinarian, and he was a bit surprised now that Buchanan did not act more assertively against the offending midshipman. In his response, Bancroft wrote that he "would readily have acquiesced if, instead of the reprimand which you suggest, you had recommended [Ochiltree's] removal from the institution and the service." But since Buchanan recommended a letter of reprimand, Bancroft supplied one. In it he warned Ochiltree and the other midshipmen that it was due to Commander Buchanan's "indulgent recommendation, and not to any disposition on the part of the Department to treat such offense with lenity," that Ochiltree avoided immediate dismissal.[22]

There was no other serious breach of discipline that fall. In December, Buchanan reacted angrily to a charge by a Mr. Denison that there had been "instances of conduct unbecoming a gentleman" on the part of several midshipmen. Buchanan hotly denied the charge, responding that the citizens of Annapolis all spoke very highly of the conduct of the

midshipmen. There was not "the slightest foundation for such a complaint," he asserted, and he felt vindicated a month later when Denison
was expelled from the First Baptist Church for "lying and obtaining
money under false pretenses." That same January, the Oldsters of Apollo
Row hosted a formal ball for the elite of Annapolis as a way of recipro-
cating the hospitality of the community.[23]

Inevitably, however, behavior problems did arise—problems of a character sure to provoke Buchanan's wrath. The cold days and long nights
of February—the "dark ages," in midshipmen's parlance—apparently led
more than one midshipman to seek solace in spiritous liquors. The most
infamous case was that of Midn. Augustus McLaughlin, who in mid-
February requested leave to visit his sick mother in Baltimore. Buchanan
readily granted it and wished the young man Godspeed. But then, that
very evening, he encountered McLaughlin playing a game of billiards in
an Annapolis tavern! What about the sick mother? he inquired.
McLaughlin claimed that he had missed his train and was waiting for
the next one. But Buchanan heard McLaughlin's slurred speech and saw
at once that the midshipman had been drinking—heavily. This time
there was no ambiguity. Buchanan filed charges, convened a court martial, and immediately approved the court's sentence of expulsion.
Although a number of McLaughlin's friends appealed to the secretary of
the navy for clemency, Buchanan argued that "no drunkard should be
tolerated in the Navy." Bancroft agreed and accepted Buchanan's ruling,
writing to him: "Your prompt course in this matter meets the entire
approbation of the Department." Alas, McLaughlin was not the only
midshipman to be discovered in his cups that month, and there were
several other charges of intoxication. Some cases led to expulsion; others provoked abject apologies and pledges of good behavior that allowed
the culprits to survive.[24]

In addition to his supervision of the midshipmen, Buchanan also had to
manage the finances of the Naval School. On this as on other issues,
Bancroft gave him wide latitude. The secretary merely asked him to send
the Navy Department an estimate of the amount of money he would
need to run the school each month. Unless Buchanan heard otherwise,
he was to consider all such submissions approved. In this manner, the
school lived month to month—much as Buchanan did in his household
expenses.[25]

Indeed, if the school's finances were often precarious, Buchanan's own accounts were nothing short of disastrous. Money had always been a problem for the Buchanan family, and with their move to Annapolis the problems multiplied. Nannie felt an obligation to make the superintendent's quarters as presentable as possible, and to entertain as well, but these ambitions ran up against their limited means. Although she attempted to save money by effecting small economies such as sewing up tears in the children's clothes rather than buying them new ones, the money nevertheless drained away. She complained to her mother that groceries in Annapolis were expensive, and she bought only what was absolutely necessary from day to day. The problem was compounded by the fact that visitors from Washington (the "great folks," she called them) arrived regularly and expected to be fed and entertained. At one point she confessed to her brother that "our bank is entirely broken," and asked to borrow two dollars in order to pay wages owed to a servant. In time she accumulated much larger debts to several Annapolis merchants. Unable to pay them in a timely manner, she was embarrassed to go back and ask for more credit. The situation got so bad that she literally had to worry about the family eating. "If I do not get some money," Nannie wrote to her mother in November, "I know nothing about what we'll do in the eating department. We are all out of supplies and I was ashamed to send to any of the merchants for a few cents worth until I can pay them bills of nearly three years standing." She had to travel to Baltimore to shop because she was loath to ask the local merchants to further extend her credit. Alas, the next month she was reporting to her mother, "I have not a cent. . . . We must try and borrow from the bank again. If you think there is any use in writing to my brothers, I'll beg you to do so." The family's strained circumstances did not, however, prevent Franklin from continued gestures of generosity to his wife. That same month, Nannie wrote her mother the news that her husband had surprised her with "a beautiful piano," confessing that "he had to borrow to pay for it."[26]

Buchanan must have felt a twinge of guilt only a few months later when he read aloud to the assembled midshipmen an order from Secretary Bancroft about the importance of personal financial responsibility. It was the policy of the department, Buchanan read aloud in the "vigorous tones" that he used in all his public addresses, to discourage midshipmen from "a disposition to incur debts beyond their means of punctual payment." He announced that henceforth, any midshipman who incurred a debt while a student at the Naval School would be considered as having failed the course of study. Moreover, any midshipman who left Annapolis while carrying a debt on the books of any local merchant would be reported to the Navy Department.[27]

Money problems or not, the Buchanans' social regimen continued. As hosts for all official events, the commander and his wife were expected to be present at the ball hosted by the Oldsters of Apollo Row in January and at the play held in town in the spring. Both husband and wife found that every waking minute was fully occupied. "We are all the time in a bustle," Nannie complained to her mother, "and I never felt so tired in my life. It seems unavoidable at times: company calling all the time." Musical parties were particularly popular. Couples would gather at one or another of the professors' homes to sing and entertain one another. The Chauvenets hosted one such affair at Christmas, and Nannie reported to her mother: "We had a most agreeable evening."[28]

In addition to her social duties, Nannie stood in loco parentis for many of the midshipmen, particularly the "Youngsters," those aged thirteen to sixteen who were mere children themselves. Midshipmen who fell ill during the school term were her particular concern; she took them into her home and nursed them as if they were her own. She wrote to their parents and consulted with Surgeon Lockwood about their condition. "Poor little dear," she wrote her mother about one of them, "he seems anxious to see [his mother] and his case, we fear, is a hopeless one." She sat up with the most serious cases, fed them soup, and called the doctor when they worsened.[29]

After only one semester, Buchanan considered the Naval School a success. More important, so did Bancroft. In his annual report to Congress in December, the secretary made a point of praising Buchanan, who, he said, "has carried his instructions into effect with precision and sound judgement, and with a wide adaptation of simple and moderate means to [achieve] a great and noble end." And if official praise was not enough, there was public praise as well. *Niles Weekly Register* reported the next month that Buchanan supervised the discipline of the midshipmen "in person with the tone, system, and energy for which he is distinguished."[30]

The following June (1846), Buchanan presided over the school's first annual exams. Fifty-two midshipmen submitted to written and oral exams administered by the usual five-man Board of Examiners, headed that year by Commodores Charles Ridgley and Matthew C. Perry. Thirty-four of the Oldsters took the lieutenant's exam. The others took interim exams. The event was conducted with great solemnity and ceremony. The professors and board members first paraded through town to the Naval School, where the professors conducted the exams while the board members watched. All midshipmen were required to pass the portion of the exam that concerned seamanship and navigation, but they could fail any other portion so long as their overall performance was satisfactory. Of the fifty-two midshipmen, twelve failed one portion or another, but only seven were found to be "not studious," and only three were "returned to their friends," the euphemism used to describe expulsion.[31]

On the whole, the examiners were pleased. They reported their satisfaction to Bancroft, who in turn lauded the school to Congress. That body responded by authorizing its usual annual appropriation of $28,000 for midshipman training, but this time stipulating that the funds could be used for "repairs, improvements, and instruction at Fort Severn." Buchanan immediately asked for an appropriation to allow him to purchase wood, paint, nails, and so on for "repairing Midn rooms, repairing and painting part of [the] Professor's houses [and] for enclosing part of the grounds." By midsummer the grounds were being transformed again as the Naval School expanded.[32]

By then, Buchanan had other things on his mind. The war with Mexico, long simmering, had finally exploded into violence along the disputed border. With real war in the offing, Buchanan applied to Bancroft for active service. The secretary turned him down, but gently, promising that he would not be forgotten. "Were it not for the important business in which you are presently engaged," Bancroft wrote back, "you would be one of the first on whom the Department would call." Buchanan was probably not surprised at this answer, but it must have been difficult for him to forward orders for active duty to his young students while he stayed behind. He even had to advance the examination date in 1846 so that his students could go off to war.[33]

Not until the spring of 1847 did Buchanan get orders to active duty. In March he left Annapolis to take command of the USS *Germantown* at Norfolk. He spent a year on the *Germantown* and saw a great deal of action, earning two commendations for his gallantry. But nothing he did in the war against Mexico approached the historical importance of his work as the first superintendent of the Naval Academy. His stern and forbidding demeanor, his commitment to order and discipline, and his almost pedantic attention to detail were precisely the strengths necessary to set the Naval Academy on a straight course. Surviving month to month financially, and coping day to day with his curious responsibilities as a combination commanding officer and headmaster, he managed to please his superiors without antagonizing his juniors. He would have been pleased to know that a century and a half later, the superintendent's home at the Naval Academy is still called Buchanan House.

~6~

WAR AND DIPLOMACY

My language was not guarded or very mild.

In thirty years of service as an officer in the U.S. Navy, Franklin Buchanan had never served on a ship that fired a shot in anger. On numerous occasions the vessel on which he was serving had fired across the bow of a suspected pirate or slaver, but in each case the suspected miscreant proved to be either innocent or elusive. As a result, he had never participated in the kind of bloody naval encounter that had inflamed his imagination as a youth. His appointment to the command of the U.S. sloop-of-war *Germantown* in 1847 promised to change that. Here, at last, was an opportunity to win fame and glory in a war against a foreign power.

The war was the result of a disagreement over the location of the Texas-Mexico border. Although Texas had won its independence from Mexico in 1836, Mexicans continued to think of that province as part of their national territory, and when the United States annexed the state in 1845, the Mexican government protested. Furthermore, Mexico insisted that the Texas-Mexico boundary was the Nueces River, not the Rio Grande, as claimed by Texas and (after annexation) the United States. Both countries sent armed patrols into the disputed territory between the two rivers, and in late April 1846 the inevitable clash took place. Asserting that "American blood had been shed on American soil," the United States declared war.[1]

Initially, the principal theater of war was along the Rio Grande. General Zachary Taylor led an American army across the river and defeated the Mexican army in several important battles in the spring and fall of 1846. But when these victories did not bring about a political solution, it became clear that complete victory could be secured only by landing an army on the Mexican coast and marching inland to occupy the capital. This shift in strategy, decided in November 1846 while Buchanan was still superintending the Naval School at Annapolis, gave the U.S. Navy a much larger role in the war. Indeed, for the navy, the war against Mexico presented strategic problems very different from those of earlier wars.

Appreciating America's great superiority in naval assets, the Mexicans did not contest command of the sea. Instead they adopted the traditional strategy of weaker naval powers: they relied on privateers to raid enemy commerce and they defended the coastline with fortifications—essentially the same strategy used by the United States against Great Britain in two wars and the strategy the Confederacy would adopt in 1861. For its part, the United States relied on the strategy traditionally practiced by the British in their wars against nonnaval powers: blockading the coast, suppressing commerce raiders, and operating against the shore—a strategy that foreshadowed Union operations against the Confederacy.[2]

The U.S. Navy found its logistic capabilities stretched to the limit in applying this strategy. One reason was simply that the United States possessed too few vessels to blockade the Mexican coast efficiently; often the blockade of a city had to be entrusted to a single vessel. In addition, it proved nearly impossible to keep the steam-powered warships supplied with coal while they operated hundreds of miles from friendly bases; the eighteen-hundred-mile round trip from Vera Cruz to Pensacola to re-coal burned up almost as much fuel as the bunkers could hold. Finally, the geography of the Gulf coast seemed to conspire against the Americans, for none of the coastal cities offered protected anchorages offshore where a blockading fleet could ride out a storm. As if to demonstrate this, the ill-fated *Somers* went down off Vera Cruz in December 1846. Rather than passively blockade, therefore, the U.S. Navy undertook to capture and occupy the important Mexican coastal cities by amphibious assault. Although he got a late start, Buchanan would play a key role in this effort.[3]

Released at last from his obligations in Annapolis, Buchanan traveled to Norfolk and took command of the *Germantown* during its commissioning ceremony on 9 March 1847, coincidentally the same day Winfield Scott's army landed on the Mexican coast south of Vera Cruz. The *Germantown* was a brand-new warship, rushed to completion after the U.S. declaration of war. Named in honor of the Revolutionary War Battle of Germantown, it was a flush-decked sloop some 150 feet in length (23 feet longer than the *Vincennes*) with a complement of 210 officers and men. The ship carried twenty-two guns, eighteen of them thirty-two-pound carronades. Buchanan wasted no time in getting under way; he sailed for the Gulf six days after taking command, and arrived off Vera Cruz on the first of April.[4]

As the *Germantown* dropped anchor in the roadstead amid the scores of transports and warships of the U.S. squadron, Buchanan could see the American flag flying above the Mexican citadel of San Juan de Ulloa, which had surrendered to the invaders only three days earlier. The sight must have evoked mixed feelings in the forty-six-year-old navy commander. He had missed the War of 1812 by a matter of days, and now, apparently, he was too late for this war as well. He need not have worried, for the war had another full year to run, and if he had missed a chance to play a role in the siege of Vera Cruz, there were other important targets on the Mexican Gulf coast.

Buchanan reported his arrival to the new American squadron commander, Matthew C. Perry, who had replaced David Conner only days before. Buchanan knew Perry not only as the late Oliver Hazard Perry's younger brother, but also because Perry had presided over the Board of Examiners at Annapolis the year before. Moreover, Buchanan knew that Perry was a man (like Buchanan himself) who preferred action to contemplation. Indeed, Perry and Buchanan saw eye to eye on most things. Both men considered themselves reformers in that they supported the adoption of new technology, and both were also traditionalists in their attitude toward discipline. Both, for example, were stout defenders of flogging, a practice that was coming under increasing criticism both inside and outside the navy. Much later, a disagreement between the two men would convince Buchanan that Perry had feet of clay, but in April 1847 he was delighted to be assigned to Perry's command, and he enthusiastically welcomed Perry aboard the *Germantown* when the commodore visited the ship on 9 April. To a friend in Annapolis, Buchanan gushed that Perry was "the most industrious, hard working, energetic, zealous, persevering, enterprising officer of his rank in our navy."[5]

Perry's orders to Buchanan were to sail at once to the mouth of the
Tuxpan River, 180 miles north of Vera Cruz. With Winfield Scott's army
safely launched on its march to Mexico City, Perry was eager to close
down the few remaining Mexican port cities not already in American
hands. He started with Tuxpan because he believed American honor was
at stake there. The previous August, the American sloop-of-war *Truxtun*
had run aground off the mouth of the Tuxpan, and its captain had been
forced to surrender. A landing party from the USS *Princeton* had burned
the *Truxtun* to keep it from falling into Mexican hands, but not before
the Mexicans successfully removed several of the ship's guns, which they
mounted in a small fort three miles up the Tuxpan River. Perry considered Mexican possession of those guns to be an intolerable insult, and
he wrote to the secretary of the navy that it was "a point of honor as well
as duty" to reclaim them.[6]

Buchanan and the *Germantown* left the anchorage off Vera Cruz on
11 April, sailing in company with the brig *Albany* and two bomb vessels,
the *Vesuvius* and the *Stromboli*. Three days later, off the island of Lobos,
the *Mississippi* joined them, and on 17 April the American squadron
dropped anchor off the mouth of the Tuxpan River. There was not a lot
to see: the Tuxpan River was narrow, with marshy banks and a shallow
sandbar protecting its mouth, and because the city of Tuxpan was six
miles upriver, there was no evidence of habitation. Halfway between the
city and the river's mouth, however, was the small Mexican fort called
La Peña (literally, "the rock"), which housed three cannon, two of them
carronades from the *Truxtun*. In response to an "All Captains" signal
from the flagship, Buchanan called for his boat and was rowed over to
the *Mississippi* to discuss the plan of attack.[7]

The plan that Perry communicated to his captains was simple and
straightforward. Because the larger U.S. vessels, including the *Germantown*, could not cross the shallow bar at the mouth of the river, the men
would embark in the ships' boats and be towed over the bar by the
squadron's shallow-draft steamers. Once opposite La Peña, the Americans would land and storm the fort. The next day, therefore, Buchanan
turned the *Germantown* over to a junior lieutenant in charge of a skeleton crew, and most of the ship's company—17 officers, 114 sailors, and 21
marines—piled into the ship's launch and three cutters. They lashed the
boats together bow to stern, like beads on a string, and tied up to the
stern of the tiny *Spitfire*, which Perry was using as a temporary flagship.

The *Spitfire*'s masts had been removed to lighten its draft. Boats from other ships in the squadron tied up to other shallow-draft streamers until the river expedition was ready: six small steamers towing thirty boats and barges filled with nearly fifteen hundred men. At noon the whole flotilla crossed the bar and entered the Tuxpan River.[8]

After slowly ascending the winding river for about an hour and a half, the Americans arrived within range of La Peña early in the afternoon. Buchanan joined Perry onboard the *Spitfire* so that he could more readily respond to the expected order to "land and storm the forts." Almost at once the thirty-two-pound guns of the small Mexican fort opened on the *Spitfire,* and, as Buchanan had hoped, Perry ordered him to land his force and lead the attack. Rejoining his men, Buchanan ordered them to cast off the towlines and put their backs into it as they pulled toward the river-bank. Then he splashed ashore and led the charge uphill. The yelling Americans, variously armed with muskets, pistols, and cutlasses, swarmed up and over La Peña's low, timber-faced dirt wall to capture the fort and reclaim the cannon lost from the *Truxtun.* This easy but exhilarating success provoked three cheers from the men still aboard the boats. If it was not exactly the equivalent of a frigate dual, it was nonetheless a most satisfactory victory, and Buchanan had several of the fort's cannonballs loaded onto the *Germantown* to take home as souvenirs.[9]

Buchanan's second major operation in the war came less than a month later and in very similar circumstances. This time, Perry targeted the city of San Juan Bautista (which the Americans called Tabasco), and once again avenging American honor was a factor in Perry's planning. The city had resisted an earlier American attack largely by refusing to acknowledge the Americans' presence. This time Perry planned to leave the defenders no recourse—he would not only capture the city, he would occupy it and garrison the town. To accomplish this, he assembled a naval force of eleven warships, including the *Germantown,* off the mouth of the Tabasco River in mid-June.

Once again, the crews of the larger warships scrambled down into the ships' boats to be towed over the bar at the river's mouth by several small steamers. And once again, Buchanan left the *Germantown* in the hands of a subordinate and joined Perry on the deck of the small river steamer (the *Vixen* this time) that he was using as a flagship. Unlike Tuxpan, which was only six miles upriver, Tabasco was eighty miles from the mouth of the river, and that necessitated a long and dangerous journey. The American flotilla had to thread its way up a river that was only eighty yards wide. One participant recalled the scene: "The clear sky and bright sunshine, the blue water rippling with the sea breeze, the green foliage and graceful palm trees on the river banks, the dark steamers and the boats crowded with men and marines . . . , with the white awnings and ensigns streaming gallantly out on the breeze, [all] formed one of those stirring scenes not readily forgotten."[10]

The Americans did not encounter any enemy resistance until mid-afternoon on the second day, when lookouts on the lead vessel heard two or three shots. This evidence of hostile forces nearby plunged the Americans into a frenzy of activity. The sailors and marines in the landing parties opened up with small arms fire, the heavy guns of the warships boomed out, and every man in the squadron began cheering, yelling, and pointing all at the same time. It reminded one officer of "the sudden bursting of a thunderstorm." But all the sound and fury signified little. The few shots from the riverbank probably came from a small party of scouts, and as soon as he could make his voice heard, Perry ordered a cease-fire.[11]

No damage had been sustained in the noisy but unproductive flurry, although there had been some near misses: a few of the marines had fired their rifles across the decks of the ships and nearly gunned down their own officers. To avoid another such fiasco, Perry decided to anchor in midstream just above a turn in the river called Devil's Bend and continue the advance at first light. One more alarm was provoked by a single shot fired from the river's edge at about midnight, but otherwise all was quiet, if uncomfortable.

By 6:00 A.M. the following morning everyone in the boats was awake and ready to proceed. Because the Mexicans had placed obstructions in the river, Perry decided to land the men at once and advance overland toward Tabasco, which was still about nine miles upriver. Once again he asked Buchanan to select a site for the landing. Buchanan chose a spot on the northern bank where scant foliage and a gently sloping bank led to a low hill crowned by seven palm trees. Seeking to soften up the landing site, Perry ordered the *Bonita* to shell the thick foliage along the riverbank. But while maneuvering to get into position, the *Bonita* ran aground. "That gunboat must be placed off the palms!" Perry said aloud. Buchanan, standing near him, said that he could do it. "Do so!" was

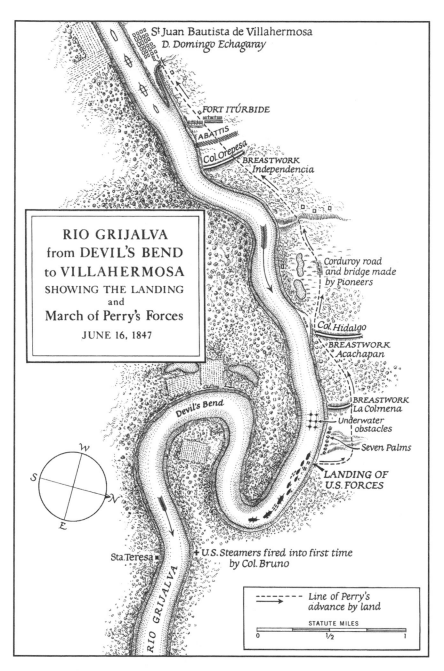

American Advance to Tabasco

From Old Bruin: Commodore Matthew C. Perry *by Samuel Eliot Morison.*
Copyright (c) 1967 by Samuel Eliot Morison. By permission of Little, Brown
and Company.

Perry's terse reply. Buchanan ordered his ship's boats to cast off from the *Vixen* and tow the *Bonita* into position. As he was returning to the *Vixen*, a flurry of small arms fire from the shore wounded several men in the boats, though Buchanan emerged unscathed.[12]

After the repositioned *Bonita* fired several rounds into the northern bank near the landing site, thus driving off the Mexican skirmishers, the barges were cut loose from their tows and the men eagerly rowed ashore, yelling enough, one witness recalled, "to frighten the Mexicans to death." The landing was unopposed, and Commodore Perry himself was among the first to set foot ashore. The sailors and marines rushed up the sloping riverbank and planted a large American flag amid the palm trees. After some self-congratulation and aimless milling about, the "naval brigade," as Perry called his landing force, was then formed up in line of march and the overland advance on Tabasco began.[13]

Buchanan now became an infantry commander. His detachment of 120 men from the *Germantown* was part of what Perry rather grandly called the "Third Division" of infantry. The pioneers (who would today be called engineers) led, clearing a path. Then came the artillery: ten six-pounders under the command of Buchanan's old shipmate Alexander S. Mackenzie, with Buchanan's detachment acting as a guard for the guns. Behind them came the armed sailors formed into two more "divisions" under the command of navy captains Samuel Breese and French Forrest. The thick chaparral made for slow going, and the hot June weather dulled the enthusiasm of the men, who were not used to long marches. Several of those assigned to pull the guns fainted and had to be left behind. Eventually, after several hours, the Americans reached the Mexicans' first serious line of defense, a fortification called Fort Acachapan, which was essentially a long breastwork defended by some six hundred infantry and cavalry and two small fieldpieces.[14]

Perry was no tactician of land warfare, but in this engagement he didn't need to be. He ordered the artillery to the front and arrayed his ragtag infantry—nearly twelve hundred strong—in a long line abreast facing the enemy's fieldworks. In an almost medieval gesture, Perry positioned himself at the center of this line, assigning a sailor to stand behind him holding aloft his commissioning pennant. After ordering his artillery to lob a few rounds toward the enemy lines, he gave his makeshift army the order to charge. Whatever this maneuver lacked in tactical sophistication it made up for in enthusiasm: the men responded with a yell and ran forward at full tilt. Buchanan ran with the rest, presumably with his sword drawn and adding his own voice to the whooping, yelling mass. It was too much for the outnumbered Mexican defenders, who broke and fled.[15]

After this nearly bloodless victory, it took awhile to restore order. Many of the Americans, desperately thirsty after their efforts, ran down toward the river to get a drink, which nearly resulted in tragedy. The American ships had worked their way upriver parallel to the marching infantry, and the men onboard, assuming that the mass of humanity charging toward the riverbank were Mexicans mounting an attack, opened fire. The error was sorted out when the men onshore waved a large American flag, and the shots were replaced by cheers.[16]

The march continued. Fatigue was a serious problem now, and large numbers of men began to fall by the wayside. The pioneers built a corduroy road of logs across the softest ground, but this was only a relative improvement, as the guns had to be bumped forward, log by log, over this surface. Progress was measured in feet. To Buchanan's disgust, some officers attempted to revive the flagging men with liquor. "Many of the officers carried canteens with liquor," he noted, "and the moment they saw a poor fellow fall they would give him 'a drop of comfort' which had an astonishing effect."[17]

Finally they came within sight of the main fort guarding the town of Tabasco. This was no temporary breastwork, but a regular fort with at least some artillery, and not likely to fall to the kind of reckless charge that took Fort Acachapan. Nevertheless, Perry was ready to try it until he espied the American flag flying from the ramparts and realized that the fort and the town had been captured by the ships of the river flotilla, which had worked their way past the obstructions in the river and arrived ahead of them, grabbing the glory. Buchanan may have been disappointed not to get the chance to lead an infantry charge against the stone ramparts of this fort, but it was probably just as well that he didn't have to try.

After this anticlimax, the rest of the campaign was routine. Perry sent the musicians to the front, and with flags flying and music playing the naval brigade entered the city. There was some drinking that night—enterprising sailors inevitably managed to find alcohol—and Buchanan established a provost marshal's guard, which was kept busy arresting the drunken sailors. A handful of men—none, Buchanan was happy to say, from the *Germantown*—broke into a house and ransacked it, pillaging closets and chests, and decorating themselves with the shawls and other finery they found inside. Discovered in the act, they were marched off to jail, wearing women's clothing, by the provost marshal's guard.[18]

The expeditionary force remained in Tabasco for a week. The Mexicans tried a few halfhearted counterattacks, which were easily driven off, but the presence of a large body of hostile forces nearby indicated that the city would be difficult to hold. That, plus the threat of yellow fever, eventually led the Americans to evacuate the town and return to the anchorage off the mouth of the river.

Buchanan returned to the *Germantown* on 19 June. Perhaps because of the activities of several members of his crew while ashore, or perhaps because he felt the need to reassert his presence onboard, he spent the next several days handing down punishments for breaches of discipline. On 28 June the crew of the *Germantown* witnessed no fewer than nine lashings: two sailors were awarded a dozen lashes each for fighting; two more got the same for "quarreling"; one man received nine lashes for doubling the grog tub (attempting to get back in line after being served once); two got a dozen each for disobedience and insolence; one got a dozen for "drunkenness and stealing grog in Tabasco"; and one got nine lashes for "not being at his station." While whipping nine sailors in a single day was a bit unusual, the familiar order for "all hands to witness punishment" was a regular refrain on the *Germantown*, as it had been on all of Buchanan's commands. He did occasionally show leniency: a ship's boy who was found guilty of "disobedience and insolence" got only six lashes, no doubt in consideration of his youth.[19]

After the two river expeditions, Buchanan and the *Germantown* returned with the rest of the squadron to the anchorage off Vera Cruz. The *Germantown* served as the squadron flagship for four months after yellow fever broke out onboard the *Mississippi* and Perry had to send it back to Pensacola. Those circumstances allowed Buchanan to cement his already close relationship with Perry. In January, with the war all but over, Buchanan and the *Germantown* left the Gulf of Mexico and returned to Norfolk, where he relinquished command to Charles Lowndes, his brother-in-law and Talbot County neighbor. Buchanan's Mexican War service had lasted not quite a year. But however brief, his efforts did not go unnoticed. Perry wrote him an unsolicited testimonial in which he asserted that "for courage, energy, and judgement he has not, in my opinion, a superior in the service." He received the formal thanks of the Maryland legislature, and was granted a section of land (160 acres) in Iowa by the national government. If it was not exactly the kind of war he had imagined when he sought his midshipman's warrant as a teenager, it was nevertheless personally and professionally gratifying.[20]

After turning the *Germantown* over to Lowndes, Buchanan returned to the Rest for an extended period of shore leave, interrupted only by occasional trips to perform lighthouse inspection duty or into Washington to serve on various courts martial. He was disappointed to discover what he, at least, concluded to be the sad state into which the Naval School had fallen. He was convinced that his successors had failed to maintain the kind of strict discipline that had been his hallmark at the school. Whenever he heard that a few middies had engaged in some "disgraceful frolic" in Annapolis, he chalked it up to an erosion in discipline.[21] He was particularly disgusted by George P. Upshur's indifferent rule over the school and was glad when Upshur relinquished command. And he tried, unsuccessfully, to talk Du Pont into taking the job. Buchanan got a chance to help set things back on course when he served on a commission to update the school's regulations in 1849. That commission also gave the school a new name: the United States Naval Academy.

Senior enough now to be considered for a major sea command, Buchanan lusted for a frigate. "I am determined to command a Frigate," he wrote to Du Pont that fall, "before I am too old and worthless." He was enough of a realist to recognize that there were far more senior officers in the U.S. Navy than there were frigate commands. His preferred solution to this dilemma was not necessarily to build more frigates— although he continued to hope that Congress would do just that. Instead, he advocated a retirement list to clear away the deadwood.

There was no provision for retirement in the navy of the early 1850s, and Buchanan felt frustrated by the top-heavy rank structure that kept him from his heart's desire. When he learned that command of the sloop *Jamestown* had been given to a captain, he complained that it was bad enough that captains got all the frigate commands; if they also got to command the sloops, there would be no good sea commands left. If captains could command sloops, he wondered sarcastically, why not allow lieutenants and commanders to command ships of the line? He began to fear that if the rank structure were not reformed, he would be a superannuated old salt before he ever got command of a frigate. "I suppose I must remain an idler for some years," he wrote Du Pont resignedly, "as I see no prospect of getting afloat."[22]

If he could not get independent command of a frigate, he decided, he would settle—if necessary—for an assignment as a flag captain. That way he could "command" a frigate even if it meant serving under the direction of an embarked commodore. Of course, much would depend on the personality of the commodore, and as Buchanan mentally scanned the Navy List, he could not conjure up the name of anyone who would be acceptable. "If there should be no increase of ships afloat," he wrote Du Pont, "I will endeavor to go as Capn under some clever Com[modor]e if such a man can now be found on the Captain's list!!!"[23]

For some time his pessimism seemed warranted. He remained ashore awaiting orders for two more years. Nannie was pregnant again in the fall of 1850, and she suffered a difficult pregnancy that ended with a miscarriage in January 1851. Then, in the winter of 1851–52, out of the blue, Buchanan received orders to ready himself to "proceed to the East Indies for the command of the U.S. Steam Frigate *Susquehanna*." This was spectacular news! The *Susquehanna* was the newest and largest of the navy's steam frigates, and arguably the best sea command in the service. His orders were a bit unusual in that the *Susquehanna* had left Norfolk for the Far East only six months before with William Inman as captain and John H. Aulick as commodore. Why was he being sent out to assume command now, while the ship was in the middle of a deployment halfway around the world?[24]

If he did not know when he first received his orders, Buchanan would have made it his business to find out. What he learned was that only weeks out to sea, while making the Atlantic crossing, Aulick and Inman had begun to quarrel. Aulick was by nature a micromanager with a tendency to provide what Inman, at least, believed was unnecessary and unprofessional oversight in the day-to-day management of the ship. Inman complained about it: first to Aulick, then formally to the Navy Department. Aulick's interference with the management of the ship, Inman insisted, made his own presence redundant. An irritated Aulick responded that if Inman felt redundant, the Navy Department should gratify him and "grant his request to be ordered to . . . some other duty." The last straw for both men came when Aulick told Inman's clerk to copy a letter for him and Inman ordered his clerk not to do it. Aulick considered that to be such an overt act of insubordination that he took the unprecedented step of dismissing his own flag captain. In Rio de Janeiro, where the *Susquehanna* made a coaling stop, Aulick ordered Inman off the ship. These awkward circumstances created the vacancy that Buchanan had been ordered to fill.[25]

If these circumstances caused Buchanan to reconsider the apparent good fortune of serving under such a man as John H. Aulick, other news from the Far East suggested that perhaps it was likely to work out after all. Aulick, it seems, had managed to alienate not only Inman, but also the American minister to Brazil, Robert Schenck, who sent his own letter of complaint to Washington. And after Aulick arrived in Hong Kong, he began to quarrel as well with the U.S. commissioner to China, Humphrey Marshall, who considered Aulick and his squadron to be tools of American diplomacy and therefore subject entirely to his orders. When Aulick declined to take orders from Marshall, the American minister wrote scathing letters back to Washington about Aulick's lack of cooperation. By then, Secretary of the Navy William A. Graham had already decided to recall Aulick. In fact, Buchanan would carry with him an order from Graham for Aulick to turn the *Susquehanna* over to Buchanan and return home at once. For a time, at least, Buchanan, a mere commander, would have independent command of the best ship in the navy![26]

Of course, a more senior officer than Buchanan would have to be sent to the Far East to serve as commodore. In the spring, Buchanan learned that Aulick's replacement would be his old commander from the Gulf of Mexico, Matthew C. Perry. Moreover, Perry would be endowed with a specific mission: the delivery of a letter to the emperor of Japan from President Millard Fillmore as the first step in a campaign to open Japan to American trade.

Delighted with these circumstances and the opportunity they presented, Buchanan supplied himself with a steward, a cook, and two seamen to act as personal servants; obtained an advance of five hundred dollars from the navy and a line of credit at England's Barings Brothers Bank; and set out from New York as a passenger on a ship bound for Hong Kong via England, the Mediterranean, Egypt, the Indian Ocean, and the South China Sea. He arranged to have his personal belongings shipped aboard Perry's flagship, the *Mississippi*. These included a rug for his cabin, "a very comfortable large chair," and other comforts of home.[27]

He left Maryland for New York in mid-August and boarded a steamer for England on the twenty-first. He was not in a hurry. After an uneventful Atlantic crossing, he spent a month in London, where he saw "nearly all the wonders of that great city" before taking passage on another vessel bound southward across the Bay of Biscay, through the Straits of Gibraltar, and into the Mediterranean. The ship deposited him at Alexandria, and Buchanan made his way in leisurely fashion across Egypt, stopping to visit Cleopatra's Needle and Pompey's Pillar, and to investigate the charms of ancient Cairo. After crossing the desert to Suez, he took passage on the sailing ship *Vancouver,* which carried him across the Indian Ocean to Singapore and up through the South China Sea. Finally, in early November, he reached Hong Kong and his rendezvous with the *Susquehanna.*[28]

Buchanan found the three-month trip "delightful," and he experienced a moment of great personal and professional satisfaction as he was rowed out to the stately *Susquehanna* resting at anchor in Hong Kong Harbor. As he expressed it to Du Pont in a private letter: "As I put my foot over the gangway of this noble ship I felt proud of my command, and anticipated much pleasure in making a long cruise in her previous to the arrival of Com. Perry." His feeling of well-being was shattered almost at once. Aulick greeted Buchanan with chilling restraint. That hardly mattered, for Buchanan knew that among the letters he carried was one from Secretary Graham that ordered Aulick to "consider himself as detached from the Command of the United States Squadron in the East India and China seas." But that same day, Aulick received another letter from Graham's replacement, John P. Kennedy, which ordered him to remain on the ship "until regularly relieved by an order." To Buchanan it was obvious that the "order" Aulick was to wait for was the one Buchanan had brought with him. But Aulick interpreted Kennedy's letter to mean that he was not to surrender his command pending further orders. In the meantime, Aulick informed him, Buchanan would serve as his flag captain. Buchanan was first astonished, then infuriated. He told Aulick "in plain language" that he was wrong, that his own orders were to take command at once and that Aulick was to go home. "If I had a cloud hanging over me," he told Aulick, "I would have rejoiced at the opportunity of going home and make my accusers face me."[29]

Aulick responded with some heat, telling Buchanan that he was not concerned about the accusations against him, and that he dared anyone to injure him. Buchanan replied with equal heat, insisting that Aulick was violating the orders of the department and interfering in Buchanan's rightful capacity as the captain of the *Susquehanna,* and that he would report him to the department. "We had quite a warm conversation," he reported to Du Pont, "and my language was not guarded or very mild." True to his word, he notified the Navy Department that "Aulick declines obeying the order from the Honorable William A. Graham," using the former secretary's full name as if to suggest the extent of Aulick's insubordination. As a result, Buchanan wrote, "I am prevented from carrying out my instructions."[30]

Aulick did not deny Buchanan's authority to assume command of the *Susquehanna.* The crew was dutifully mustered and Buchanan read his orders, formally assuming command on 10 November. But Aulick continued to treat Buchanan as merely one of his subordinate officers. And as he had with Inman, he continued to micromanage shipboard activities. Buchanan was especially outraged when Aulick opened letters that were addressed to "the commanding officer of the *Susquehanna.*" For his part, Aulick saw Buchanan as an irritating daily reminder of the charges he would sooner or later have to face.

Aulick's difficulties multiplied in January when he began to suffer from excruciating stomach pains and severe diarrhea. By February he weighed less than a hundred pounds; he was unable to rise from his cot, or even to write. He continued to hope that the department would relent and allow him the honor of returning to the United States in his own ship. The *Susquehanna* needed repairs, he asserted through an amanuensis, and the ship probably would not be able to participate in the forthcoming expedition to Japan. Given that, why not order it back to the United States? Aulick suggested that Buchanan be left behind in Hong Kong to await Perry's arrival, for he was "not needed" onboard the *Susquehanna.* Aulick literally begged the department to let him stay in command. Piteously he wrote: "I shall probably never live to reach home."[31]

Eventually, in spite of his pleas, Aulick had to accept the inevitable. On 11 March he turned the *Susquehanna* over to Buchanan, simultaneously turning the squadron over to Comdr. John Kelley of the *Plymouth,* who with Aulick's departure became the senior officer on station. A mere shadow of his former self, Aulick then took passage in the Pacific & Orient steamer *Singapore* bound for the long run around Cape Horn. The voyage enabled him to recover his health, and eventually he managed to explain his way out of his difficulties and retained both his commission and his good standing in the navy.

Among those who were happy to see Aulick go was Humphrey Marshall, the U.S. commissioner to China, whose letters of complaint had contributed to Aulick's fall from grace. With Aulick now out of the way, Marshall appealed to Commander Kelley to assign him a warship in support of his diplomatic duties. Kelley gave him the best he had: Buchanan's *Susquehanna*. Only ten days after Aulick's departure, Buchanan welcomed Marshall aboard with a salute of seventeen guns (four more than Aulick had rated when he departed), and the *Susquehanna* steamed north from Hong Kong to Shanghai, near the mouth of the Yangtze River, arriving there on 26 March. Marshall went ashore to communicate with the imperial representative and with members of the Western merchant community. Both the government and the merchants appealed to Marshall to use the *Susquehanna* to protect them from the Taiping rebels who had recently occupied Nanking, some 150 miles upriver, and now threatened Shanghai. Marshall was susceptible to these pleas, but it was not to be. On 25 April the USS *Plymouth* arrived with a message for Buchanan from Commodore Perry, who had arrived in Hong Kong on the sixth and had been very disappointed to find that his best ship—indeed, the vessel he planned to use as his flagship—had been quite literally "shanghaied" by Humphrey Marshall. Perry's orders were for Buchanan to wait where he was; the commodore would bring the rest of the squadron to Shanghai. Marshall urged Buchanan to reject those orders and instead carry him another 800 miles north to the Peiho River for an expedition to Peking. But Buchanan had no doubt about where his responsibilities, and his loyalty, lay; he stayed in Shanghai to await Perry.[32]

Perry arrived in early May and transferred his flag and his suite from the *Mississippi* to the slightly larger *Susquehanna,* on which Buchanan had erected, in accordance with orders, a spacious deck cabin that Perry used as his fleet headquarters. Marshall tried to convince Perry that the situation in China was so precarious that he should discard or at least postpone his planned expedition to Japan, but Perry declined. He left the sailing sloop *Plymouth* behind in Shanghai as a token of America's interest there, but on 23 May the *Susquehanna* and the *Mississippi,* each towing a sailing ship, left Shanghai for a historic rendezvous with the mysterious empire of Japan.[33]

❧ 7 ❧

THE MYSTERIOUS ORIENT

We hope that Japan and the United States will always be friends.

The idea of "opening" Japan to Western trade was hardly new. But the Tokugawa shogunate, which had ruled in Japan since 1600, steadfastly resisted contact with foreigners. The Japanese quest for stability and security fed a suspicion—even a fear—of outsiders that bordered on the paranoid. None but the Dutch, who operated a small trading "factory" at Nagasaki, had managed to crack the lacquered veneer of Japanese resistance to the outside world. Perry's mission in 1853 would change that forever. Perry went to Japan with three goals: (1) to secure an arrangement for the rescue and care of Western sailors who might be shipwrecked on Japan's coasts, (2) to obtain permission for U.S. ships to take on water and coal at selected Japanese ports, and (3) to urge the Japanese to open their ports to Western trade. His orders called for him to be "courteous and conciliatory, but at the same time firm and decided." As an opening gambit, he carried a letter for the Japanese emperor from President Millard Fillmore, now a lame duck since Franklin Pierce's election in November. The letter itself was a work of art: written on heavy parchment and sealed with wax and ribbons, it rested in an inlayed rosewood box with gold hinges. The idea was to impress on the Japanese the high station of the president as well as the strength and wealth of the American visitors.[1]

There was virtually no chance that Perry, or any foreigner, would be allowed to negotiate with, or even to see, the emperor himself, a figure so remote that his very existence was uncertain. In fact, the Japanese did not even allow foreign ships to enter their harbors. Only at the designated port of Nagasaki could foreign vessels enter the sacred waters of the Japanese Empire, and only in that port were foreign communications received. Moreover, the Japanese routinely dispatched low-level functionaries to receive all such communications, few of which ever actually reached the decision makers in Japan's government. The emperor maintained his lofty distance from mere mortals by sending others to speak in his name.

But two could play at that game. The "firm and decided" Perry planned to ignore the requirement that foreign vessels could visit only the designated port of Nagasaki. Instead he would steam boldly into Edo Bay (Tokyo Bay) and demand that he be allowed to present President Fillmore's letter at the imperial capital. Moreover, he would adopt the Japanese strategy of remaining out of sight and allowing others to carry out the day-to-day business of negotiating his demands. In this way he could represent himself as a personage as mysterious and powerful in his own way as the divine emperor himself. Of course, this strategy also meant that the burden of conducting the negotiations with the Japanese representatives would fall on Perry's subordinates, and in particular on the captain of his flagship. Thus it was that Franklin Buchanan became the unlikely central figure in a delicate game of international diplomacy.

The five-ship American squadron left Shanghai on 23 May and arrived at Okinawa, which was at the time was known as Lew Chew (or Loo Choo), three days later. Perry hoped to establish a coaling station there, and he used his visit to try out his negotiating strategy. He refused to meet with the dignitaries who rowed out from the town of Naha to greet him, and instead ordered Buchanan to inform them that the American commander in chief would meet only with "the principal dignitaries of the island." The visitors returned the next day, this time bearing presents, but once again Buchanan turned them away. The Okinawans were perplexed; what visitors didn't want presents?[2]

On the third day, a barge came alongside, and Buchanan again met it at the gangway. This time an elderly man with a long white beard introduced himself as the regent to the ruling prince of the island, who was only eleven years old and too ill to make a visit. Buchanan welcomed the regent and his suite aboard the *Susquehanna,* and even ordered a salute of three guns in his honor. The noise so startled the visitors that they dropped to their knees at the sound of the first gun. With much fanfare, including a musical contribution from the ship's band, Buchanan escorted the regent to Perry's cabin. There the commodore and the regent of Lew Chew held a short and polite conversation, made longer by the necessity of translating from the local dialect to Mandarin, to English, and back again. At the end of the audience, Perry declared that he would return the regent's visit soon. The regent appeared to be distressed by this announcement and claimed that the palace was not prepared to welcome the American commodore with the hospitality he deserved. Nevertheless, Perry insisted, even announcing the date of his visit—6 June.[3]

On the appointed date, Perry did indeed travel to the local palace, and he did so in style. Noting that the regent had arrived at the boat landing in a sedan chair, Perry resolved to use a similar conveyance when he returned the visit, and he ordered the ship's carpenter to build one. Although some members of the lower deck wondered if Perry wasn't putting on airs, it was all part of a calculated strategy. Perry's sedan chair led an impressive procession that included "a number of officers, the Guard of Marines, a field piece, and the band." The cavalcade wound up the hill from the boat landing to the palace, where Perry was received in appropriate style after all.[4]

Three days later, Perry, Buchanan, and the *Susquehanna* (towing the *Saratoga*) left Okinawa for another visit that was a preliminary to the main event. Eight hundred miles east of Okinawa, just north of Iwo Jima, was Peel Island in the Bonins, another place Perry hoped to establish a permanent American coaling station. Buchanan joined Perry on an exploring expedition around the island, and they gathered samples of the local flora, including several kinds of exotic fruit. The run out to the Bonins and back took two weeks, and on 23 June the *Susquehanna* was back in Naha. Perry issued an invitation for the regent to dine aboard the *Susquehanna,* and on 28 June, Buchanan once again greeted the regent and his party at the ship's gangway.[5]

The dinner was a great success. It was held in Perry's specially built cabin, the only space large enough to accommodate the entire party. Perry sat at the head of the table with the regent on his right hand, and

Buchanan sat at the other end with the mayor of Naha on his right. The Americans wore their best uniforms, and the guests were attired according to their rank in grass cloth of purple or white, with large gold pins holding their long hair in place on top of their heads. The two cultures accommodated one another: after some experimentation, the guests made do with knives and forks, and when, after dinner, the guests lit their pipes, the Americans accepted with some hesitation the invitation to participate. The mayor of Naha handed his pipe to Buchanan, who dutifully took several puffs before returning it. The dessert, consisting of fruits collected in the Bonins, was a great success, and the guests bundled up the leftovers in their voluminous robes to take them home.[6]

Satisfied with what had been accomplished during these preliminary visits, Perry ordered the squadron northward on the first of July for the main event. The *Susquehanna* led the fleet out of the harbor, slowing its engines and banking the boiler fires to wait for the *Mississippi* to take its station; then, with each of the steamers taking a sloop in tow, the four-ship American squadron set a course for Japan. It took a week to raise the headlands off Uraga, the entry to Edo Bay. The weather was thick and hazy, and the wind was dead calm as the American ships approached the shore. The local Japanese fishermen were astonished to see these strange vessels, apparently on fire with black smoke spewing from amidships, passing by at nine knots in a dead calm.[7]

The *Susquehanna* led the way into the bay and dropped anchor off the southern headland, setting out kedge anchors on spring lines so that the ship's broadside faced the batteries onshore. Its arrival caused a near panic among the local dignitaries, not only because foreign vessels were banned from entering any port except Nagasaki, but also because these were the first steam-powered ships the Japanese had ever seen. Perry's biographer, Samuel Eliot Morison, likened the Japanese reaction to what one might expect in the modern era if "delegates from another planet" arrived suddenly in Washington, D.C.[8]

Edo Bay was protected by several batteries, but the Japanese did not open fire with the smooth-bore fieldpieces they had obtained from the Dutch. Instead, dozens of small guard boats filled with armed men put out from the shore and swarmed around the American ships. The boats bumped alongside the *Susquehanna,* and the men aboard them grabbed onto the chains with the apparent intention of boarding. But Perry had issued orders not to allow this, and the would-be boarders were kept at a respectful distance by sailors wielding long pikes. Finally one boat that was larger than the others approached the *Susquehanna*. An officer in the boat held up a large sign in French: "Depart immediately and dare not anchor!" When that did no good, one of the Japanese officers indicated a wish to talk to the ship's master. Buchanan explained through an interpreter that the American commander in chief would not to talk to anyone but a high official representing the emperor himself. Once this was understood, the boats withdrew.[9]

Informal negotiations began the next morning when a man who identified himself as Kayama Yezaimon, and who purported to be the governor of Uraga province, came aboard the *Susquehanna*. He was elaborately dressed in "a rich silk robe of an embroidered pattern resembling the feathers of a peacock, with borders of gold and silver." Buchanan greeted him at the gangway just as he had met the regent of Lew Chew, but this time he did not escort him to Perry's cabin. Perry had decided that in this negotiation, Buchanan and Capt. Henry Adams of Perry's staff would deal with any functionaries who came onboard. Perry would orchestrate events from his cabin like an unseen puppeteer, but Buchanan would bear the burden of conducting the day-to-day discussions. This proved to be wise, for although the Americans never discovered it, Kayama was actually a *yoriki,* or governor's assistant, sent by the governor to find out what the men on the "Black Ships" wanted. In effect, both Buchanan and Kayama negotiated on behalf of others who were too exalted to participate directly.[10]

Kayama was accompanied by interpreters who spoke Dutch and Japanese; Buchanan's interpreters spoke Dutch and English. The need for a double translation created a certain awkwardness in communicating, and it certainly prolonged the discussions, but it also allowed each side to consider its response carefully. Given Buchanan's tendency to shoot from the hip, this may actually have worked to his advantage.

Buchanan informed Kayama of the reason for the squadron's visit: The American commander in chief, he said, had a letter for the emperor from the president of the United States and wished to deliver it to Edo. Kayama explained that this was impossible. "These communications . . . could not be received here without a violation of Japanese laws," he explained patiently. "They must be sent from Nagasaki through the regular channel." Buchanan was insistent: "The Commodore had orders to deliver the letters at Yedo and nowhere else," he said firmly. "It would be an insult to our Government to refuse receiving them, which would be properly resented." Kayama was equally insistent, saying that "it was against their laws and they could not do it."[11]

Having reached this impasse, Buchanan tried another tack. He brought out copies of the letter and showed them to Kayama, explaining that they had been copied into several languages, and that the president himself had placed the national seal on the original. Kayama wavered; this was clearly over his head. Could he send to Edo for instructions? he asked. Buchanan wondered how long it would take. Kayama was unsure. Buchanan told him that the American commodore would wait three days—no longer. If he did not receive an answer by noon on 12 July, Buchanan told him, he would consider it "an insult to the U.S. Government and take measures accordingly."[12]

Kayama returned two days later. During those two days, ship's boats from the *Susquehanna* and the *Mississippi* had been busy sounding the bay, seeking the best anchorages. Kayama was very nervous about this, but he had good news. It was very likely, he said, that the letters could be received at Edo rather than Nagasaki. But he also noted with alarm that the American ships had moved farther up the bay, and that the small boats were sounding even further upriver. It was his duty to prevent foreign ships from even entering Edo Bay, much less moving about at their pleasure, as these seemed to be doing. He expressed a hope that the Americans would go no farther. Buchanan took advantage of Kayama's obvious distress to imply that if Kayama could not manage to get the president's letter accepted, the Black Ships might force their way to Edo and present it at the muzzle of a gun.[13]

The implied threat may or may not have influenced the news that Kayama brought the next morning. The letter could be delivered ashore at Edo Bay, he reported, and a "high official person" would come from Edo to receive it in a special ceremony. Buchanan agreed that the unofficial copies could be sent in this way, preliminary to the subsequent presentation of the original at Edo. Kayama then left, but he returned again in the afternoon. Apparently his political masters were unsatisfied with the solution Buchanan had suggested. Kayama asked why the original could not be presented at the same time as the copies.

"That is impossible," Buchanan declared, his natural combativeness emerging. Kayama became plaintive: "Can you not contrive to manage it?" he asked. Very likely his own future—indeed, perhaps his life—

depended on his ability to get Buchanan to compromise on this issue. But Buchanan would not bend; he, too, had orders from his superior. "It cannot be done," he insisted. But after further laborious discussion through the interpreters, he relented. "Will the high officer, who will come here, come accredited from the Emperor?" Oh, yes, Kayama assured him, eagerly. "Will he have any proof to show that he is so authorized?" Yes, he can prove it, Kayama insisted, seeing a ray of hope in Buchanan's line of questioning.

While the interpreters bent their heads together to figure out exactly how to translate the title of the high official who would come from Edo, Buchanan slipped out of the cabin to talk to Perry. The commodore gave him permission to make a deal if Buchanan was satisfied that the representative from Edo was sufficiently exalted. When Buchanan returned to the meeting, he insisted that the representative from Edo "must have a paper signed by the Emperor stating that he is empowered to receive the letter." Kayama reassured him: "He will have a document properly signed."[14]

The agreement put Kayama in a good mood. He and his entourage stayed late, and it was after seven in the evening when they finally departed, leaving, as always, "with their usual graceful courtesies, bowing at every step and smiling in an amicable yet dignified manner."[15]

Kayama brought the letter bearing the emperor's seal the next day. Much like Fillmore's letter, it was wrapped in velvet and lay in a sandalwood box. Buchanan put out his hand to receive it, but Kayama explained that "the letter of the Emperor may be seen, but it must not be delivered out of our hands." In short, you may look, but you cannot touch. The Japanese and the American were playing the same game: each man treated the letter from his head of state as if it were a holy relic deserving of only the most reverent treatment.[16]

The meeting to deliver Fillmore's letter took place the next day (14 July) in a formal and carefully choreographed ceremony onshore. The two American steamships anchored off the beach where the presentation would be made, again laying out kedge anchors on spring lines so as to present their broadsides to the beach. Perry was taking no chances that the Japanese might try to ambush his landing party. Then Buchanan led the first wave of Americans ashore, some 250 sailors and marines in their best uniforms. Buchanan was the first to land; according to the official narrative of the expedition, he "sprang ashore." The first American to land on Japanese soil then shouted out commands for the sailors to land and form two lines parallel with the beach, facing the flagship. Only then, at precisely ten o'clock, did Perry leave the *Susquehanna* to be rowed ashore. As he set foot on the landing, escorted by two very large black American sailors and followed by two of the ship's boys carrying the president's letter in its rosewood box, the *Susquehanna*'s band broke into "Hail Columbia!" and the marines and sailors fell into line behind the commodore. If there was no sedan chair this time, the whole nevertheless made a grand procession from the water's edge to the small building the Japanese had erected for the ceremony.[17]

The ceremony itself was short and straightforward. The exalted officials from Edo sat silently in their chairs assuming an air of "statuesque formality." Perry presented the letter, which was placed in a scarlet dispatch bag, box and all; and a Japanese official handed him a memorandum, which stated that "as the letter has been received you can depart." There was then a procession back to the landing, and Perry was back onboard the *Susquehanna* by eleven o'clock. Just as he had been the first ashore, Buchanan was also nearly the last to depart. Kayama told him: "We are happy that everything has passed off well and favorably." Equally pleased, Buchanan replied, "We hope that Japan and the United States will always be friends."[18]

After two more days of surveying the harbor, which caused the Japanese on the shore additional anxiety, the American ships finally left Edo Bay on 17 July. After a stop at Okinawa, they steamed back to Shanghai, where Perry planned to pass the winter before returning to Japan in the spring. Commissioner Humphrey Marshall had other plans. He picked up where he had left off in May, insisting that the unrest in China provoked by the Taiping rebellion should be Perry's first concern. Perry did what he could to assuage the demanding American minister, sending ships to various cities along the China coast to show the flag in support of American merchants, but he knew that the State Department in Washington considered the opening of Japan to have a higher priority.

Before he did anything else, however, there was some tough negotiating to be done in Shanghai. The imperial regent was reluctant to allow American sailors the run of the city or to allow the establishment of a coal reserve on shore. When talks over these issues faltered, Perry hinted that he might land a force of armed men, capture the imperial palace, and hold the next negotiating session there. This hint worked wonders, and the regent gave way on all fronts. This was precisely the kind of negotiating posture Buchanan approved of, and no doubt Perry's firm stand elevated the commodore even higher in Buchanan's eyes. In August there was another brief trip out to Okinawa, then a sojourn down to British Hong Kong, where shipboard activities took on the aspect of a carnival. The *Susquehanna* hosted several social events for the international community, including a formal concert ashore by the *Susquehanna*'s band and a "theatrical production" afloat.[19]

Reinforcements for Perry's fleet began to arrive, including storeships carrying the presents Perry intended to offer when he revisited Edo in the spring. One event that would affect Buchanan in particular was the arrival in October of the new American commissioner to China, Robert M. McLane, who would replace Humphrey Marshall. McLane was less imperious than Marshall, but he shared Marshall's view that U.S. interests in China were at least as important as opening Japan, and he urged the State Department in Washington to order Perry to make at least one ship from his squadron available to provide substance to McLane's efforts in China. In the meantime, Perry had decided to advance the date for his return trip to Edo Bay, largely because of news that a Russian expedition to Japan was also being mounted. In January, just as the American squadron was preparing to depart, Perry received a letter that caused him "deep disappointment and mortification." A Navy Department order dated the previous October instructed him to turn one of his ships over to McLane in Hong Kong. Privately, Perry decided to let McLane have Buchanan's *Susquehanna,* but he chose to delay the execution of the order until he had completed his primary task.[20]

The American squadron, including the *Susquehanna,* left Shanghai in January and steamed east to Okinawa. There, Perry prepared to transfer his flag from the *Susquehanna* to the *Powhatan* by ordering the deck cabin on the former to be dismantled and reassembled on the *Powhatan.* Perry did not transfer his flag, however, until after the squadron arrived in Edo Bay.

The Americans returned to Edo Bay in February, and on 8 March Perry landed in Japan for the second time, this time near Yokohama, to hear the Japanese response to the president's letter. Even though Perry had transferred his flag to the *Powhatan,* Buchanan once again orchestrated the landing. And once again it was more like a pageant than a military operation. Buchanan's line of boats rowed toward the shore in a line abreast as if it were an invasion force. The boats touched the beach more or less simultaneously, and a double column of sailors and marines formed a respectful gauntlet for the commodore to pass through. As Perry left the *Powhatan,* a seventeen-gun salute banged out from the new flagship, and as the commodore's foot touched the beach, the band struck up the *Star Spangled Banner.*[21]

Buchanan was not involved in the negotiations this time. He learned later that the Japanese readily gave way on the issues of helping ship-wrecked sailors and opening a port for an American coaling station, but they wanted no part of opening trade with the West. Perry did not press it, although he successfully urged the Japanese to allow the establish-ment of an American consulate in Japan, which in the end proved to be a foot in the door for an eventual trade agreement.[22]

On 12 March, with his business completed and the terms of the treaty accepted by all parties, Perry authorized the squadron to bring ashore the presents he had brought. The most spectacular of these was a minia-ture eighteen-inch-gauge railroad, complete with circular track, engine, and a string of cars. The Japanese were charmed and fascinated by this splendid toy, and most of the dignitaries took turns riding on the tiny engine. Although language was still a barrier, the Americans and Japan-ese attempted to converse. American marines marveled at the size and strength of the local sumo wrestlers; the Japanese expressed wonder at American beards and clothing. The door to Japan, locked for 250 years, was at last ajar.[23]

After sharing in the diplomatic triumph in Japan, Buchanan had an opportunity to achieve a similar, if less spectacular, success on his own in China. The civil war between the adherents of the Manchu dynasty and the Taiping rebels continued to rage. As was often the case in wars of rebellion, neutral merchants eager to trade with both sides were fre-quently caught in the middle. The new American commissioner, Robert McLane, was determined to protect the interests of American merchants in China. He wanted to warn both the Manchus and the Taipings to respect American rights; obviously, such a warning would carry much greater weight if delivered from the deck of a warship. Eight days after the celebratory presentation of presents at Yokohama, therefore, Perry detached the *Susquehanna* from the squadron and ordered Buchanan to report to McLane at Hong Kong for such service as the commissioner might request.[24]

McLane reported onboard the *Susquehanna* soon after it arrived in Hong Kong in early April. That same day, Buchanan took his steam frigate out of the harbor and turned north toward Shanghai. That city was still under imperial authority, and thanks in part to Perry's firm stance, imperial officials there did not bother American merchants. But 150 miles upriver, just below Nanking, imperial authority gave way and the Taiping rebels were in charge. Little was known about the attitude of the Taipings toward Western merchants; no Western power had attempted to open discussions with them—until now.

For a month, while new air pump beam shafts were installed in the *Susquehanna*, Buchanan and McLane explored Shanghai in the *Confucius*, a small steamer that McLane chartered. Then, on 22 May, with the *Confucius* acting as a tender, the *Susquehanna* began the ascent of the Yangtze. Such a move was not only politically dangerous, it was physically dangerous as well, for no ship the size of the *Susquehanna* had ever attempted to steam up the Yangtze. Buchanan's charts were old, and the river's channels shifted constantly. The huge *Susquehanna* worked its way upriver very slowly, grounding occasionally on uncharted sandbars.[25]

The political dangers soon manifested themselves as well. At Chinkiang (Zhenjiang), where the *Susquehanna* arrived on 25 May, Buchanan exchanged salutes with the imperial fleet. But just beyond its anchorage, a fort onshore fired a shot across his bow. Buchanan stopped the ship and sent an officer ashore to demand an explanation. The officer returned without a reply, and Buchanan took pen in hand, writing to "the Commander of the forces at Chu Kiang fu." He minced no words: "If the fullest and most satisfactory apology is not made by you in response to my demand, I shall not hesitate on my return from Nanking to resent the insult offered to the flag of the United States." But before he could send the letter ashore, a Chinese official arrived with an effusive apology.[26]

The representatives of the Taiping government at Nanking proved far less pliable. After the *Susquehanna* arrived there on 27 May, Buchanan sent another message ashore, this one addressed to "the Commander in Chief of the Military Forces at Nanking." The note informed that official of the ship's arrival at Nanking with the American commissioner onboard and expressed a wish "to communicate with His Excellency."

Buchanan got back a most extraordinary reply, one guaranteed to provoke his natural combativeness: "From you, Buchanan, there has been
received a public Document in which a desire is expressed to come & see
the Eastern King's Golden face, but we, the Ministers of State, on reading what is contained therein find that you have presumed to employ
terms used in correspondence between equals. This is not in conformity
with what is right." Buchanan's astonishment metamorphosed into
anger as he read on. The ministers, it seemed, were willing to be lenient
in light of the fact that "Buchanan" resided "on the Ocean's borders" and
could not be expected to know the "ceremonies of the Celestial Court."
In consideration of this the ministers were willing to grant him indul-
gence and allow him "to bring tribute." By the time he finished reading
this letter, which was titled "A Mandatory Dispatch," Buchanan was
probably ready to load the tribute into a cannon and deliver it at once.
But McLane, who was determined not to provoke a confrontation,
calmed him down.[27]

Instead, therefore, Buchanan replied with a restrained but firm note
to "the Ministers of State at Nanking," in which he stated that the message he had received was "so peculiar and unintelligible as to cause me
much astonishment." He repeated the wish of the American minister to
communicate with the authorities at Nanking about the rights of Americans caught in the Chinese civil war. He closed with: "He also desires
me to inform you that the Government of the United States in their
intercourse with Foreign Governments, neither pay tribute nor acknowledge any superior pretensions on the part of other Nations." Buchanan
also sent a drawing of the U.S. flag "to prevent any future misapprehen-
sion on your part."[28]

While the ministers of state to the "Celestial King" thought this over,
Buchanan took the *Susquehanna* upriver beyond Nanking. No Western
ship had ever ascended the Yangtze beyond Nanking; indeed, no ship as
large, and no steamship of any size, had ever penetrated so far into
China. But whatever satisfaction Buchanan may have taken from playing the role of a pathfinder was lessened by his fury at having to put up
with the pretensions of the Taiping government. To Perry, Buchanan
reported that the United States should put no faith in the leaders of the
Taiping rebellion. As usual, he was candid to a fault: "A more worthless,
degraded class of beings I cannot think exists in this world."[29]

After McLane completed his business at Nanking, where he finally managed to deliver his message of American neutrality, the *Susquehanna* successfully maneuvered back down the Yangtze to Shanghai, and eventually back to Hong Kong, where in September McLane left the ship to join Perry on the *Powhatan*. The U.S. commissioner was full of compliments for "the cheerful spirit and consummate skill" with which Buchanan had performed his service, "involving as it did great difficulties in the matter of the navigation of the River, and very delicate relations to the two belligerent parties that occupied different points of it."[30]

Buchanan's time in the Far East was now drawing to a close. In September the *Susquehanna* lifted anchor at Hong Kong for the last time and steamed eastward across the Pacific to Honolulu, where it arrived on 18 October. While he was there, Buchanan entertained the Hawaiian king, Kamehameha III, at a dinner aboard the ship. From Hawaii, the *Susquehanna* headed east again to San Francisco, then south to Acapulco, Mexico, and south again to Valparaiso, Chile, making the passage between those cities in a record twelve days. From Valparaiso, Buchanan rounded Cape Horn for the third time in his life, and arrived at the Philadelphia Navy Yard on 10 March 1855, completing a circumnavigation of the globe two and one-half years after he left.[31]

Although Buchanan was not suited by instinct to the conduct of international diplomacy, his tenure of command on the *Susquehanna* had been almost entirely successful, and his partnership with Perry a happy one. Alas, both the cruise and that relationship ended on a bitter note. It had to do partly with shipboard discipline, and partly with Buchanan's conception of his professional perquisites and his honor as an officer.

Both Perry and Buchanan had reputations in the navy as advocates of reform. Both men had supported the adoption of steam navigation; both had supported the establishment of the Naval Academy; both favored a retirement program to clear the Navy List of superannuated officers. But neither man was a reformer when it came to questions of discipline— Perry and Buchanan were both unapologetic advocates of the lash. When in September 1850 Congress banned the use of the cat-o'-nine-tails on navy ships, both men had worried that the decision would make it difficult to maintain discipline aboard ship. Before he left for the Far East, Buchanan had received a letter from Perry in which the commodore mused that "we shall be obliged to govern in some measure . . . by moral suasion."[32]

Buchanan may have thought at first that Perry was being sarcastic, but as the mission lengthened, he began to suspect that he had been entirely serious. The commodore's alternative to flogging was an active program of ship-sponsored theatricals, races, and other such entertainments as a carrot for good behavior. Buchanan's response, which was far more typical among the officers of the day, was to find alternate forms of punishment. The problem was that most of the officially approved forms of punishment were dramatically less effective than flogging. Confinement—either in irons or on bread and water, or both—seemed to be the only realistic alternative. But it did not fully answer, for sailors often saw confinement, even on bread and water, as a break from work. Flogging had been so satisfactory precisely because the sailor could be back at work the next day. Besides, the spectacle of the punishment itself was a wonderful deterrent for the other hands. The sight of one of their own resting in jail while they worked was much less so.[33]

Buchanan experienced this reality firsthand while the *Susquehanna* was in Shanghai between visits to Japan. For gross insubordination, Buchanan sentenced marine private James Chapman to solitary confinement for thirty days and a dishonorable discharge without pay at the end of the cruise. But after serving his thirty days, Chapman refused to take any orders or do any more work. He knew that he was going to be dishonorably discharged, and he wasn't going to be paid, so why work? Buchanan would no doubt have loved to have the marine sergeant trice him up at a hatch cover and lay on a dozen or more first-rate stripes, but that was no longer an option. Instead, he ordered Chapman confined again and declared that he would remain confined in single irons until he agreed to do his duty. What else could he do?[34]

If Buchanan assumed that Perry shared his frustration about the limits placed by Congress on a commanding officer's authority, he may have misunderstood his man. Several times during the cruise, Perry interfered (as Buchanan saw it) with Buchanan's disciplinary decisions. On the first occasion, Buchanan presided over the court martial of Seaman Philip Daugherty, who had committed the grievous offense of assaulting an officer, Lt. John Duer, while Duer was placing him in irons for a minor offense. Buchanan sentenced Daugherty to be placed in double irons and to exist on bread and water for the duration of the cruise. Concerned that such a regimen might kill the sailor before the *Susquehanna* returned to the United States, Perry added a stipulation that the ship's surgeon was to visit the prisoner regularly to check on his health. If Seaman Daugherty showed any signs of physical deterioration, the surgeon was authorized to augment his diet.[35]

If Buchanan objected to such mollycoddling, he left no record of it. But he did object, and vociferously, to Perry's interference in the case of Coal Heaver William Thompson. Thompson's crime was the most serious of all: he had not only verbally threatened an officer of the ship (the ubiquitous Lieutenant Duer), he had drawn a weapon against him. During the ensuing fracas, Thompson had called out for all to hear: "Come on, you son of a bitch; you would not let me go ashore and want to treat me like a dog." Before being subdued, Thompson wielded an auger, an eyebolt, and even a musket. This was nothing short of mutiny. Nor was there any question about his guilt; there were literally dozens of witnesses. Clearly, Thompson had to be dealt with firmly and quickly as an example to the crew before such mutinous attitudes became endemic.[36]

At his court martial, Thompson readily confessed his crimes. Under such circumstances, the verdict of the court was certain, and there was only one prescribed punishment—death. Because there was no dispute over the facts, Buchanan did not call any witnesses. He merely heard Thompson's confession and then polled the court for its decision. To no one's surprise, the court found Thompson guilty, and Buchanan announced the sentence: Thompson was "to be hung by the neck until dead to the fore-yard arm of the United States Frigate *Susquehanna*."[37]

Perry changed the sentence. Perhaps he did not want the cruise to end on such an ugly note. Or perhaps (as one authority suggests) he remembered the outcry that had followed the execution aboard the *Somers* a decade earlier. In any case, he decided to seek legal as well as political advice, and he sent his flag lieutenant, Silas Bent, into Hong Kong to talk with Commissioner Robert McLane, who was also a lawyer. McLane responded that the sentence was perfectly legal, but he also noted that "it is very unusual to convict & sentence a man—particularly in so grave a case as the one in question—upon his simple 'pleading guilty.'" McLane concluded that "it is always better to have the corroborative testimony of witnesses." Thus advised, Perry decided to mitigate Thompson's sentence to life imprisonment.[38]

Buchanan might have been able to accept Perry's decision, but he could not accept Perry's public explanation for it. Perry wrote that the court had failed to do its full job: "The court did not take sufficient time to reflect upon a question of so grave a character," he wrote. "Evidence should have been taken upon all of the particulars in the case, notwithstanding the plea of the prisoner. . . . The Court . . . should have admitted his defense as evidence." Worst of all, Perry had this decision read aloud before the ship's company, thus chastising Buchanan publicly before his own command. For that, Buchanan would never forgive him.[39]

And he would not let it go. After he returned to the States, Buchanan took up the issue with the secretary of the navy. He charged that Perry had "overstepped the bounds of his privilege and propriety by addressing the conduct of the Court in language as illogical as untrue, and impugning my Character as a Member of the Court, to which I cannot submit in silence as a man of Honor." Prone as ever to flights of hyperbole whenever he felt that principle was at issue, he begged the secretary to rescue his reputation "from the ungenerous, unjust, and wanton abuse of Official Authority." Alas, he got no satisfaction from a Navy Department that was thoroughly pleased with Perry's handling of the whole Far East expedition. The only long-term fallout of this event was that it poisoned his relationship with Perry.[40]

In the half decade that straddled the midpoint of the nineteenth century, fate and chance conspired to place Franklin Buchanan at the center of events that characterized the two roles of the U.S. Navy. He was a warrior in Mexico, where he twice participated in the storming of an enemy fort; and he was a diplomat in both Japan and China, where he had to deal with a far subtler foe. In both assignments, he demonstrated his characteristic aggressiveness and his equally characteristic punctiliousness. But once again, his touchiness about matters of personal honor and his combative nature led him to undermine much of what he had gained by a pointless protest over a question of personal prerogative. The legacy of his protest would affect his standing in the navy. Franklin Buchanan divided most of humanity into two categories—"high toned" and "worthless." Mentally he consigned Perry to the latter category.

~8~

The Immortal Fifteen

We want to get rid of indifferent worthless officers.

For the rest of the 1850s, Franklin Buchanan was shorebound, a duck out of water living the life of a gentleman farmer on Maryland's Eastern Shore. Worse, he suffered intermittent bouts of ill health (a legacy of his long sojourn in the Far East) that frequently kept him bedridden. When not confined to the house, he contented himself with tending to his lands around the Rest, supervising minor repairs on the house and outbuildings, and planning the next year's crops. He also spent time with his family. After her miscarriage in 1851, Nannie gave birth to another daughter, and their last child, in 1853, completing a family of eight daughters and one son.

Buchanan's rural retreat was interrupted in the summer of 1855 by an appointment to serve on a board of navy officers charged with compiling a list of officers who would be compelled to retire. This was a reform Buchanan had long advocated, and he eagerly embraced the opportunity to play a role in it. The duty itself occupied only about five weeks, but the repercussions of the assignment dogged him for years and demonstrated just how political navy affairs could be when personnel issues were involved.

Buchanan had always conceived of himself as a tough-minded, forward-looking advocate of reform and efficiency. Despite his disdain for the so-called reformers who had abolished flogging, his self-image as a "high-toned" and progressive officer never wavered. In this case, a certain amount of his support for "reform" was the product of simple self-interest. He was convinced that there were too many superannuated, morally weak, or simply incompetent senior officers clogging up the Navy List and preventing the promotion of more energetic and talented men—men such as himself. Of course, he never couched his protests in such terms. He invariably presented his advocacy of reform as evidence of his concern for the efficiency of the service.

In Buchanan's view too many charlatans and opportunists already held commissions in the U.S. Navy. He had vigorously opposed granting commissions to veterans of the Texas navy in the aftermath of the annexation of that state in 1845; and in much the same spirit he opposed granting regular navy commissions to surgeons and pursers (including his brother McKean) who served at sea. He was perfectly willing to allow them in the wardroom, so long as it was clearly understood that they were subordinate to line officers and that they could never exercise command. He also advocated the forced retirement of any serving officer whose performance failed to meet the navy's standard of excellence.[1]

There was no such thing as retirement in the pre–Civil War navy. Unlike the Royal Navy, whose captains were required to retire at age fifty-five, in the U.S. Navy of the 1850s the *youngest* captain was fifty-six. Officers served (or at least they were kept on the Navy List) quite literally until they died. Some senior officers who continued to draw full shore pay had not had an assignment of any kind, ashore or afloat, for decades, and they had come to look on their positions as titled sinecures.[2]

It was Samuel F. Du Pont who first suggested in the fall of 1850 the idea of creating a "retired list" that would allow the navy to retire selected officers from the service and grant them some sort of pension. Buchanan thought it a splendid idea. "We want to get rid of indifferent worthless officers," he wrote to Du Pont, "and fill their places by worthy men, and I don't care how that object is attained as long as they do not starve those they retire." Thus assured of Buchanan's support, Du Pont shared with him a proposed draft for legislation that would turn the proposal into law, and even a prospective list of those who should be purged.[3]

Nothing came of their efforts at the time, but in 1855, after Buchanan returned from the Far East, Du Pont resurrected the idea. This time he found a ready audience in Franklin Pierce's secretary of the navy, James

C. Dobbin, and the chairman of the Senate Naval Affairs Committee, Stephen R. Mallory (D-Florida). At Du Pont's urging, Mallory introduced "An Act to Promote the Efficiency of the Navy" in January 1855. The act required the president to appoint fifteen officers—five captains, five commanders, and five lieutenants—to a special board that would "make a careful examination" of all active-duty officers and report the names of those who were "incapable of performing promptly and efficiently all their duty both ashore and afloat." Those named would then either be placed on a retired list or furloughed, or in a few cases, dropped entirely. It seemed a reasonable enough proposition at the time, and it passed Congress easily—unanimously in the Senate and overwhelmingly in the House—on the last day of February. Who, after all, could be opposed to efficiency?[4]

The selection of the fifteen officers who would serve on the board was crucial. Du Pont was convinced that the moral courage to vote one's conscience was at least as important as professional competence. He intended for the knife to cut deeply, and he wanted colleagues on the board who would not quail when it came time to make the hard call. He and Buchanan had discussed in some detail those whose participation would be most desirable to achieve their objective, and Buchanan was therefore not surprised when he received orders to report to Washington in May.

The board met for the first time on 20 June in a sultry, muggy Washington that had been abandoned by most government servants. Buchanan found himself part of a distinguished group. The captains on the board included Matthew C. Perry, William Shubrick, Charles McCauley, Cornelius Stribling, and Abraham Bigelow. Besides Buchanan, the other commanders were Samuel S. Barron, Andrew H. Foote, G. J. Pendergrast, and, of course, Du Pont.[5]

The board first examined the cases of passed midshipmen, masters, and lieutenants. In each of these cases all fifteen board members, including the five lieutenants, could vote. The five lieutenants on the board then withdrew, and the ten captains and commanders took up the consideration of the active-duty commanders; after that, the five captains considered the cases of their peers. In this way, although board members could vote on the fate of officers of their own rank and below, they could not vote to retire officers above them. On the other hand, Buchanan and the other commanders exercised considerable influence on all the decisions of the board by offering testimony and asking questions, and in that respect every member of the board shared in all of its decisions.[6]

Two contending factions emerged almost at once. One group, composed mostly of senior captains and led by Matthew Perry, expressed sympathy for those under examination, many of whom were personal friends, and voted only with the greatest reluctance to strike their names from the active list. The other group, led by Du Pont, urged a kind of pragmatic ruthlessness for the good of the service. The board did not constitute a court, and its proceedings were administrative rather than legal in nature. Although the board heard evidence from a variety of sources, its deliberations were secret, and most of the information presented was hearsay. Little, if any, of the "evidence" collected would have been admissible in a court anyway. In effect, the members of the board simply told one another what they knew or had heard about a particular officer. If the individual was unknown to them, they asked trusted friends for their opinions. In this manner they examined the cases of 712 officers in a little over five weeks.

The authorizing legislation did not specify the criteria to be applied by board members in reaching their decisions. Each member was therefore free to make that determination for himself. For Buchanan, issues of character predominated: Did the officer under consideration maintain strict discipline aboard ship? Did he have a reputation for truthfulness? Was he loyal to his friends? Did he shirk his duty? Did he drink? A man's professional competence or accomplishments carried little weight with Buchanan if he was not also a man of impeccable personal standards. In applying such criteria, Buchanan was a man on a mission, convinced of the correctness of his vision and of the need to trim away the rotten branches so that the healthy tree might grow stronger. His role did not cause him any apparent emotional agony; as he saw it, he was simply doing his duty. But he did feel another kind of agony. He suffered a return of what he called "my old China complaint"—probably severe diarrhea—and had to miss several meetings of the board. Even when he was present he was not as assertive as he otherwise might have been in urging his views on the committee. Nevertheless, he suffered through the sessions stoically, and by the third week in July the board had finished its work.[7]

For the most part Buchanan and Du Pont had their way. The board recommended that 71 officers be placed on a "Reserved" list and granted half pay; that 81 others be retired with "furlough pay" (a quarter of their full pay); and that 49 men be dropped altogether, their names to be simply removed from the Navy Register without further ceremony or compensation. A total of 201 officers were thus to be retired or shelved—not quite 30 percent of the entire officer corps. The ax fell hardest on the most senior. Fully four-fifths of all those recommended for retirement or dismissal came from the upper half of the Navy List. A cynic might argue that the board members were simply clearing the way for their own promotions. On the other hand, where else was one to find "deadwood" except at the top of the tree?[8]

Buchanan returned to the Rest at the end of July satisfied with what had been accomplished, but his physical torment had become so severe that he had to take to his bed at once. He could not leave it unaided, and he remained in bed several days, racked by intestinal pain and hardly able to move. At the end of the week, when he was strong enough to travel, he acted on his doctor's advice to retreat to Red Sweet Springs in Allegheny County, Virginia, to take the waters. There, as his health gradually improved, he scanned the papers for the latest navy news, and particularly for any public reaction to the board's recommendations. Several well-known names were on the list of those to be retired, and many of them had powerful friends in Congress. It soon became evident that there was going to be a fight to confirm the board's recommendations.[9]

The public controversy began almost at once. Those whom the board had voted to retire received their rather perfunctory letters of notification in the third week of September. Within days a virtual firestorm of protest erupted as one after another of them wrote to his congressman or senator to protest the decision. The most celebrated case was that of Lt. Matthew Fontaine Maury, a well-known hydrographer who had built an international reputation as a scientist, but who was physically crippled and on that basis had been recommended for retirement. Ironically, Maury himself had long been an advocate of reform through mandatory retirement, but it had never occurred to him that he might end up one of its victims. In any event, he was not going to take his forced retirement lying down. He sent letters to influential friends protesting what he called "this monstrous inquisition," urging them to use their influence to get the board's decision reversed.[10]

The protests from Maury and others unsettled a nervous Congress.

Senators had been happy to vote for "efficiency" in general terms, but they had never anticipated that more than two hundred officers would be affected. When letters from outraged constituents began to arrive, they could see that moving from the theoretical to the particular carried a stiff political price. As member after member rose in the Senate to present memorials from disappointed naval officers, the focus shifted from a consideration of the individual cases to accusations about the process. After all, the officers under investigation had never had a chance to defend themselves, or even been allowed to hear the charges against them. They had been charged, tried, and found guilty without ever knowing what shortcomings had been imputed to them.

The press, too, emphasized the inequity of the process. The *New York Journal* suggested that all the "retired" officers should be immediately restored to duty, "then if any charges rest against them on the records of the Navy Department, let them be tried, and, if found guilty, condemned. But it is absurd to believe that fifty percent of the Navy has been for years inefficient, immoral, and worthless."[11]

But "worthless" was exactly the word Buchanan used. As his health improved, so did his combativeness. Despite the complaints from the officers slated for retirement (or perhaps because of them), he began to wish that he had pushed for even more mandatory retirements. To Du Pont he wrote, "It is [a] matter of much regret to me now that I was so unwell while sitting as a member of the Board. . . . By exercising a little more tact with the Captains of the 'Board' we could have induced them to lay aside a few more of their grade." It was mortifying to him that there were still "several men on the list who are useless to the Service." He named a half dozen additional captains, John Aulick among them, who "ought to be retired." As for those who complained that the board had been unfair, Buchanan was utterly unsympathetic. It would be "an outrage on the Service," he wrote, if any of those named by the board were returned to the active list.[12]

There was some good news. While in Virginia, Buchanan learned that he had been nominated for promotion to captain. Indeed, all five of the commanders who had served on the board had been selected for promotion, a fact that attracted public notice and added fuel to the controversy. Those officers whose careers had been cut short (as they saw it) by the "Board of Fifteen" argued that it smacked of crude self-interest that members of the committee who had voted to force them into retirement were now to be rewarded with promotions. It did not help that the promotions were announced on the very day following the publication of the board's findings. This had all the trappings of a political deal. The *New York Journal* editorialized that it was at least suspicious, and perhaps dishonorable, that the members of the board could dismiss their competitors in closed session while board members themselves avoided "the ordeal of a secret inquisition." The *New York Herald* heaped sarcastic praise on the "fifteen Spartans" for inflicting a "Thermopylae defeat" on 201 of their fellow officers, by which heroic action they "promoted themselves." In backing Maury's claim to reconsideration, *Scientific American* noted archly that it was evident that the members of the board "all took very good care to look out for Number 1."[13]

Whether or not Buchanan's promotion was intended as a reward for his willingness to prune the service of inefficient officers, the ensuing furor over both the board's report and his pending promotion had two consequences: first, the board's recommendations were put on hold; and second, Buchanan's promotion was delayed. It would be a full year before he could put on the uniform of a navy captain.

Buchanan returned to the Rest in the first week of October and settled back into the life of a country farmer. He kept in touch by mail with his friends in the Navy Department and Congress, and eagerly followed developments in Washington. He also began to receive letters from those whom he had voted to retire. A few of them, including Maury, demanded that he explain and justify his vote. Buchanan refused to be drawn into a debate over individual cases, and for the most part he replied that he had simply done his duty. To one officer who insisted that Buchanan answer a list of questions about that officer's moral and professional fitness, Buchanan replied coldly that because his answers "would neither benefit nor gratify" the man, he declined to respond. To Maury's inquiry he did not reply at all.[14]

Buchanan professed to have no second thoughts about his behavior—neither on the merits of the issue nor on whether the ensuing controversy would affect his own eventual promotion. His friends assured him that it was only a matter of time before the decisions of the board—and his promotion—were confirmed by Congress. He simply had to stick it out. To Du Pont he wrote, "We must expect some hard rubs from various quarters, but as we are satisfied that we did our duty tolerably well, I don't think we need fear the result." Indeed, he insisted that if given a second chance, he would "apply the knife a little deeper."[15]

But as time passed and no decision was forthcoming, he grew more concerned. At midwinter he confessed to Du Pont, "I am anxious to know what the Naval Committee intends to do." He even began to wonder what status he would have in the navy if his promotion were not confirmed. Would he remain a commander, or would he be in the navy at all? On the question of the retirements he remained unyielding. "I have not hesitated to say in every letter I have written to my friends since our action that if the duty was to be performed over again, my vote would be given to retire more than were retired, for we certainly left many worthless men on the active list who ought not to be there."[16]

Buchanan's precarious health interrupted his routine again in the early winter when he caught a severe cold while supervising the collection of ice for his icehouse. He recovered in time to enjoy Christmas at home, but fell ill again with his "old China complaint" in the new year. He could not keep any food down and began losing weight dramatically. For a period of weeks there was some concern that he might not survive the winter. But his appetite gradually returned, and by March he was nearly recovered.

While he lay prostrate in his Eastern Shore home, Congress took up the issue of navy retirements, and a general debate broke out on the floor of the Senate. Robert Toombs of Georgia took the lead in criticizing the Retirement Board's action. He objected most of all to the apparent arbitrariness of its decisions, and claimed that it had exceeded its jurisdiction by considering questions of character as well as professional competence—precisely those issues that Buchanan had emphasized. Because the board members had exceeded their jurisdiction, Toombs argued, "I believe that this proceeding was illegal; that the law was not properly executed; [and] that the action of the board is void."[17]

The crusty and avuncular Sam Houston spoke several times on the question, not only to defend those whom he characterized as victims of the purge, but even more to criticize those who had conducted the purge. He asserted boldly that they acted from selfish motives and implied that if their own careers were subjected to the same kind of secret and malicious scrutiny that they had focused on others, they would be exposed as being no better, and in many cases far worse, than those whom they had voted to retire. On 18 March 1856, Houston spoke for more than three hours before a full Senate and a packed gallery. He characterized the work of the board as a deliberate conspiracy designed "to strike down chivalrous and gallant men and give position and promotion to those who grasped the scepter in their hands and wielded it with despotic sway." The entire proceeding, he said, was a devious plot by a group of self-interested officers, and he named Du Pont as chief among them.[18]

Mallory defended the board as best he could, but he was on the defensive, and for a while it seemed that the board's recommendations would be thrown out entirely. Several of those who had served on the board traveled to Washington to justify and explain their decisions, but Buchanan was not among them. Still bedridden, he apologized to Du Pont that he could not help in the effort to defend the board's decisions from Houston's slanderous assaults. "It has been a serious annoyance to me, my worthy friend, that I have been prevented from assisting you all in Washington in quieting these blustering ignorant Senators, many of whose speeches are made for 'bunkham,' who are so much disposed to support worthless men and blackguards."[19]

Buchanan did eventually have an opportunity to reply to Houston. One afternoon months later, he was standing in the Capitol with several other officers when the Texas senator walked up in the company of a few others. Buchanan offered him a "Good afternoon," and Houston replied cordially, saying that he was glad to see him.

"I don't know that General," Buchanan replied pleasantly. "You abused us so much in your speech last winter."

At that, Houston took a closer look, then said, "Oh, you were one of the Board."

"Yes, I was," Buchanan replied. "And if I had the duty to perform over again, I would give my vote to retire more."

Houston, who was sixty-four years old and slightly hard of hearing, replied "Oh, if you had it to do over again, you would do better."

Buchanan wanted to be sure that the aging senator got the point. "Yes," he said, "by *retiring more*."[20]

Buchanan had an opportunity to discuss the situation with more sympathetic senators when Judah P. Benjamin (D-Louisiana) and Thomas Pratt (D-Maryland) visited Edward Lloyd at Wye House. Both senators had supported the Board of Fifteen in the floor debate, and Buchanan took the opportunity to talk with them about naval affairs generally.

Looking out, as always, for his own professional prospects, he broached not only the question of his own pending promotion to captain, but also another issue. During the expedition to Japan, he told them, he had been a commander in rank but he had borne the duties and responsibilities of a captain. Since he had done the job of a captain, wasn't he also entitled to the pay of a captain? The two senators were sympathetic to this argument, and Buchanan took their assurances to mean that he would not only soon be promoted, but that he was likely to get some welcome back pay as well.[21]

Congress eventually hammered out a compromise on the retirements. Mallory proposed a new bill that would allow retired and furloughed officers to appeal their cases, and in January 1857 Congress passed "An Act to Amend 'An Act to Promote the Efficiency of the Navy.'" Buchanan viewed this as less a compromise than a retreat. He saw little wisdom in giving ground to pedantic blusterers. "We must take a bold stand," he wrote to Du Pont, "and state our reasons and authority for our acts, and name the officers from whom we received information." If the Navy Department wanted to restore an officer out of a sense of "clemency & forgiveness," that was one thing, but to imply that the board had somehow done these men a wrong was entirely unacceptable. It would impute error—or even worse, dishonor—on the part of the members of the board. In his usual contentious tone, he wrote Du Pont, "We must not for a moment let the Sec'y or President suppose that we will submit tamely to any thing that can reflect upon our honor." He predicted that "the whole affair will be a total failure."[22]

Buchanan expected to be ordered to Washington to provide testimony before the new boards. When such orders were not forthcoming, he went anyway. He left Easton on 25 February 1857 and took the steam ferry to Annapolis, stopping to dine with his brother-in-law William Goldsborough before taking the afternoon train to Washington, where he checked into the Ebbitt House.[23]

He called on Commodore Shubrick to discuss the arrangement of the boards and who would serve on them. Buchanan emphasized the importance of finding officers who were not only advocates of reform but who also had unassailable records of personal and professional behavior— "none who have ever lived in glass houses" was the way he put it. Shubrick's first notion was to create three boards, one for each category of retired officer (retired, furloughed, or dropped). But Buchanan suggested that it would be better to arrange the boards (and the cases) by seniority, so that junior men did not find themselves judging their seniors, a nicety that had not overly concerned him when he had argued (though, of course, not voted) for the retirement of dozens of navy captains.[24]

He stayed in Washington for several weeks, testifying in more than a dozen cases and urging in each that the original decision of the board be confirmed. He became increasingly depressed, however, and convinced that politics, not considerations of competence, would rule the day. The disappointed officers simply had too much political clout. Senators came to the defense of their constituents without concerning themselves overmuch about the merits of their cases. Some implied that every officer who had been recommended for retirement by the board was the victim of a vicious cabal, and characterized the Board of Fifteen as a kind of Court of Star Chamber.[25]

Buchanan recognized that he was fighting a losing battle. Many of the officers called to testify before the courts suffered from a convenient amnesia. Board member Charles McCauley professed not to know anything at all, good or bad, about one officer, despite having lived and served with him for years. Likewise, Thomas ap Catesby Jones (himself originally slotted for retirement by the board in part because of rumors about his fondness for boys) claimed to know nothing whatsoever about the moral character of any of the officers with whom he had served. Worst of all, in Buchanan's view, was the behavior of Matthew Perry, who not only testified on behalf of many of the men he had voted to retire, but now claimed that he had opposed their retirement and had simply been outvoted. Perry even published a letter in the *New York Herald* claiming that he had protested the retirements to the president. Buchanan was disgusted. "It is nothing more than I expected from old Perry," he wrote to Du Pont. "I knew he had not the manly courage and independence to adhere to his acts . . . he is as culpable as the rest of us." Buchanan was pleased, however, when his own nephew Charles S. Winder positively "disgorged" before the committee, providing it with more than enough evidence (in Buchanan's opinion) to sustain the board's decision in a number of cases.[26]

Even when the court sustained a board decision, however, that decision still had to be approved by the secretary of the navy and confirmed by the Senate. Buchanan was particularly disgusted with the new secretary

of the navy, Connecticut-born Isaac Toucey, who replaced the North
Carolinian Dobbin in March. Buchanan wrote Du Pont that Toucey was
"the poorest Secretary we have ever had!" In language that hinted at his
growing sectionalism, he charged that "Our Sec'y is a Yankee through."[27]

In the spring, Buchanan was informed that his testimony was no
longer required. "I heard and saw enough to disgust any man of proper
Naval pride," he reported to Du Pont. "I was rejoiced when I found I was
not required any more." The announcement of the court's findings soon
followed. A total of 118 of the original 201 officers who had been nominated for retirement by the board had chosen to appeal their cases. Of
those 118, just over half (64) were returned to duty by the court of
inquiry. One of them was Maury, who was promoted to commander. Of
the remaining 54, 29 were elevated from one-quarter pay to half pay, 8
withdrew their appeal, 1 failed to appear before the court, and 1 died.
Counting those who chose not to appeal, a total of 137 of the 201 officers
recommended for retirement by the Board of Fifteen were, in fact,
retired. It would be easy to count this as a victory for reform.

But Buchanan was not happy. Half a loaf was not good enough. He
believed that by restoring "incompetent" men to positions of responsibility, the court had done more mischief to the navy and the nation than
any other tribunal in the country's history. Although Mallory and other
"friends of the Navy" had tied to prevent confirmation of some of the
most questionable cases, "the Senate took the matter out of their hands
and after a very acrimonious debate, confirmed the whole batch." As
Buchanan saw it, the cowardly Senate confirmed the findings, and the
equally spineless president signed them. "The President did not examine one record," Buchanan complained, he "just looked at the finding."
It was enough "to disgust all those who feel the proper interest in the
service, and have a proper sensitive pride in all matters relating to their
profession."[28]

Although disappointed that weak men in the government had failed
to sustain their good work, Buchanan was proud of his service on the
Board of Fifteen. For the rest of his life, he remained convinced that he
and Du Pont had pursued the correct course. Indeed, his behavior
throughout the entire process demonstrated his tendency to choose a
side and defend it with unwavering commitment. There was little room
for nuance in Buchanan's universe. Like most issues, the fight over the
recommendations of the Retirement Board became for him a matter of

right versus wrong—even good versus evil. Likewise, the participants in the discussion were either friends or enemies. Those, like "Old Perry," who quailed or backed away from the hard calls were nothing more than cowards; the others, those who held fast and took the heat, were heroes. Buchanan felt a bond with them akin to that formed by men who fought side by side in a bloody battle. For the rest of his life he remembered with pride and fondness the work of what he called "the immortal fifteen."[29]

⚜9⚜

WAR CLOUDS

The Negro is the cause of it all.

I
n spite of his disgust at the political gamesmanship that had watered down the recommendations of the Retirement Board, Buchanan's professional prospects were never higher than in the last few years of the 1850s. He was finally confirmed in the rank of full captain—the highest rank then possible in the U.S. Navy—and he could look forward to the command of either a squadron overseas or a navy yard at home. Even better, his health had finally returned. "I am quite myself again," he wrote to Du Pont in the summer of 1856, "perfectly well and nearly as stout as ever, eat well and drink as usual." That same month, he applied to the Navy Department requesting "active service at sea." No orders were forthcoming until the spring of 1859, however, and in the meantime he remained at the Rest living the life of a country gentleman.[1]

During those years, events in Kansas and elsewhere intensified the sectional debate, edging the nation ever closer to the brink of disaster. Buchanan deplored the sectional bickering, and he particularly resented the preachy tone of northern abolitionists, whom he held responsible for the climate of confrontation. That resentment, combined with a hardening of his own views about slavery and an increasing antagonism toward all things "Yankee," led him to side with the southern position on most national issues. His close association with the Lloyds contributed significantly to this process. In time, these views would lead him to the most fateful decision of his personal professional life.

Buchanan's daily regimen was dominated by the responsibilities of superintending the grounds at the Rest and by the activities of his large family. Sallie, the oldest, turned twenty in December 1855 (the same month Buchanan received his promotion to captain); Letitia was eighteen; Alice was sixteen; the twins, Nannie and Ellen, were fourteen; Elizabeth was eleven; Buchanan's only son, Franklin Jr., was nine; Rosa was five; and the youngest, Mary Tilghman, was almost three. His time was also taken up by the charms (and demands) of the wider circle of his family and friends throughout Talbot County, a circle that included several brothers-in-law and that was presided over by his wife's brother Edward, who had returned from his unsuccessful attempt to establish new plantations in the Deep South to resume his roles as the master of Wye House and the unchallenged patriarch of Talbot County. Wye House once again became a political and social salon for Maryland's cognoscenti. Buchanan was naturally part of this society, and he had frequent opportunities to engage in lengthy discussions with Edward Lloyd about family affairs, farm management, navy news, and, of course, national politics.

Throughout most of his adult life, Buchanan had been a Whig, the traditional party affiliation of the propertied classes. But he had broken with the Whigs in 1852, declining to vote for General Winfield Scott because he did not think Scott was "a Navy man," and because he did not believe him to be "any safer on the slavery question than [Franklin] Pierce," even though Scott was from Virginia and Pierce was from New Hampshire. By 1856 Buchanan no longer had the option of voting for a Whig for president, for the party had been torn asunder by the growing national quarrel over slavery in the territories. Lacking a Whig candidate on the ballot, antislavery Whigs gravitated to the new Republican Party, while proslavery Whigs, like Buchanan, became Democrats.[2]

Edward Lloyd, too, was a Democrat. In his case, it was a family tradition. His own father had been a Democratic governor of Maryland and a Democratic U.S. senator. But in addition, Lloyd was a Democrat because of what one contemporary called "a belief that in the supremacy of that party lay not only the national welfare but the security of his property in slaves." By 1856 Edward Lloyd had come to measure national political candidates in terms of their soundness on the slavery question.[3]

Buchanan owned only six slaves—family servants rather than field hands—but he, too, often assessed national candidates for office on the basis of their commitment to the defense of slavery. He was horrified by the emergence of the Republican Party in 1856 and the presidential candidacy of John C. Frémont. Although Buchanan's father had expressed public opposition to slavery in the 1790s, and had even participated in meetings of the Maryland Society for Promoting the Abolition of Slavery, such views were anathema to the son. In the increasingly confrontational political climate of the late 1850s, Buchanan foreswore the legacy of his father's opposition to slavery and embraced the proslavery doctrines of his in-laws.

Given Buchanan's tendency to view issues in terms of moral absolutes and to ignore the more ambiguous middle ground, it is not surprising that he ascribed only the basest motives to the opponents of slavery, and saw himself and other defenders of slavery as the guardians of honor and stability. The principal problem in American society, he believed, was "the rascally Northern interference with the institution of slavery," and particularly the ranting of northern abolitionists, who ought to mind their own business instead of trying to enforce their perverse views on the rest of the country. Frémont was not an outright abolitionist, but he was the next best (or worst) thing, for he opposed the right of slave owners to take their slaves into the western territories—territories that had been won at least in part by the sacrifice and bloodshed of men from the slaveholding states. Moreover, Buchanan believed that Frémont lacked the high moral character to be expected in a president. After hearing stories from friends about Frémont's grandstanding and incompetence in California during the war with Mexico, the judgmental Buchanan wrote off "the Pathfinder" as a simple charlatan and opportunist. The election of such a man, he believed, would tear the country apart. "If Fremont is elected," he wrote to Du Pont, "which I cannot believe, there will be no certainty how long the U. States may hold together."[4]

In the election held that fall, Buchanan voted *against* Frémont at least as much as he voted *for* the Democratic candidate, who, coincidentally, was also named Buchanan but was no relation to him. James Buchanan was a Pennsylvanian, but one who relied heavily on southern support, a political arrangement that led his enemies to pin on him the pejorative epithet "doughface," meaning that he was a northern man with southern principles. For his part, Franklin Buchanan was pleased that the new president-elect was "sound on the slavery question," and he was satisfied "to wait and see what the administration of Mr. Buchanan could do to allay this unpleasant feeling in the country."[5]

He was generally disappointed by Franklin Pierce's State of the Union message in December. He was pleased that the lame duck president declared that the work of the Retirement Board had been "attended by the most advantageous results." But Pierce spent most of his annual message outlining the sectional dispute over slavery, and especially the violence in Kansas. Although the president put most of the blame on northern fanaticism (correctly, in Buchanan's view), Buchanan nevertheless feared that the president's remarks would re-ignite the dispute. "I do not like that portion of the President's message that dwells so long on slavery and the acts of Northern fanatics," he wrote to Du Pont. "He has caused an unnecessary excitement in the country . . . , and the whole session will be expended in long excited speeches which can do no good."[6]

An important insight into Buchanan's hardening attitude about slavery can be detected in his response to Maryland's effort to define the legal status of its growing population of free blacks. Maryland was a slave state, but it was also a "border state" with the nation's largest population of free blacks. These facts affected the local debate over the "peculiar institution" in two important ways. First, its border-state status made Maryland a particular target of abolitionist literature. That angered and irritated Maryland's slaveholding population, including Buchanan, and kept the issue percolating. Second, the state's large free black population seemed to many slaveholders—Buchanan among them, but more particularly Edward Lloyd—a tangible and proximate threat to their interests and even their safety. Both of these factors drew Buchanan increasingly into the local, and eventually the national, debate over slavery.

Within Maryland, the agricultural Eastern Shore, and especially Talbot County, was the area most strongly committed to slavery. Even there, however, free blacks constituted a significant—and growing—percentage of the population. The 1850 census revealed that almost half of the county's total population (48 percent) was black, and, further, that free blacks made up a significant proportion of that black population (2,593 of 6,727, or 38 percent). Indeed, during the decade of the 1850s, even as the number of black slaves in the county declined by 10 percent (to 3,725), the free black population increased by more than 14 percent (to 2,964).[7] Many slaveholders found that trend deeply troubling.

One problem particularly affected large planters such as Edward Lloyd: the natural increase of his slave population (which also increased his capital wealth) meant that additional work had to be found to keep this growing labor force from idleness. In Maryland and Virginia, however, most of the arable land was already in use. Most slaveholders confronted by this problem sold their "excess" slaves to planters in parts of the country still in need of labor—Alabama and Mississippi in particular, and also the trans-Mississippi West. That is precisely why the closure of the West through the Missouri Compromise had been so troubling to men like Edward Lloyd.

In the 1830s, Lloyd had sought to resolve his excess labor problems by buying substantial tracts of land in Arkansas, Louisiana, and Mississippi where his slaves would have plenty of work. He had spent many years in Mississippi attempting (unsuccessfully) to make the new plantations pay for themselves. More recently, he had begun to "sell his slaves South," consigning them to dealers who sold them for a profit in the Cotton Belt. In the late 1850s, Lloyd sold off more than a hundred of his slaves, though he remained by far the largest slaveholder in the county.[8]

For smaller slave owners, however, selling "excess" slaves was often not a viable solution. Lacking access to national markets for the internal slave trade, some simply freed their slaves; others rented them out under conditions that allowed the slaves, over time, to purchase their freedom, a practice that contributed to the growing number of free blacks in the county. The growth of the free black population was worrisome to slave owners for three reasons. First, it put the lie to the argument that slavery was the natural condition of the black race—one of the principal justifications for slavery put forward by southerners. Second, it undercut the financial underpinning of the institution by depressing the price of slaves on the open market. And third, it seemed to many to constitute a social threat as well. The presence of a large population of free blacks, answerable to no one but themselves, was a prospect that troubled many, if not most, whites. As the historian Barbara Fields has noted, "The rise of two free populations in Maryland, one white and one black, challenged the political, moral, and ideological coherence of slave society."[9]

Concerned about this issue, a score of Eastern Shore slave owners organized a convention that met at Snow Hall, in Worcester County, in

the fall of 1858. The ostensible purpose of the meeting was to devise better security for the management of slaves. Angered by the steady northward flow of runaways, some delegates supported increased punishments for escapees, including torture and death, although the moderates
in attendance opposed such proposals. When they found themselves
unable to agree, the delegates issued a call for each of the Eastern Shore
counties to send representatives to another convention to be held in
Cambridge, in Dorcester County, in November.

Although there is no evidence to suggest that he sought the assignment, Buchanan was one of twenty delegates elected from Talbot
County to attend this conference. In the first week of November, he traveled to Cambridge, where his vote helped elect his brother-in-law
William Goldsborough president of the convention. After much discussion, the delegates adopted a resolution decrying the presence of free
Negroes on the Eastern Shore and the "evils resulting therefrom." The
resolution asserted that "free negroes and slavery are incompatible with
each other, and should not be permitted longer to exist in their present
relations side by side within the limits of the state." The solution offered
was as simple as it was draconian. Free blacks would be presented with
an alternative: "go into slavery or leave the state."[10]

Such a doctrine—that all blacks who lived in a slave state must be
slaves—was characteristic of only the most assertive and combative slave
cultures of the Deep South. That Buchanan would support it proves how
far he had gravitated away from the antislavery doctrines of his father.
His Whiggish moderation had given way to an assertive property rights
doctrine that was not dissimilar to that of southern fire-eaters in Mississippi or South Carolina.

Another aspect of Buchanan's growing sectionalism in the 1850s was his
increased antagonism toward all things northern, and particularly
toward anything that could be labeled "Yankee." This was ironic in two
ways: first, because it flew in the face of Buchanan's lifelong patriotism,
wherein he had celebrated "Yankee" victories over foreign foes; and second, because in his personal life Buchanan was something of a Puritan.
His often expressed disgust at any evidence of human weakness—drunkenness, licentiousness, even simple greed—would have been fully appreciated by the scions of Plymouth or Salem. But by 1858, "Yankeeism" had
come to mean something very different to him. It no longer meant hard

work, personal responsibility, and self-denial. Instead it stood for a sharp deal, a cut corner, a shirked responsibility.

He was disgusted, for example, with recent events in China. In order to prevent the Chinese from interfering with Western trade on the Pearl River, the British, with French support, had declared Canton to be under blockade. The British had invited the United States to join in the effort, but the United States had declined. To Buchanan, that decision was worse than simple cowardice, it was scheming calculation. "We must come in for the same advantages without having spent a *cent* or sacrificed a *life* to accomplish it," he wrote disapprovingly. Although some argued that this was merely wise policy, Buchanan saw it as calculating and pusil-lanimous, a policy unworthy of a great nation. "*Cute Yankee tricks*," he wrote, "cannot elevate the character of any country." "If this is not *Yan-keeism* what is it?" Victories in war, or in statecraft, should come fairly and forthrightly by dint of sacrifice and bloodshed, not be won by sleight of hand or careful calculation. Such calculation was unheroic, if not unmanly, and demonstrated an insufficient concern for principle.[11]

Buchanan's lengthy hiatus awaiting orders finally ended in the spring of 1859. He had twice requested sea service, and Secretary of the Navy Isaac Toucey had promised him that he "would not be overlooked." He had hopes, even expectations, of getting orders to "a fine ship," and was astonished when instead he was ordered to take command of the Wash-ington Navy Yard. There were always many contenders for this plum job, and Buchanan had not even asked for it. He was in Annapolis sitting on a board of examination for midshipmen when the orders arrived to pro-ceed to the Washington Navy Yard "without delay" and assume com-mand. He arrived in Washington two days later, "assembled all hands, made a short speech, and took command."[12]

Buchanan's ascension to command of the Washington Navy Yard should have been the pinnacle of his career. While his duties were largely administrative, the assignment validated his importance and influence. He and Du Pont (who got command of the Philadelphia Navy Yard) were now at the very top of the navy hierarchy. Ever since their midshipman days together on the old *Franklin*, they had talked about how they would reform the navy if and when they achieved positions of command authority. Now they had them.

Buchanan's satisfaction in this accomplishment was fleeting, however. Although the administration of the navy yard kept Buchanan fully occupied, the accelerating sectional crisis soon dominated his thoughts. In October, news arrived of John Brown's raid on the government arsenal at Harpers Ferry, Virginia, and Buchanan was cautioned by his superiors to be wary of saboteurs and insurrectionists. The following summer, the pending presidential election excited the passions of even the most apolitical.

Buchanan considered Abraham Lincoln's candidacy almost an insult. In Maryland, the presidential race was a contest between John Bell, the Constitutional Unionist from Tennessee, whose platform was to rely on the Constitution to safeguard the interests of the South, and John C. Breckinridge, the sitting vice president, who advocated a more hard-line defense of southern rights. Statewide, Breckinridge won a narrow victory over Bell (45.7 percent to 44.9 percent), with Stephen A. Douglas picking up most of the rest of the votes. In Talbot County, Breckinridge ran even stronger, winning an absolute majority; almost certainly Buchanan and the rest of the extended Lloyd clan voted for him. Just as certainly none of them voted for Lincoln, who received only two votes in Talbot County.[13]

Lincoln was elected nonetheless, and that event, widely expected, triggered an immediate secession ordinance from South Carolina. The Union, southern newspapers declared, was dissolved. Buchanan was perplexed by these events. Was the Union permanently dissolved, or was this merely another bump on the road to the next compromise? "Matters may become reconciled," he wrote to Du Pont the day after Christmas, "but there are none here who think so." There was a suggestion of a less-than-absolute commitment to the old flag in his assertion that "we can never again feel as proud of the flag we sail under, as we have felt during our naval careers."[14]

The success of South Carolina's gambit depended on the reaction of the rest of the South. In the first weeks of the new year, six other Deep South states followed the Palmetto State's example, and on 4 February, delegates from those states met in Montgomery, Alabama, to form a southern Confederacy. James Buchanan, now a lame duck president, was unwilling to precipitate a crisis and did nothing, or at least nothing that was likely to lead to hostilities. Franklin Buchanan was still an officer of the U.S. Navy, and he remained committed to his duty. Three days before the Confederate Congress met, he issued orders to those under his command specifying their obligations in case the yard was assailed by an armed mob: "This yard shall not be surrendered to any person or persons except by an order from the Hon. Secretary of the Navy, and in the event of an attack, I shall require all officers & others under my Command to defend it to the last extremity."[15]

A month later, Abraham Lincoln took the oath of office as president, adopting a conciliatory but uncompromising tone in his inaugural address. He asserted that the secession ordinances were "legally void" and avowed his determination to protect and defend all federal territory—including, by clear implication, Fort Sumter. The new administration toyed with a variety of plans to reassert national authority. Along with Fort Pickens near Pensacola, Fort Sumter in Charleston Harbor was at the center of most of these plans. The new navy secretary, Gideon Welles, ordered Buchanan to prepare the steam sloop *Pawnee* for sea as part of a relief effort for the garrison of Fort Sumter. He was to ensure that it had a month's provisions onboard and that it was ready by 6 April. On that date, Buchanan dutifully reported that the *Pawnee* had left that morning for Norfolk "in obedience to its order."[16]

During this critical period, as the nation teetered on the brink of war, Buchanan hosted a wedding. One of the twins—Nannie, who was now twenty—married Lt. Julius E. Meiere of the U.S. Marine Corps. The wedding took place at the navy yard on 3 April, and Buchanan's exalted status was validated by a glittering guest list that included Abraham Lincoln himself. The Buchanan-Lloyd clan was not altogether certain that the president did them any honor with his presence. Buchanan himself was professionally correct, but Elizabeth, then fifteen, declared that she would not shake hands with the man. But the cheerful demeanor and friendly manner of the tall, lean president, who smiled at her and called her a "little rebel," convinced her to shake hands after all. After the ceremony, Lincoln escorted the bride in to dinner.[17]

Nine days later, on 12 April, Confederate authorities fired on Fort Sumter, and three days after that, Lincoln responded by calling for volunteers to suppress "combinations" of men "too powerful to be suppressed by the ordinary course of judicial proceedings." Lincoln's announcement, taken as a declaration of an intent to "coerce" the South back into the Union, prompted four more states to side with the southern Confederacy: Arkansas, Tennessee, North Carolina, and, most important of all, Virginia. That brought the crisis very close to home—

not only to Buchanan's professional home at the Washington Navy Yard, now across the river from what was putatively a foreign country, but also to his ideological home, the slave state of Maryland.[18]

Many Marylanders, especially those in Talbot County and the rest of the Eastern Shore, expected to follow Virginia out of the Union. A week after Fort Sumter, on 19 April, that expectation seemed about to be fulfilled when a Massachusetts regiment marching along Pratt Street in Baltimore en route to the nation's capital was attacked by a mob of citizens. The troops fired on the crowd, killing twelve. Southern papers trumpeted their outrage at this massacre of innocent citizens by the minions of abolition. The whole tenor of the discussion over Maryland's future changed in a day, and secession seemed imminent.

The mood in Washington was all but hysterical. The clerk of the House of Representatives sent to the Navy Department for "seventy-five revolvers" so that the officers of the Congress could defend themselves. Welles was more concerned about the safety of the navy yard. He sanctioned the organization of militia companies made up of yard workers until Buchanan complained that such acts stripped him of his labor force at a time when he needed it badly. Welles then ordered Buchanan to place as much valuable material as he could aboard the USS *Anacostia* to ensure a quick getaway if necessary. The important thing, he wrote to Buchanan, was "to prevent public property [from] falling into the hands of lawless persons." Privately, Welles believed it might be necessary to destroy the yard, and he ordered Captain John A. Dahlgren, at Norfolk, "to confer immediately with Captain Buchanan."[19]

For his part, Buchanan assumed that Maryland's exit from the Union was certain—that, as he expressed it later, "she was virtually OUT of the Union." There were rumors that federal forces were about to shell Baltimore, and he convinced himself that "every Marylander should be at his post." He had relatives in Baltimore, and he decided that he ought to be there too "to render all the assistance in [his] power."[20]

Three days later he walked into the office of Secretary of the Navy Gideon Welles and presented his resignation. Hard as it was, he had no doubt at the time that he was doing the correct thing. Within days, however, he realized that he had acted too hastily. Maryland did not secede, nor did it appear likely to do so. Somewhat sheepishly, he wrote to Welles from his self-imposed exile at the Rest to recall his resignation. That same day (4 May) he admitted to a friend that he regretted resigning, that he was not a secessionist, and that he would be unhappy out of the service. When he received Welles's curt reply that his name had been struck from the Navy List, however, Buchanan's resentment flared anew. As he nursed that resentment, he found additional reasons to justify his resignation.[21]

Buchanan considered his abrupt dismissal by Welles an uncharitable and ungrateful act. After all, he wrote to a nephew in Baltimore, he had never done anything to earn the suspicion of the government. "I am as strong a Union man as any in the country," he asserted. "I am no secessionist, I do not admit the right of secession, but at the same time I admit the right of revolution." But Union man or not, his hurt feelings and truculent mood were evident in his next lines: "I have never written or sent a message South to secure a situation there," he wrote, "but I have been told I could get one without the least difficulty." Buchanan apparently considered the Lincoln administration to be on probation. "My intention is to remain neutral," he wrote. "But if all law is to be dispensed with . . . and a coercive policy continued which would disgust barbarians, and the South literally trampled upon, I may change my mind and join them." For the moment, however, his dominant emotion was sadness. "The deed is done," he wrote, "and I am made an unhappy man."[22]

His sadness changed to anger after Buchanan had a small, but very personal, brush with the minions of Lincoln's government. In June a small party of soldiers landed at his private dock and began to remove the arms and ammunition from the armory in Easton. He would have resented this in any case, but he was positively infuriated when he looked out a window of his home and saw a party of men removing the decorative cannonballs from atop his gateposts—cannonballs that he himself had captured from the Mexican fort of La Peña at Tuxpan. He stormed outside, confronted the officer in charge, and peremptorily ordered him to put the cannonballs back.[23]

When the young army captain in charge of the party claimed that he was merely following the orders of Colonel Smith of the Brooklyn Volunteers, Buchanan immediately set off to find Colonel Smith and set him straight. Smith affirmed that indeed he had ordered the removal of the cannonballs, as well as any other arms that might be found. Buchanan employed his quarterdeck voice to insist "in strong language" that the colonel's men were "stealing" his private property and that he wouldn't stand for it. Confronted by this blustering and outraged citizen,

Smith tried to bluster back and threatened to confine him if he did not control himself. Buchanan dared him to do it but warned him of the dire consequences that would ensue should he try.

Smith now began to wonder just who it was he was dealing with. "Who are you?" he asked. "I don't know you."

Buchanan walked straight up to him, "as mad as a hornet," and told him: "I am a *gentleman* and the owner of the property your men are *stealing,* that is enough for you to know."

Although Smith had a company of men at his disposal, he decided that discretion was called for and gave way. He ordered his men to put the cannonballs back on the gateposts. Then it was reported that two of them could not be found. Buchanan remained outraged. To him the whole episode was an indication of the kind of tyranny and blustering incompetence to be expected from an administration of Yankee lowlifes. The soldiers, he said, were "of the lowest order of mankind," thieves and liars and blackguards, and their officers were no better. In short, they were exactly what one would expect of northern soldiery.

This event, plus his continued perusal of the northern papers, did much to sustain Buchanan in a nearly constant state of moral outrage. He claimed now that he wouldn't take his commission back under any circumstances. While in part this may have been sour grapes, his curt dismissal by Welles, his anger and frustration at Colonel Smith's imperiousness, and his unwillingness to be left out of the great events of his age all led him to consider going south to fight for the Confederacy.

He was still mulling it over in the second week of July even as armies from both sides moved toward Manassas, Virginia, for the first great battle of the war. He took up his pen to explain himself to his "worthy friend" Frank Du Pont. Du Pont had written to say that he could understand, maybe even appreciate, Buchanan's unwillingness to fight *against* the South, but surely, Du Pont added, he did not intend to fight *for* the South? To fight against the old flag? Buchanan responded with an explanation that provides a window to his thinking at this critical moment in his life.

Buchanan insisted that a "common sense view" of the matter would show what was at the root of the entire national crisis. "The Negro is the cause of it all," he wrote; what the country now faced was "a war of *races.*" The vile Republicans intended nothing less than the emancipation of all the slaves, an event that would lead to race war and the extermination of the whites. The Yankees would then divide up the land of the murdered southerners among themselves. In such a time, he wrote, each person must follow his own conscience and judge for himself. Buchanan insisted that he had no doubt about which side was in the right. His commitment to slavery and the racial doctrine that underpinned it led him to view the pronouncements of northern abolitionists as the onset of a cataclysmic holocaust, and he made no distinction between the most radical of their pronouncements and the more moderate assurances of the new president. "Look at the tone of the miserable President's message," he urged Du Pont, "and the Northern papers: 'War to the death,' 'Slavery must be abolished,' 'Slavery is a sin,' 'Annihilation of all slave holders,' 'Subjugation of the South,' 'Slaves must be set free, and the land divided among the northerners.'"

"I am now so thoroughly and completely disgusted with the present administration and the vile party which is governing the country," he wrote, "that nothing now, my worthy friend, could induce me to accept my former situation in the Navy." The only solution to the crisis, he insisted, was for the U.S. government to acknowledge the southern Confederacy. If the peace conventions did not compel a peace, the intervention of Britain and France "to a certainty" would do so.

He did not finish his letter in one sitting. He put it down and picked it up again two days later. In that short time his opinions had crystallized. Lyman Trumbull's proposal that the government should consider emancipating the slaves in the seceded states, a proposal that was well ahead of both public opinion and administration policy, seemed to Buchanan evidence of a vile northern conspiracy "to cause an insurrection in those states, to cut the throats of their masters, the land to be given to Northerners, etc."

"Good God, Du Pont, can this government last under such rulers? My worthy friend, that flag which I have served under faithfully many years, and had hoped to die under, no longer exists; it has been degraded, disgraced and torn to pieces by those who rule the country." Even now, however, he could not bring himself to see where his rhetoric was taking him. He did not appreciate that it would be impossible to revile the country, its cause, and its flag, and not alienate those who continued to serve all three. "It is no reason why we should not remain as warm friends," he wrote to Du Pont. "Let me hear from you."

He never got a reply.

Franklin Buchanan at about age twenty-five in the uniform of a U.S. Navy lieutenant. *Painting by Rembrandt Peale, courtesy of Louise Meiere Dunn (Mrs. Paxton Dunn)*

Ann Catherine Lloyd (Nannie) in her mid-twenties at about the time of her marriage to Franklin Buchanan. *Painting by Rembrandt Peale, courtesy of Louise Meiere Dunn (Mrs. Paxton Dunn)*

The parlor at Wye House in a modern photograph, but looking very much as it did in the 1830s when Lieutenant Buchanan courted Nannie Lloyd. *Photograph by the author*

Buchanan's first command, the sloop-of-war USS *Vincennes*. Buchanan cruised the Caribbean and Gulf of Mexico in the *Vincennes* from 1842 to 1844 searching for pirates and slavers and becoming entangled with U.S. policy in Mexico. *Print by Nathaniel Currier in 1845, courtesy of U.S. Navy*

The Naval School at Annapolis as it appeared in 1845–47 when Buchanan served as its first superintendent. Fort Severn is the circular battery at right; the buildings behind it are the cadet quarters and the recitation hall. *Courtesy U.S. Navy*

A photograph of the steam frigate USS *Susquehanna*, which Buchanan commanded during Matthew Perry's expedition to Japan in 1853–54 and during a cruise up the Yangtze River in China in 1854. *Courtesy U.S. Navy*

In 1860, only months before Buchanan resigned from the U.S. Navy, he hosted this delegation of visiting Japanese officials at the Washington Navy Yard. Buchanan is in the officer's cap standing at right center. To his right, in the top hat, is his friend Captain Samuel F. Du Pont. *Courtesy U.S. Navy*

Buchanan as a U.S. Navy captain. This photograph was probably taken at about the time that Buchanan took command of the Washington Navy Yard in 1859. *Courtesy U.S. Navy*

The ironclad CSS *Virginia* (formerly the steam frigate USS *Merrimack*) under way in Hampton Roads. *Courtesy U.S. Navy*

The USS *Cumberland* heels over to port after being rammed by the *Virginia* in this modern portrayal of the Battle of Hampton Roads. Buchanan ordered the bow gun to fire at the moment of contact. Within minutes the *Cumberland* began to settle, threatening to take the *Virginia* down with it. *Courtesy U.S. Navy*

An artist's depiction of the opening phase of the Battle of Mobile Bay (ca. 7:00 A.M.). Fort Morgan is on the left. A mine has just exploded under the *Tecumseh* (right center) while Buchanan's *Tennessee* (lower left) steams to

confront Farragut's *Hartford* (at right). *Painting by J. O. Davidson, courtesy of Anne S. K. Brown, Military Collection, Brown University*

The latter phase of the fight in Mobile Bay at about 9:00 A.M., just prior to the surrender of the *Tennessee*. Buchanan's flagship is surrounded by enemies and unable either to steer or to fight back effectively. Within minutes, Captain Johnston would raise a white flag ending the fight. *Courtesy U.S. Navy*

Buchanan's Eastern Shore home, the Rest, as it appeared after being rebuilt in a Victorian style following the war. Buchanan died here on 11 May 1874. *Courtesy Mrs. Oliver Reeder*

Franklin Buchanan after the war. This photograph may have been taken during the time he served as president of the Maryland Agricultural College, 1868–69. *Courtesy Mrs. Oliver Reeder*

Buchanan's ivy-covered final resting place in the Lloyd family cemetery at Wye House. Nannie's grave is next to his, and beyond it lie three of their children. Near Buchanan's footstone are two of the iron cannonballs he brought back from the Mexican War. *Photograph by the author*

Part Two

REBEL GRAY

~ 10 ~

THE CONFEDERATE NAVY

My heart, feelings, and sympathies are all with the South.

I n his last letter to his lifelong friend Frank Du Pont, Buchanan wrote that it was "folly, pure folly, for any sensible man to suppose that the South can be subdued." He penned those words on 11 July. Ten days later, as if in fulfillment of that prophecy, Confederate armies in Virginia defeated federal forces along Bull Run Creek in the first great battle of the war. Only days later, Franklin Buchanan decided to cast his lot with the Confederacy. Although his decision was driven by outrage— at the policies of the Lincoln administration, at his treatment by Welles, and at the behavior of federal troops on his own property—it was nevertheless a calculated one.[1]

Buchanan's dilemma was shared by most, if not all, southern officers. In the secession spring of 1861, there were 571 officers in the U.S. Navy (captains, commanders, and lieutenants), of whom 253 (44.3 percent) were southern born. Buchanan, interestingly, was not among them. Since his family had been living in Philadelphia when he accepted his midshipman's warrant, his state of record was Pennsylvania. Of the 253 who did list southern states as home, almost exactly half (126) resigned from the navy to go south. The rest—a bare majority, but still a majority— stood by the flag. For some it was a difficult call. William Shubrick of

South Carolina, who had served with Buchanan on the Retirement Board, was seventy-one years old. He considered resigning to go with his state, but he decided in the end that the tiny Confederate navy was unlikely to have a job for a septuagenarian and stayed in the U.S. Navy, eventually becoming a rear admiral. David Farragut, whose state of record was Tennessee, and who had grown up in New Orleans, never considered resigning. His view was that he served the United States collectively, not any one of them individually. Indeed, such a view—that officers served the whole country—was much more prevalent in the navy than in the army, whose officers were more likely to go with their states. In part, perhaps, this derived from the fact that navy officers frequently represented the Stars and Stripes overseas (as Buchanan had done in the Mediterranean, the Caribbean, and the Far East), and therefore conceived of themselves as representatives of the national government. Army officers, by contrast, served mostly in fixed forts or army posts where they became closely integrated into the local culture. For them, state loyalty or family loyalty frequently predominated.[2]

The decision was complicated further for Marylanders by virtue of the fact that while Maryland was a slave state, it was also a Union state. Many southern sympathizers argued that Maryland *would* have seceded if Lincoln and Maryland governor Thomas H. Hicks had not conspired to keep it in the Union against its citizens' will. Certainly this was the view of navy commander (and Maryland native) Raphael Semmes. In February 1861, two months before Confederate forces fired on Fort Sumter, and well before federal soldiers fired on civilians on Pratt Street in Baltimore, Semmes responded to an invitation from the Confederate government in Montgomery by telegraphing: "Dispatch received; I will be with you immediately." It was six months more before Buchanan decided to follow a similar course.[3]

Another useful comparison to Buchanan's circumstances is the case of Capt. Isaac Mayo, another Marylander. In language remarkably similar to Buchanan's, Mayo submitted his resignation to Welles in May 1861 (one week after Buchanan) in protest of what Mayo conceived to be Lincoln's coercive policies. "For more than half a century," Mayo wrote to Welles, "it has been the pride of my life to hold office under the Government of the United States. It was the hope of my old age that I might die, as I had lived, an officer of the Navy of a free Government. This hope has been taken from me. . . . As one of the oldest soldiers of America, I protest—in the name of humanity—against this 'war against brethren!' I cannot fight against the Constitution while pretending to fight for it. You will therefore oblige me by accepting my resignation." But Welles did *not* accept it. Instead he responded to Mayo in exactly the same way he had replied to Buchanan: he sent him a short note informing him that he was dismissed from the navy. In both cases the imputation was unmistakable: individuals who would not stand by the flag in this crisis were no longer to be entrusted with a commission. Denied the honor of resigning, they were dismissed as unworthy. Buchanan was outraged; Mayo killed himself.[4]

Angry as he was at treatment that he considered both unwarranted and unjust, Buchanan never considered such a drastic act as Mayo's. Indeed, until he received Welles's curt note of dismissal, he had desperately tried to retrieve his resignation. He claimed that the circumstances that had induced him to resign "no longer existed," and because of that, he was perfectly willing—even eager—to retain his commission. He wrote Welles that he was "ready for service," although he later insisted that he planned to ask for orders that would have sent him to foreign stations so as not to have to fight against the South, a request that surely would have been denied. Unlike Semmes, who decided at once that he would commit himself to the Confederacy; or Farragut, who was equally committed to the Union; or even Mayo, who opposed government policy but could not bear the ignominy of dismissal, Buchanan wanted to have his cake and eat it too—to keep his commission and at the same time avoid fighting against the South on behalf of a Yankee administration. Welles was not going to let him have it both ways.[5]

Buchanan did not at once resolve to go south after receiving Welles's dismissal. It is possible that, like Shubrick, he worried that there would be no place for him in the Confederate navy. He had alluded to such a possibility back in December 1860, when he wrote Du Pont: "If each state walks out on her own hook, all of us cannot be employed." At first, he avoided any direct contact with Confederate authorities. Perhaps he nursed a hope that Lincoln and Welles would change their minds and restore his commission; if so, that hope soon faded. As spring turned into summer, Buchanan became increasingly bitter about his situation; he conceived of himself as the innocent victim of the calculated ill will of a Yankee administration. In mid-July he asserted to Du Pont that nothing could induce him to accept his "former situation in the Navy," and by mid-August he had opened communications with Richmond about obtaining an appointment in Confederate service.[6]

What he learned from his contacts in Richmond is that, by Confederate law, any U.S. Navy officer who resigned his commission to fight for the South was entitled to a commission in the C.S. Navy at the same grade as the one he had held before resigning. Thus encouraged, he made a special trip in late August to the Talbot County seat in Easton in order to transfer the legal title to his land—and his six slaves—to his wife and children. If the Lincoln administration subsequently labeled him a traitor and tried to confiscate his property, it would discover that legally, at least, he had none.[7]

After evaluating his options at length and deciding that only one offered both challenge and opportunity (and, he would have said, honor), Franklin Buchanan left the Rest on or about the last day of August 1861. Saying good-bye to Nannie, who stayed behind, he crossed the Chesapeake Bay and headed south. Very likely he avoided Washington and crossed the Potomac well downriver from the capital in a small boat, probably at night. Once he stepped on Virginia soil, there was no going back. For better or worse, he was now committed to the Confederacy.

When Buchanan arrived in Richmond on or about 4 September, he encountered a city in the midst of a dramatic transformation. The population had expanded spectacularly during the previous three months as officeholders and office seekers (both civilian and military) vied for space with wounded soldiers from Bull Run, Yankee prisoners, and opportunists of every sort. What had been a relatively quiet southern town was now a jostling national capital. Hotels and boardinghouses were overflowing, as were the taverns, bars, and bawdy houses. Citizens deplored the erosion of manners and civility. The new arrivals elbowed matrons off the sidewalks, and prostitutes plied their trade with increased brazenness. The alarmed editors of the *Richmond Examiner* called the city a "bloated metropolis of vice."[8]

Buchanan made his way along the crowded sidewalks to the Mechanics Institute Building on 9th Street between Main and Franklin. There, in a second-floor office where the new government had established its Navy Department, he reported to the Confederate secretary of the navy, Stephen R. Mallory, his old friend and ally from the days of the "Committee of Fifteen." Mallory, who had been expecting him, at once offered him not only a commission as a C.S. Navy captain, but a plum job as well: chief of the Bureau of Orders and Detail—the highest administrative post in the infant Confederate navy.[9]

Like its federal counterpart, the Confederate navy was organized on the bureau system. This meant that instead of relying on a hierarchical command structure with a senior officer at the top, the administrative responsibilities were parceled out to a handful of autonomous bureaus, each headed by a captain, and each responsible for some aspect of navy management. Buchanan's Bureau of Orders and Detail had authority over personnel questions: recruiting enlisted men, assigning officers to various duties, determining ranks and promotion, and courts martial. Other bureau chiefs managed Provisions and Clothing, Medicine and Surgery, and Ordnance and Hydrography. In time, Buchanan's office would assume responsibility for other aspects of the navy that didn't seem to fit elsewhere, such as the supply of coal and the fitting out of ships. Indeed, in terms of its duties and responsibilities, the Office of Orders and Detail was clearly the first among equals, and in recognition of that, Buchanan often worked closely with Mallory as his unofficial navy adviser.[10]

If Buchanan's assignment was an important one, it was also relatively mundane. According to Confederate navy regulations, it was the job of his bureau to maintain the service records of every officer in the Confederate navy. The bureau kept track of each man's duty assignments, any requests for assignment (and any orders that were declined), any noteworthy accomplishments (or failures), and any charges preferred against him and "any other facts which will aid the Department in forming a correct opinion of the availability of this officer." Based on these service records, Buchanan's office nominated officers to various assignments in the navy, including command.[11]

In addition, Buchanan had to maintain the service records of the navy's enlisted force, an archive that had to be assembled from the monthly reports submitted to him from all across the Confederacy. These detailed each sailor's enlistment date, his initial assignment and subsequent transfers, his rating (as seaman, landsman, coal heaver, or boy), and, of course, any crimes he may have committed as well as the punishment he received. Receiving and maintaining these records, and prodding operational commanders to submit them monthly, were not activities likely to generate much enthusiasm in a warrior like Franklin Buchanan.

Even more depressing, perhaps, was the fact that the Confederate navy, which had to be created quite literally from the keel up, had so few assets. The nineteenth-century naval historian James Russell Soley wrote that "it would be hardly be possible to imagine a great maritime country more destitute of the means for carrying on a naval war than the Confederate States in 1861." The Norfolk Navy Yard was a treasure, but the South could point to little else that would be useful in building or sustaining a naval force: shipyards, ropewalks, smelting works, ordnance foundries, or powder mills. Most important of all, the South lacked ships. Moreover, few in the Confederacy seemed to think that it mattered very much. In part this was because the euphoria of Bull Run still hung over the capital, but in addition, many seemed to believe that southern independence was more likely to be won by the army than the navy. The Confederate army had already proved its mettle on the banks of Bull Run Creek, whereas the navy had no triumphs to exalt. One officer who later served under Buchanan wrote that "the position of a naval officer was decidedly uncomfortable" in the fall of 1861. "The people were full of the promises of the army, but were unreasonable concerning the navy. We were expected to do everything with nothing." Or nearly nothing. As Buchanan discovered in attempting to establish a professional and businesslike system within the bureau assigned to him, the only thing the Confederate navy had in surplus was officers.[12]

When it first established the Navy Department in the spring of 1861, the Confederate Congress had authorized a 38-man officer corps: 4 captains, 4 commanders, and 30 lieutenants. As noted above, however, some 126 U.S. Navy officers resigned to support the Confederacy, and there were simply not enough billets in the infant C.S. Navy for all those who were legally entitled to them. The Confederate Congress soon enlarged the Navy List to include 4 admirals, 10 captains, 31 commanders, and 125 lieutenants—a total of 170 officers. But even if every applicant with the right to claim a commission was allowed to do so, these commissioned officers could not be productively employed. Some officers waited around hoping that something would turn up; many more became disgusted and accepted commissions instead in the Confederate army.[13]

Not only were there too many officers for too few commands, but many of the more senior officers were somewhat long in the tooth. Rather uncharitably, Raphael Semmes commented that many of the naval officers who offered their services to the Confederacy brought with them little more than their patriotism and their gray hair. Not a few of them were the very ones that Buchanan had sought to consign to the retired list—including sixty-five-year-old French Forrest, the crippled hydrographer Matthew F. Maury, and sixty-seven-year-old Lawrence Rousseau, whom Buchanan succeeded as bureau chief. If they were not entirely "worthless" (the word Buchanan would have used), neither were they the energetic and innovative cadre that the South would need to contend successfully in a naval war with the United States.

The Confederate navy's greatest need was ships for its officers to command. The U.S. Navy had some ninety warships at the start of the war; the Confederate navy had literally none. One southern officer called on his colleagues "to bring with you every ship and man you can, that we may use them against the oppressors," but none did. Instead, southern-born U.S. Navy commanding officers brought their ships into port, turned them over to the proper authority, then made their way south. The only exception to this was a half dozen revenue cutters that were assigned to the Treasury Department (the forerunner of the modern Coast Guard) whose commanders turned them over to state authorities and which were eventually taken into the Confederate navy. Those six, plus the venerable side-wheeler *Fulton,* more than two decades old, and the partially destroyed hull of the steam frigate *Merrimack,* abandoned when the federals fled Norfolk, constituted the entire C.S. Navy in the summer of 1861. By the time Buchanan arrived in Richmond that fall, the seagoing armada of the Confederacy consisted of some three dozen cutters, armed tugs, and harbor patrol craft. All of them were small, most of them were armed with only a single gun, and none of them carried a crew of more than a few dozen.[14]

By contrast, thanks to its virtually unlimited assets, the U.S. Navy had expanded from ninety ships to more than two hundred in just a few months, and that number was growing daily. Promotions in the old navy were also coming thick and fast. Buchanan learned in September that his old friend Du Pont had been named a flag officer and appointed to command the South Atlantic Blockading Squadron. By itself, Du Pont's squadron boasted more guns afloat than the entire Confederate navy.

Thus, instead of running a navy, Buchanan found himself supervising minor, even petty, issues. Contractors and prospective commanding officers wrote to him asking for everything from fire brick for the boilers to sperm oil for the binnacle lamps, and most of the time Buchanan had to answer that he had none to send, and that officers would have to improvise. More serious was the shortage of trained sailors—or even untrained sailors, for that matter. Buchanan tried to recruit men in Norfolk, where he opened a "naval rendezvous," but his principal hope was to get men from the army. That proved difficult, not only because the army was reluctant to let them go, but also because there was little interest in naval service in the aftermath of the army's victory at Bull Run. Service in the army was patriotic; service in the navy struck most southerners as quaint at best. When Comdr. John R. Tucker asked Buchanan to send a marine contingent for his squadron, Buchanan answered bluntly: "There are no Marines to send you."[15]

While Edward M. Tidball, the chief clerk, supervised much of the paperwork in the office, Buchanan and Mallory discussed what the Confederacy might reasonably attempt to accomplish given its limited assets. It was simply not possible to challenge the U.S. Navy for command of the seas—certainly not with conventional means. The traditional recourse for an underdog naval power was to defend its own coast with a combination of shore fortifications and floating batteries, and to conduct a campaign of commerce raiding against the enemy's merchant trade. This had been the strategy of the United States in its two wars against Great Britain, and, more recently, of Mexico against the United States.

Accordingly, one of the first acts of the infant Confederate government was to authorize letters of marque, documents that gave private ship owners the authority to attack vessels of the enemy—a practice known as privateering. Most Western nations had declared privateering illegal in the 1850s, but because the practice had proved so useful in the past, the United States had declined to sign the protocol. Thus, European powers had little sympathy in 1861 when the United States protested the Confederacy's decision to issue its own letters of marque. But while Mallory knew that commerce raiding might help to convince the northern states that a lengthy war could cost them more than they were willing to pay, he also knew that relying on private vessels to carry out such a campaign was a thin reed. It would take more than a handful of private entrepreneurs, however enthusiastic, to ravage the worldwide commerce of the United States. He therefore began at once to contract with English shipyards for the construction of modern steam-powered raiders to attack Union merchant shipping.[16]

Defending the southern coastline was the second element of Mallory's strategy. Lincoln had declared a naval blockade of the southern coast on 19 April, and the Union navy immediately sought bases along the Atlantic and Gulf coasts to support that blockade. On 4 September, the very day that Buchanan arrived in Richmond, Mallory spent much of the afternoon closeted with Jefferson Davis discussing the Union's capture of Hatteras Inlet on the North Carolina capes. Then, only two months later, while Buchanan wrestled with mountains of paperwork in his 9th Street office, his old friend Frank Du Pont led a naval squadron into the roadstead at Port Royal, South Carolina, and pummeled the two Confederate forts there into submission. Landing an occupation force, Du Pont then secured Port Royal as a base for his South Atlantic Blockading Squadron. Much alarmed, Mallory ordered Buchanan to go personally to the South Carolina coast and report to the senior army officer there, Robert E. Lee.[17]

By the time Buchanan arrived at the rail stop of Coosawhatchie, near the headwaters of Port Royal Sound, the situation had stabilized. He discussed the strategic circumstances with Lee, and both men agreed that the lesson of Hatteras Inlet and Port Royal seemed to be that steam-powered ships armed with heavy rifled guns could easily overpower the wood-and-earth forts that guarded most southern ports. Lee's recommendation, therefore, was to choose a handful of critical seaports where the geography or other special circumstances provided unusual protection, and let the rest of the South's coastline go by default.[18]

Back in Richmond, Buchanan shared Lee's idea with Mallory. The navy secretary did not disagree with Lee's assessment, but which ports were "critical"? Certainly the navy yard at Norfolk had to be kept; it was too vital to lose. Other sites, too, were critical: Charleston, Savannah, Mobile, and New Orleans, among them. But to protect these cities, Mallory argued, it would be necessary to make at least some effort to contest the seas around them. The Confederacy could hardly hope to construct fleets large enough to stand up to the powerful squadrons of warships that the Union could deploy. Instead, the South would have to compensate for inferior numbers by relying on innovation. Mallory expressed his policy in a letter written to his wife in August 1862: "Knowing that the enemy could build one hundred ships to one of our own, my policy has been to make such ships so strong and invulnerable as would compensate for the inequality of numbers." The ship that would make the trial of this policy was the CSS *Virginia*, which began life as the USS *Merrimack*.[19]

The origin of the vessel that became the *Virginia* is a story in itself. Originally laid down in the summer of 1854 as a wooden-hulled sailing frigate with an auxiliary steam engine, the *Merrimack* was launched and christened a year later in June 1855. The name, of Indian origin, derived from the Merrimack River in New Hampshire. The *Merrimack* was one of the so-called river-class steam frigates, like Buchanan's former command, the *Susquehanna*, and Perry's *Mississippi*. It cruised through an indifferent career on the European and Pacific stations before being decommissioned and sent to the Norfolk Navy Yard for an engine overhaul in 1860. It was still there in the spring of 1861, its engines disassembled, when Virginia's secession put Norfolk's future in question. When Virginia militia forces, more noisy than dangerous, threatened the navy yard on 20 April, the panicky federal commandant, sixty-seven-year-old Commo. Charles McCauley, ordered that the yard be evacuated and that the seven warships there, including the disassembled *Merrimack*, be scuttled to prevent them from falling into unfriendly hands. A last-minute attempt to wreck the ships was inefficiently performed, and although much was destroyed in the hasty Union evacuation, much of value was left behind, including the partially burned hull of the frigate *Merrimack*.[20]

The Confederacy's chief naval engineer, John L. Porter, was the first to propose that the Confederacy build a casemated ironclad warship. But it was Lt. John M. Brooke, an ordnance specialist who had served aboard the *Merrimack* during its earlier European deployment, who suggested that the damaged steam frigate could be salvaged and converted into an ironclad modeled on Porter's design. The construction of an ironclad warship was a creative but not entirely original notion. France had launched the ironclad *Glorie* with great fanfare a few years earlier in 1859, and the English were even then building an iron-hulled warship, the *Warrior*. In late June, while Buchanan was facing down the federal militia who were stealing his decorative cannonballs at the Rest, Mallory authorized Porter and Brooke to collaborate on the conversion of the *Merrimack* into an ironclad.[21]

Buchanan had little to do with the conversion. Porter was responsible for salvaging the hull and cutting away the charred timbers. It was

Porter, too, who designed the interior arrangements and laid a new gun deck over the old hull. William P. Williamson overhauled the engines, and Lieutenant Brooke assumed responsibility for the iron plate and the battery. Lt. Catesby ap R. Jones joined the team as the ship's designated first officer in November. For nearly eight months, the hopes of the Confederate navy, and a significant percentage of its assets, went into the *Merrimack* as it was raised up, pumped dry, cut down, patched over, redesigned, armored, and armed.[22]

As the reconfigured vessel took shape, it was soon evident to all that it would be an unusual, if not entirely revolutionary, warship. Its key design characteristic was its armored casemate, an oblong fort that rested atop the frigate's hull. The casemate was constructed of pine timbers that were laid across one another to a thickness of twenty inches, then encased in four inches of oak and covered over again by two layers of two-inch-thick iron plate. The original plans had called for the use of multiple layers of one-inch-thick plate, but experiments conducted on Jamestown Island proved that two layers of two-inch plate were significantly more resistant to heavy shot. This decision resulted in more delay, largely because the Tredegar Iron Works was the only place in the Confederacy that could roll two-inch plate. Then there was trouble in transporting the plate from Richmond to Norfolk. The last shipment did not arrive until 12 February, a mere five days before the ship was launched.[23]

Although the *Merrimack* had carried fifty guns as a frigate, it would carry only ten as an ironclad: four rifled guns of Brooke's own design, and six nine-inch Dahlgren smoothbores. Four guns faced out to each broadside, and one gun pointed forward and one aft. The strange-looking vessel was finally launched, with virtually no ceremony, on 17 February 1862, and rechristened the *Virginia*.[24]

Throughout the winter, as the *Virginia* emerged phoenix-like from the charred remains of the *Merrimack*, Buchanan remained in Richmond managing the day-to-day work of his bureau. But he was aware as early as January that he was likely to be tapped for command of the peculiar vessel. His selection for the coveted post was due almost exclusively to Mallory, who, recognizing the experimental nature of the *Virginia*, did not want a merely competent officer in command, but rather one who was also aggressive and willing to take calculated risks. An appointment based strictly on seniority would have given the *Virginia* to French Forrest, then commandant of the Norfolk Navy Yard, a man who looked every one of his sixty-five years, and who was unlikely to provide the spark of aggressive leadership that Mallory felt necessary. At sixty-one, Buchanan was no youngster, but Mallory knew him well enough to know that the same combative spirit that had been evident in their political wars was likely to manifest itself at sea as well. Buchanan, he thought, would be daring without being foolhardy. Mallory resolved the seniority problem by appointing Buchanan to the command of the James River Squadron, which included five small wooden gunboats as well as the *Virginia,* then designating that command as separate from Forrest's command of the navy yard.[25]

The optimism that had dominated Richmond through the late summer of 1861 dissipated during the fall and then evaporated altogether when a string of bad news arrived in February. To the south, Roanoke Island, in North Carolina's Pamlico Sound, fell to the enemy on 7 February. Out west, Fort Henry on the Tennessee River fell the same week; Fort Donelson on the Cumberland fell a week later. In all of these disasters, a key factor had been the presence of U.S. Navy war craft acting in coordination with Yankee soldiery. The dominant mood of self-congratulation so evident in midsummer gave way to carping, whining, and fault finding, much of it evident in the pages of the anti-administration *Richmond Examiner.*

In such a mood, official Richmond assembled for the inauguration of Jefferson Davis as the first "permanent" president of the Confederacy on 22 February, George Washington's birthday. Davis had been acting in a provisional capacity since the spring, but now he was to begin his formal six-year term. Buchanan was almost certainly somewhere in the large audience that gathered near the equestrian statue of Washington in the public park outside the capitol building. The ceremony ought to have been a celebration of self-government. Instead, its bleak aspect mirrored the mood of the populace. It rained throughout the ceremony, and Davis spoke gloomily of sacrifices made and sacrifices yet to come. The only hopeful notes in his address were references to the likelihood of imminent European intervention and Maryland's probable entry into the war. Yet even before that day was over, more bad news arrived: Confederate armies in Tennessee had evacuated the state capital at Nashville and were still falling back.[26]

. . .

Two days later, Buchanan received orders detaching him from the Office of Orders and Detail and assigning him to the command of the James River Squadron, including the new ironclad *Virginia*. Mallory and Buchanan both hoped that this experimental warship might be the instrument that would turn the tide and sweep away the wave of despair that had engulfed the South. A victory now would act as a tonic on public opinion. Mallory challenged Buchanan to be creative: "The Virginia is a novelty," he wrote. It "is untried, and its powers unknown, and the Department does not give specific orders as to her attack upon the enemy. Her powers as a ram are regarded as very formidable, and it is hoped you may be able to test them." The secretary then added a call to battle that he knew would appeal to a man of Buchanan's character and outlook: "Action—prompt and successful action—now would be of serious importance to our cause." He urged Buchanan to be bold, suggesting "a dashing cruise on the Potomac as far as Washington." Energized by such orders, and no doubt eager to leave his desk for the deck of a warship, Buchanan left Richmond for Norfolk the next morning.[27]

❧ II ❧

IRON AGAINST WOOD
The Battle of Hampton Roads

The eyes of the whole world are upon you.

Franklin Buchanan spent fifty years as a naval officer, but he is often best remembered for the five days he spent in command of the ironclad ram CSS *Virginia* in the spring of 1862. For a man whose most salient characteristic was eagerness—indeed, almost desperation—to confront the enemy, those five days offered the best opportunity yet in a long and varied career to fulfill his dream of commanding a battle fleet in a desperate fight against a professional foe. The opportunity brought him a glorious victory, promotion, and public honors. But even as he secured that victory, his volatile personality and his fragile sense of personal honor provoked him to commit a foolish act of bravado that removed him from the historical stage on the very eve of the dramatic climax.

Buchanan arrived in Norfolk on the afternoon of 25 February and immediately went to the navy yard, where he watched the *Virginia* take on its initial load of coal. He had seen the vessel under conversion in dry dock, but this was his first glimpse of it afloat. Nearly 270 feet in length from iron ram to stern, the *Virginia* was a dozen feet longer than the *Susquehanna*, which he had commanded on the China station, and sixty feet longer than the largest U.S. sailing warship ever built—the ship of the line *Pennsylvania*. It looked smaller, however, because much of its hull was all but submerged. The armored casemate that gave the *Virginia* its peculiar silhouette was 170 feet long at its base, with walls that tapered upward and inward at a thirty-six-degree angle (calculated to deflect enemy ordnance) to a flat roof consisting of iron grating two inches thick. One sailor described the *Virginia* as "a floating Mansard roof with guns peeping out the windows." The ship's great weakness was its engine plant, which consisted of essentially the same machinery whose indifferent performance had sent the *Merrimack* into the shipyard for a refit two years earlier. Indeed, the average vacuum maintained in the boilers was only about half of what was considered minimal in other steam plants, and produced a paltry 18 pounds of pressure per square inch (psi), as compared with other ships whose engines operated routinely at 100 psi or higher.[1]

The five wooden steamers that made up the rest of Buchanan's command were far less imposing. Two of them (the *Raleigh* and the *Beaufort,* each with only one gun) were alongside the *Virginia* and serving essentially as tugs. The other three—the *Patrick Henry* (six guns), the *Jamestown* (two guns), and the *Teaser* (one gun)—all under the command of Capt. John R. Tucker, were trapped up the James River by two large federal frigates at Newport News Point, which effectively blockaded them in the river. Even if those three gunboats could be brought into action, the *Virginia* would be a giant attended by pygmies; whatever was to be achieved by the grandly named James River Squadron would be achieved by the *Virginia,* whose capabilities at this point were still a matter of speculation.

In his orders, Mallory had challenged Buchanan to be bold. Buchanan was hardly a man to shrink from a call to boldness, but he knew that Mallory's notion of conning the *Virginia* up the Potomac River to place Washington under fire was a pipe dream. The ship was simply too unseaworthy to trust to the open waters beyond Hampton Roads. So he dashed cold water on Mallory's vision and proposed instead a more limited attack on the two federal frigates at Newport News Point. Mallory accepted Buchanan's assessment and shelved, albeit reluctantly, his more ambitious dreams.[2]

Buchanan reported aboard the *Virginia* on 4 March—the first anniversary of Lincoln's inauguration—and took command in a formal address to the crew. Word had circulated onboard that Buchanan had waited six months before joining the Confederate cause, and as a result, some crewmen had expressed concern about his loyalty and commitment. Aware of these concerns, Buchanan offered a patriotic and impassioned call to battle. He avowed his determination to do his full duty, noting that he expected the same of every man aboard. A witness recalled that "his words completely offset several well circulated reports then current regarding both himself and the ship." He impressed one of the ship's officers as "an energetic and high toned officer"; another, in an assessment that Buchanan would have appreciated, described him as "a typical product of the old-time quarter deck, as indomitably courageous as Nelson, and as arbitrary."[3]

Buchanan's officers consisted of seven lieutenants and six midshipmen. The executive officer, Lt. Catesby ap Roger Jones, was a capable and energetic forty-year-old ordnance expert who had cherished hopes of being named to the command himself, especially because he had presided over the vessel's reconfiguration since the previous November. He knew the ship better than anyone, including, perhaps, its designers. One noted historian of the battle states bluntly that "Jones should have commanded the *Virginia*." But if Buchanan's relative lack of seniority to Forrest had concerned Mallory, he had far more serious qualms about nominating a mere lieutenant for the command. Perhaps because he was aware of this, Jones accepted his subordinate position with stoicism.[4]

Only hours after assuming command, Buchanan began to consider his initial sortie. As Buchanan laid it out for Mallory, the plan called for the *Virginia*, accompanied by the two tugs, to assault the two enemy frigates off Newport News Point. That would free the three gunboats up the James River to join in the fight; at the same time, General John B. Magruder's forces would attack the federal shore batteries from the rear. Buchanan quickly learned a lesson in the perils of combined army-navy operations when Mallory informed him that Magruder would not cooperate in such a scheme. Magruder claimed that he was outnumbered, that the roads were bad, and that all in all, he did not think the plan a very good one. Lacking the authority to order Magruder to cooperate, Mallory could do no more than write to Buchanan that "it will be impossible for General Magruder to act in concert with or render you any aid in the plans agreed upon to attack the enemy at Newport News."[5]

Aware now that he would have no help from the army, Buchanan revised his plan. He would ease the *Virginia* out of port in the middle of the night, move slowly down the Elizabeth River under cover of darkness, and be in position to attack the two federal frigates at first light. This plan, too, met with disappointment, due this time to the unwillingness of the pilots, on whom Buchanan depended to guide the *Virginia* downriver, to accept the responsibility. They pointed out that the ship's deep draft (twenty-two feet), its uncertain and untested engines, the narrow channel, and the absence of navigational lights made a nighttime sortie unacceptably dangerous. They refused to do it. Buchanan fumed, but he had to acquiesce. The *Virginia* would sortie in broad daylight, then, its purpose evident for all to see. If he had to fight without the help of the army and the element of surprise, his ship and his crew would simply have to make up for it with increased determination.[6]

The eighth of March 1862 marked a milestone in the history of naval warfare, but few besides Buchanan were aware that anything historic was in the offing when the sun came up that day, for he had kept his plans mostly to himself. He had confided the secret to the captains of the two armed tugs, telling them to add a new signal to their books: the numeral 1 hoisted over the commodore's flag, he told them melodramatically, would mean "sink before you surrender." On his own ship, only two others knew that Buchanan intended to take his experimental vessel directly into battle on its shakedown cruise: Jones, his second in command, and Robert D. Minor, his flag lieutenant. Others may have guessed Buchanan's intentions from the intensity of his preparations, which included coating the sides of the iron casemate with wax to help deflect enemy shells. But officially Buchanan maintained that he was merely preparing for a trial run to see how the engines worked and what flaws, if any, could be discovered in the *Virginia*'s design.[7]

Indeed, the engine plant was the focus of much of Buchanan's concern. The ship's chief engineer, H. Ashton Ramsay, later testified that "a more ill-conceived, spradling and unreliable pair [of engines] were never made." And those engines had never been fairly tested—the *Virginia* was still at anchor in the same berth it had occupied since its launch less than three weeks before. Buchanan asked Ramsay if he thought the engines needed a trial run before the ship could be committed to battle. Ramsay replied that the trip down the Elizabeth River would provide an ample test. That was just the kind of answer Buchanan liked to hear from his subordinates, and he tried another question: Did Ramsay think the engines could survive a collision with another vessel? Ramsay said yes, that the engines were well braced and likely to survive any collision. Nodding with satisfaction, Buchanan then included Ramsay in the small group of officers who were privy to his plans, and instructed him to be prepared to throw the engines into full astern at the exact moment he felt the impact of collision.[8]

Buchanan based his tactical plan on a consideration of the firepower of the enemy vessels. Although originally sister ships, one of the two federal "frigates" at Newport News Point, the *Cumberland,* had been recently reconfigured as a sloop, and though it now carried only twenty-two guns to the *Congress*'s fifty, those guns were larger and more dangerous, and at least some of them were believed to be rifled. Since large-caliber rifled guns were the only weapons capable of penetrating the *Virginia*'s iron casemate, Buchanan determined to bypass the nearer and larger *Congress* and run straight into the *Cumberland* with his ram. If the ram did not prove fatal, Buchanan was prepared to lead a boarding party and take the sloop in hand-to-hand combat.[9]

The morning dawned clear and bright, with blue skies and gentle breezes—a good omen. At eleven o'clock Buchanan hoisted his admiral's pennant and ordered the lines cast off, and the *Virginia* moved slowly into the Elizabeth River, a movement announced by a signal gun fired from the navy yard. Thus alerted, civilians began to gather along the riverbanks to watch. There was a festival atmosphere as the crowd grew. Men doffed their hats and women waved handkerchiefs. One witness estimated that "nearly every man, woman and child in the two cities of Norfolk and Portsmouth" gathered on the shore to watch the ungainly ironclad make its slow passage downriver assisted by the wooden tugs. Other spectators watched from the decks of dozens of small craft that accompanied the *Virginia* in its stately progress. William H. Parker, captain of the armed tug *Beaufort,* recalled that "everything that would float, from the army tug-boat to the oysterman's skiff, was . . . loaded to the water's edge with spectators." Buchanan allowed the men to go topside and man the rails, standing uncovered in mute acknowledgment of the tribute.[10]

The big ship moved slowly, ponderously, amid this escort of the anxious and the merely curious. The engines labored, but seemed to be working satisfactorily. Buchanan ordered the crew piped to dinner; it would take nearly two hours to navigate the ten miles from the *Virginia*'s berth at the navy yard to the mouth of the Elizabeth River beyond Craney Island, and he did not want the men to fight on empty stomachs.

At about one o'clock, approaching Craney Island, the helmsman reported that the ship would not answer its rudder. There was so little water under the hull that the heavy *Virginia* was wallowing uselessly. Buchanan ordered the *Beaufort* to come alongside, and the crew passed a line to the little tug so that it could tow the *Virginia* into deeper water. As the *Virginia* emerged under tow into the relatively open waters of Hampton Roads, Buchanan could see across the roadstead to the looming bulk of Fortress Monroe dead ahead, and beyond it the channel that led into the Chesapeake Bay. He ordered the towline cast off and put the helm over to turn the ship slowly to port, away from Fortress Monroe and toward the two federal frigates off Newport News Point.[11]

Buchanan's intentions were now evident to all—including those aboard the federal warships across the sound. When the *Virginia* emerged from the Elizabeth River, the two frigates were festooned with drying laundry. It was Saturday—wash day—and the routines of naval life were being observed. The crewmen aboard the *Virginia* could see the laundry being taken down and bundled below as the two federal warships cleared for action.

Buchanan ordered the boatswain to pipe the hands to muster, and the crew lined up on the port side of the ship facing the officers, who were similarly arrayed across from them. They waited silently for the expected speech, and Buchanan did not let them down. "Sailors," he called out in his booming quarterdeck voice, "in a few minutes you will have the long-looked-for opportunity to show your devotion to our cause. Remember you are about to strike for your country and your homes. The eyes of the whole world are upon you this day, and in the name of Virginia, let every man do his duty. Beat to Quarters!" And with that, the drum and fife sounded the call to quarters, a call almost instantly echoed by the *Congress* and the *Cumberland*.[12]

There would be no stealth in this attack. The *Virginia*'s sortie in midday, its imposing size, its deliberate speed, and the clouds of black smoke issuing from its stack banished all thoughts of subterfuge. Buchanan raised the signal for "close action" and kept it flying throughout the day, making no other signal by flag hoist. He did not bother with fleet tactics; he simply aimed his command at the enemy and relied on each ship commander to do his best.

The two enemy warships that awaited his attack mounted more than seventy guns to his ten, although Buchanan hoped that his armor walls

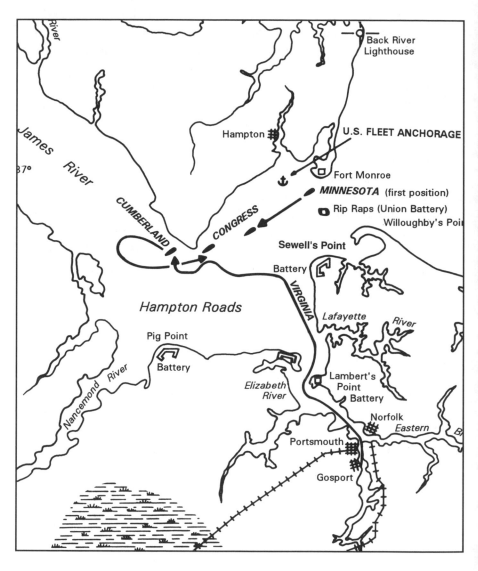

Battle of Hampton Roads
From Craig L. Symonds, The Naval Institute Historical Atlas of the
U.S. Navy *(Annapolis, Md.: Naval Institute Press, 1995).*

would even the odds. Even if they didn't, he was determined to push the issue. Steering carefully to clear the Middle Ground Shoal, he steadied the *Virginia* on a course toward the *Cumberland,* which was anchored broadside-on, thus "capping the T" of the charging *Virginia.*

The *Congress* came within range first. Somewhere on that ship was Buchanan's brother McKean, but Buchanan had no time for such considerations now. The *Congress* fired a full broadside as the *Virginia* passed. The shells slammed into the iron casemate dramatically and noisily—a "terrible noise" one gunner recalled—but without doing any perceptible damage. Buchanan fired a four-gun broadside in reply but did not change course or speed. With the *Congress* slipping away to starboard, he ordered the *Virginia* to steady on course for the *Cumberland,* picking out a spot just forward of amidships on its starboard side. The *Cumberland* fired raking broadsides with its nine-inch Dahlgren guns as the *Virginia* closed, but once again the enemy shells did little damage. The *Virginia*'s great weight (3,200 tons) and underpowered engines held it to a top speed of only about six knots in this curious slow-motion charge. Just before the ships struck, Buchanan ordered the seven-inch bow rifle to fire. According to one witness, that first shot "opened a hole in the *Cumberland* large enough for a horse and cart to drive through."[13]

Buchanan's main fear was that when he struck the *Cumberland* his ship's momentum would embed the ram's prow so deeply in the sloop's wooden hull that he would not be able to withdraw. At fifty yards, with the distance closing rapidly, he ordered all stop and allowed the *Virginia* to glide forward under the momentum of its long run. He called out to the crew: "Lookout men, I am going to Ram that ship." Everyone braced for the collision.[14]

A floating barrier of timbers had been erected around the *Cumberland*'s bow to protect it from a torpedo attack. The *Virginia*'s iron prow smashed through that barrier like an icebreaker gliding through a thin crust of ice, and Buchanan, as well as everyone else onboard, could distinctly hear the crash below the water line as the fifteen-hundred-pound iron ram ripped into the sloop's wooden hull. One officer wrote later that it felt as if the *Virginia* had run aground. Buchanan's flag lieutenant, Bob Minor, was so excited that he ran along the length of the gun deck to pass the word: "We've sunk the Cumberland!"[15]

Not yet. As planned, Ramsay had thrown the *Virginia*'s engines into reverse at the moment of collision, but despite the straining engines, the ship's single screw had no perceptible effect on its motion. The *Cumberland* began to settle almost at once as tons of water rushed into the gaping hole in its side, and the downward pressure of the stricken ship carried the embedded prow of the *Virginia* down with it. Buchanan could feel the deck below his feet cant forward; water washed over the foredeck and in through the bow gun ports.[16]

All this time the men manning the guns on both ships had continued to fire. One shot, lucky or well aimed, struck squarely on the muzzle of one of the *Virginia*'s nine-inch Dahlgren guns and broke it off two feet from the muzzle, the explosion killing one man and wounding several others. The *Virginia*'s bow continued to settle, and it seemed that the mortally wounded *Cumberland* would drag its assassin down with it. But even as the *Virginia*'s ram held fast inside the crippled *Cumberland*, its stern slewed around until the two vessels were nearly parallel. That movement created an irresistible torque on the *Virginia*'s ram, and with another subsurface crash the ram broke loose. The *Virginia*'s bow heaved up, then settled back again as it was released from the jaws of the *Cumberland* and regained buoyancy. The *Virginia*'s seventeen-foot propeller found purchase in the water, and the ironclad slowly backed away from its rapidly sinking enemy, whose guns were still firing and whose flag was still flying.[17]

The behavior of the *Cumberland*'s crew provoked grudging admiration from the men on the *Virginia*. Buchanan himself noted in his report that "she commenced sinking, gallantly fighting her guns as long as they were above water. She went down with her colors flying."[18]

Having disposed of the *Cumberland,* Buchanan turned his attention to the *Congress*. It was only three o'clock, and there was plenty of daylight left to finish the job. His problem was the sluggish maneuverability of the *Virginia* in the confined waters of Hampton Roads. To close with the *Congress,* he had to maneuver up the James River to find sufficient deep water for his giant vessel to turn about, then conduct a slow turn to port around the compass before steadying again on an eastward course. It took more than half an hour, with the *Virginia*'s keel scraping bottom frequently, simply to turn the ponderous vessel 180 degrees. Onboard the *Congress,* the Union gunners saw the *Virginia* turn away and concluded that it was giving up the fight. They raised three cheers and tossed their caps, but the cheers died on their lips as they saw the *Virginia* continue its slow turn to port and move in their direction.[19]

The destruction of the *Cumberland* had released the three Confederate gunboats in the James River, and they now entered the fight. Buchanan later praised their gallant efforts, but in fact they made little difference. Unarmored and outgunned, they were little more than targets. Early in the fight, a shell from one of the federal guns ashore ripped through the boiler of the *Patrick Henry,* the largest of the wooden gunboats, scalding four men to death and forcing the ship to retire from the action. The single gun onboard the *Raleigh* slipped from its carriage, making it incapable of offensive action. Although both vessels later returned to the fight, their participation was more a gesture of bravery than anything else.

Buchanan conned his iron monster, its engines straining, toward the *Congress.* "We were some time in getting our proper position," he wrote later in his official report, "in consequence of the shoalness of the water and the great difficulty of managing the ship when in or near the mud."[20]

Indeed, the attack on the *Congress* posed a different tactical problem. Ramming was not possible, not only because the *Virginia* had lost its iron ram, buried inside the doomed *Cumberland,* but also because the *Congress* had fled into shoal water and had run aground. The *Virginia,* with its much greater draft, simply could not reach its foe. Buchanan therefore maneuvered his ship carefully to take a dominant position off the stern of the *Congress* from which he could blast the wooden frigate to pieces with his heavy guns. All this time, the Union shore batteries, of much smaller caliber than the naval ordnance, maintained a constant harassing fire. Buchanan returned fire and took some satisfaction in watching the damage done to the batteries by his own counterbattery fire. "We silenced several of the batteries and did much injury on shore," he wrote. "A large transport steamer alongside the wharf was blown up, one schooner sunk, and another captured and sent to Norfolk. The loss of life on shore we have no means of ascertaining."[21]

Once in position, Buchanan's big guns hammered away at the *Congress* from a range of only about 150 yards. More than once an enemy shell carried away the colors on the short flagstaff of the *Virginia.* Finally, Lt. John R. Eggleston climbed out onto the exposed deck and secured the colors to a tear in the metal smokestack, and there they stayed. For a time the *Congress* replied to the *Virginia's* fire with its two stern guns, but both of these were soon put out of action and the *Congress* became a passive target, hard aground and unable to return fire. At a few minutes past four, the Union flag fluttered down and a white flag appeared in its place. A second white flag was run halfway up the mainmast.[22]

Buchanan ordered the gunners to cease firing. In the relative quiet that followed, the *Virginia*'s crew climbed out onto the exposed upper deck to observe their defeated enemy. "After being housed up for some hours it was quite refreshing to stand on the upper deck," one recalled. They could see the destroyed *Cumberland* resting on the bottom with men still clinging to its exposed masts. They could see, too, the grounded *Congress*, its stern a complete wreck and two surrender flags flying from its rigging. It was a triumphant moment. Buchanan signaled Lieutenant Parker to bring the *Beaufort* alongside and called out verbal instructions. As Parker later remembered it, Buchanan ordered him "to go alongside [the *Congress*], to take the officers and wounded men prisoner, to permit the others to escape to the shore, and then to burn the ship."[23]

Buchanan watched as Parker's small tug ran alongside the *Congress*. From his distant vantage point, however, he could not witness the controversial drama that played itself out on the deck of the *Beaufort*. After arriving alongside the *Congress*, Parker sent an officer to request its captain to come onboard. Not one captain, but two, presented themselves. Lt. Austin Pendergrast was the commander of the *Congress*, but with him was William Smith, the former captain, who was awaiting orders and who had stayed onboard as a volunteer. Parker, who was a career navy officer and familiar with the conventions of sea warfare, asked for the captains' side arms as token of their capitulation, but they had none to offer, and Parker made them go back onboard the *Congress* to get them. It rankled Parker a bit when Pendergrast returned with a ship's cutlass rather than a ceremonial sword, but he accepted it nonetheless.[24]

This formality had hardly been completed when a fusillade of small arms fire swept across the deck of the *Beaufort*. Several men fell to the deck. Parker himself received three shots through his clothes, had his cap shot from his head, and was wounded in the knee. He claimed later that "every man on the deck of the *Beaufort*" except the two federal officers "was either killed or wounded." An entire regiment of Union infantry had taken up position on the shoreline, barely two hundred yards away, and at that range their marksmanship was alarmingly good. Pendergrast, himself in the line of fire, "begged" Parker to hoist a white flag to stop the firing, but Parker would have none of it. He told Pender-grast to order the men onshore to stop shooting. But Pendergrast, a navy officer, had no command authority over the soldiers; and it was not likely that they would have obeyed him in any case. Instead he offered to go back aboard the *Congress* to help expedite the evacuation of the wounded. To that, Parker readily assented. But soon the small arms fire made remaining alongside the *Congress* impossible, and Parker ordered his crew to sheer off and move out of range. With so many wounded onboard, he headed for the relatively safe waters off Sewall's Point, where he could send the wounded ashore, but he did not first return to the *Virginia* to tell Buchanan what had happened.[25]

Watching from the *Virginia*, Buchanan saw the *Beaufort* sheer off from the *Congress* and assumed that his orders had been carried out—that Parker had removed the wounded and fired the ship—and he waited to see the rising smoke that would tell him that the *Congress* was on fire. But soon it was evident that the *Congress* was not on fire, and that the *Beaufort* had been driven off by hostile fire—hostile fire from an enemy that had surrendered!

Buchanan was outraged. The *Congress* was a surrendered prize of war flying not one, but two, white flags; its captain had offered his personal surrender and tendered his side arm in token of defeat. It was a gross violation of the traditions of sea warfare, not to say a breach of honor and simple decency, for the enemy to reopen hostilities. But the fire in this case came from the Union infantry on the *shore*. The soldiers there had not surrendered, and the traditions of the sea did not impress them in the least. Buchanan was in no mood to consider such hairsplitting legalities. His sense of order and discipline was offended. "That ship must be burned!" he exclaimed aloud to no one in particular.[26]

Hearing him, his loyal flag lieutenant, Bob Minor, offered to under-take the assignment himself—to run the gauntlet of fire from the shore in one of the *Virginia*'s boats and plant incendiaries onboard the grounded and surrendered *Congress*. Buchanan gave his assent. He watched as Minor and his volunteer crew of eight men raised a white flag and rowed to within a hundred yards of the *Congress*. He was horri-fied when renewed fire from shore wounded Minor and several others and the boat's crew had to reverse course. He exploded in righteous fury. "Destroy that damned ship!" he called out. "She's firing on our white flag!"[27]

Technically this was not true. Although a few participants subsequently claimed that some return fire came from the *Congress,* most, if not all of it, came from the infantry onshore. Nevertheless, the gunners on the *Virginia* set to work with a will, methodically smashing the *Congress* to pieces and setting it afire in several places with hot shot heated in the furnaces of the boiler room and hauled up to the gun deck on a trivet. The few remaining crewmen on the *Congress* jumped overboard and made for shore. "Dearly did they pay for their unparalleled treachery," one Confederate officer on the *Virginia* wrote later. "We raked her fore and aft with hot shot and shell till out of pity we stopped without waiting for orders."[28]

There were no orders to cease firing for two reasons. First, Buchanan wanted the shelling to continue until the *Congress* was utterly destroyed beyond any hope of salvation. Jones later speculated that Buchanan's determination to finish off the *Congress* derived in part from his unwillingness to allow anyone to suggest that he had spared the ship for his brother's sake. But in addition, Buchanan could not give the order to cease firing because he was a casualty of the battle. As he watched the cannonade from the exposed deck atop the casemate, his anger unabated, Buchanan seized a musket from the ship's small arms locker, put the weapon to his shoulder, and fired at the offending Yankee infantry, aiming particularly at the officers who had ordered the gross breach of the rules of war. One witness recalled that "Captain Buchanan remained on deck of our ship all the evening firing his rifle at the enemy's officers whenever he could get a chance." The riflemen onshore returned fire, and Buchanan slumped to the deck, shot through his left thigh, high on the leg near his groin.[29]

Eventually the wound, or more likely the passage of time, allowed Buchanan to appreciate how foolishly he had behaved in exposing himself to enemy fire by trying to take on an infantry regiment personally. All that he would say in his official report was: "I was disabled and transferred the command of the ship to that gallant intelligent officer, Lieutenant Catesby Jones, with orders to fight her as long as the men could stand to their guns."[30]

Buchanan was carried from atop the *Virginia*'s casemate down to his quarters and laid on his cot near where Bob Minor also lay wounded. The bullet had passed perilously close to Buchanan's femoral artery, and there was some concern that he might bleed to death. But it soon became apparent that, however painful, the wound was not life threatening. As he was carried to his cabin, he turned command over to Jones, ordering him "to fire hot shot into the Congress and not to leave until she was afire."[31]

In the aftermath of the fight, both sides hurled accusations of dishonorable behavior at one another. Buchanan's view never wavered. The *Congress* had surrendered in accordance with the traditions of naval warfare. Its officers had raised the white flag and tendered their side arms. Twice, however, they had then fired on vessels that had come to complete the surrender—the second of them flying a white flag. And when Buchanan learned that Pendergrast and Smith, each of whom had surrendered to Parker, had subsequently jumped ship and made their way ashore, he saw this as further evidence of Yankee perfidy. In his view, his decision to destroy the *Congress* by hot shot was therefore a reasonable, and indeed a necessary act, made so by the treacherous behavior of the Yankees themselves.

Not surprisingly, federal authorities did not see it that way. The infantry fire against the *Beaufort,* which was a legitimate target of war, came from the shore, not from the *Congress.* Pendergrast and Smith had returned to the *Congress* with Parker's approval to aid in the removal of the wounded. When the *Beaufort* then abandoned them onboard the *Congress,* they came under renewed and heavy fire from the *Virginia.* They could hardly have stayed there, and they fled to shore to save their lives. In their view, it was Buchanan who was guilty of firing on a flag of truce, blasting away at the grounded and helpless *Congress,* which was flying two white flags.[32]

Sometime after five o'clock, with the *Congress* in flames and with Jones now in command, the *Virginia* made a few halfhearted attempts to continue the fight by engaging the Union frigate *Minnesota,* which had also run aground nearby. But it had been a long day, the *Virginia*'s engines were laboring, and the crew was exhausted. The pilots onboard protested that the ship must be safely anchored before dark or risk running aground itself. Jones decided that the *Minnesota* would still be there tomorrow. He steered the *Virginia* toward Sewall's Point, firing a long-range broadside at the USS *St. Lawrence* en route, and dropped anchor.

That evening the officers gathered in Buchanan's cabin. Their commanding officer lay on his cot, pale from loss of blood and looking every one of his sixty-one years. The men discussed the fight in hoarse voices. On the whole it had been a grand victory. Two enemy warships, each of them officially more powerful than the *Virginia,* at least in armament, had been destroyed. The ship's questionable engine plant had held up; the armor had proved effective. Even as they talked, the *Congress* continued to burn, the flames, "running from mast to mast and falling in showers of sparks," reflecting off the dark surface of Hampton Roads. Occasionally a loaded gun fired off as the heat of the flames reached it. A few minutes past midnight, the flames reached the magazine and the *Congress* exploded in a giant fireball. It had paid in full for the zealousness of the soldiers onshore. In a voice "filled with emotion," Buchanan said: "My brother, Paymaster Buchanan, was on board the Congress." After that, the discussion died out and the officers drifted away, leaving Buchanan to fall into a restless sleep.[33]

The next day, the ninth of March, would go down in history as marking the first-ever duel between two ironclad warships. Buchanan would play no part in it. He was reluctant to leave the *Virginia* and announced his intention to share its fate in the continuing fight, but his officers convinced him that he and Minor occupied space that would be needed to treat any future wounded. Convinced by this argument that it would be nobler to go ashore than to remain aboard, he allowed himself to be taken off the ship. That morning, with the *Virginia* still at anchor off Sewall's Point, he and Bob Minor were carried gingerly up the ladders and handed down the sloping side of the casemate into the only ship's boat that was still undamaged. It ferried them to shore, where they were transferred to a steam launch that carried them eventually to hospital beds in Norfolk.[34]

Buchanan was still on his way to the hospital when he heard the sound of renewed gunfire. Surely he would have assumed that the *Virginia,* with Jones now in command, was destroying the grounded and hapless *Minnesota.* Not until later did he learn that en route to the *Minnesota,* Jones had encountered the newly arrived ironclad *Monitor,* which had interposed itself in front of the grounded federal frigate. For more than four hours the two prototype ironclads battled each other to a standstill. Afterward, each side proclaimed victory. Confederates noted that the *Monitor* twice fled into shoal water: once to bring more ammunition into the turret from the magazine below the waterline, and again after its captain was temporarily blinded when a shell burst against the pilothouse. For their part, federals pointed out that it was the *Virginia* that headed back into port at the end of the day. With the bulkheads of its armored casemate sagging inward from repeated pounding, with its engines laboring, and with the tide falling, Jones decided that the *Virginia* should retire to effect repairs. Although it would sortie again, it would never engage in another fight. No one knew it at the time, but for all practical purposes, the *Virginia*'s career was over.[35]

~12~

CONFEDERATE ADMIRAL

I am fast breaking officers & men into proper man-of-war discipline.

uchanan spent two months in the hospital at Norfolk. In some ways those two months represented the pinnacle of his professional career, for even as he suffered from the physical agony of his wounded leg, he basked in torrents of praise from the public media, from fellow officers, and from the government for his conduct in the Battle of Hampton Roads. Moreover, the triumph of a single ten-gun warship over *two* enemy warships which together mounted more than seventy guns seemed to forecast the inevitability of the South's final triumph over similar odds elsewhere. It was not immediately clear, especially to southerners, that the arrival of the *Monitor* had effectively neutralized the offensive potential of the *Virginia,* and for some time they continued to hope that the Confederate ironclad might still turn the war around. The news that the *Virginia* had failed to destroy the grounded *Minnesota* or chase away the impertinent *Monitor* was disappointing, but Buchanan, like most others, assumed that it was only a matter of time before the ship sortied again to finish off the Union fleet. Perhaps he even entertained the hope that he would be back in command when it did.

Buchanan's physical pain was eased by dozens of letters of congratulation, including the formal thanks of Congress, voted him on 12 March 1862. The congressional resolution, which praised Buchanan and his men for their "unsurpassed gallantry," was especially welcome. Buchanan ordered that the proclamation be read aloud to the officers and crew of the *Virginia*, who assembled in the sail loft at the navy yard for the ceremony. Buchanan could not attend because he was still bedridden, but he sent the men his own written "thanks for the gallantry, perseverance, and determination with which you sustained the honor of the flag and the country."[1]

The congressional reference to Buchanan's gallantry was gratifying on several levels. Not only was gallantry a key component of the southern cultural and psychological value system, but in this case it had political and even legal significance. Buchanan knew that according to law, all promotions to the rank of admiral in the Confederate navy would not be based on seniority but earned by "gallant and meritorious conduct." If this knowledge raised in him a hope that his recent performance might win him such a promotion, he kept the thought to himself. Others were less circumspect. Josiah Tattnall, who succeeded Buchanan in command of the James River Squadron, wrote to congratulate him on his brilliant achievement. It "will carry your name to every corner of the Christian world," he said, "and be on the tongue of every man who deals in salt water." Tattnall concluded by asserting that he hoped "Congress will make you an admiral and put you at the head of our navy."[2]

Buchanan began working on his official report of the battle in Hampton Roads as soon as he was able. He could not write it himself, for he could not yet sit up; his leg and hip were swathed in bandages, and he was compelled to lie prone for most of the day. Clerks sat by his bed while he dictated. The final version of the report was dated 27 March, three weeks after the battle, and Buchanan devoted most of it to praising the actions of virtually every officer who had been on the *Virginia*, with special accolades for his executive officer, Lt. Catesby Jones. The report was direct and appropriately modest, setting just the sort of professional "high tone" Buchanan had always admired in others. Accordingly, he had praise for his gallant enemy as well. He noted admiringly that the men on the *Cumberland* had continued to fire their guns even as their ship sank beneath them.[3]

He remained angry, however, over the craven deceit of those who had continued to fire on the *Virginia* after the *Congress* had struck its flag. He was angry as well with Lieutenant Parker of the *Beaufort*, who (as Buchanan saw it) had abandoned the fight and run to safety without fulfilling his duties. It was Parker's dereliction of duty that had compelled

Buchanan to send Bob Minor in a ship's boat to do the job Parker ought to have done. In Buchanan's mind, Minor's injury was as much Parker's fault as if he had fired the shot. Not wanting to sully his official report with such charges, Buchanan sent them on to Mallory in a separate letter. In it he stated bluntly that "Lieut. Commanding W. H. Parker is unfit to command." Not only had Parker failed in his duty to burn the *Congress*, Buchanan asserted, but he had demonstrated poor judgment by opening fire when he was more than a mile beyond effective range. "An officer who can be thus delinquent in his duty, is not, in my opinion, fit to command."[4]

Mallory ignored the criticism of Parker and forwarded Buchanan's official report on the battle to Jefferson Davis, adding a gratifying endorsement: "The dashing courage and consummate professional ability of Flag Officer Buchanan and his associates achieved the most remarkable victory which naval annals record." A few days later, Mallory notified Buchanan that he planned to recommend him for promotion to the rank of admiral. For once in his life, Buchanan objected to receiving a promotion. He responded that he was "honored and gratified at the very complimentary language you are pleased to use," but he declared that "a sense of justice" demanded that Josiah Tattnall, and not he, should have the first rank in the Confederate navy. "He is my senior in the service," Buchanan wrote, "and an officer of high tone, bearing, and gallantry. . . . I therefore sincerely hope he may be placed above me." Just how sincere Buchanan was in his self-effacing protest can only be guessed. He knew that Tattnall had already declared his support for Buchanan's promotion, and perhaps he felt that some demonstration of professional modesty was called for here. In any case, Mallory ignored his protest and sent Buchanan's name to President Davis later that summer. Franklin Buchanan would become not only the *first* full admiral of the Navy, but, as events would prove, also the *only* one.[5]

Praise and promotion were gratifying, to be sure. But physically, Buchanan was having a difficult time of it. He was, after all, sixty-one years old, and he had suffered a grievous wound. As if miraculously guided, the bullet had missed not only the femoral artery, but also the femur and the pelvic bone. It had, however, torn away the musculature and sinews in his upper leg. There was probably nerve damage as well, for Buchanan reported that at times he had no control over, or feeling in, his left foot. His injuries kept him bedridden and immobile, but he maintained a stoic demeanor. When Bob Minor's brother visited a week after the battle, he reported that although Buchanan was "suffering from his wound, . . . he never murmurs, [and] those around him may think that he is easy & doing well." It was painful that Nannie could not be with him—she remained in Maryland throughout the war—but several of their children were there. Nannie's namesake, the young woman whose wedding Abraham Lincoln had attended just over a year earlier, was in Richmond with her husband, Capt. Julius E. Meiere, who had resigned from the U.S. Marine Corps to fight for the South. She and Alice, who also came south, took turns sitting by their father's bed. For a while he seemed to improve, bolstered, perhaps, by the flow of congratulations. Then he suffered a relapse. In the second week of April, more than a month after the battle, he was suddenly far worse—unable to walk, or even to sit up. His body seemed to be wearing down. He dictated his letters to one of his daughters or to a clerk, and could barely sign his name at the bottom.[6]

As he lay in his hospital bed, bad news arrived from several fronts. A federal fleet under David Farragut had steamed past the forts below New Orleans and captured the Crescent City. Closer to home, a sustained buildup of Union troops at Fort Monroe suggested that the enemy was planning to use the Virginia peninsula for an advance against Richmond itself. That advance, which got under way in early April, threatened not only Richmond but also the Confederate hold on Norfolk. For nearly a month, Joseph E. Johnston's Confederate army at Yorktown stalled the enemy advance, but on 3 May Johnston evacuated his Yorktown line and fell back to Williamsburg. His withdrawal uncovered Norfolk and necessitated its immediate evacuation. The Confederates decamped from the city with nearly as much haste as the federals had shown a year earlier. The *Virginia*, too, had to be given up. At first the pilots said they could save the ship if Tattnall could reduce the draft to eighteen feet so that it could ascend the James River. But when, after much effort, that was accomplished, the pilots then said that it was not enough. With time running out, Tattnall ordered the ship destroyed on 11 May. Just as federal troops had burned the *Merrimack* when they abandoned Norfolk the year before, so now did Confederate troops destroy the *Virginia* as they too evacuated the city.

Of course, the evacuation of Norfolk also meant that Buchanan had to leave the Norfolk hospital. Still bedridden, he was lifted onto a litter and carried to the train station, where he took the cars for Greensboro, North Carolina, on 6 May. His doctor had recommended Greensboro because of the fresh country air, and indeed, within a few days Buchanan was feeling much better. Within three days he was able to get out of bed and take a short walk using his new crutches, and by the end of the month he was writing Mallory, in his own hand, that he would be able to assume the command of a squadron within ten days.[7]

Taking him at his word, Mallory ordered him to Memphis to take command of the Mississippi River Defense Fleet; but Buchanan had to admit that he had been too optimistic. "I regret to say that I decided prematurely," he wrote to the new chief of the Office of Orders and Detail, French Forrest. "My lameness still continues, and I suffer much pain in my left foot & leg." Three days after Buchanan wrote that letter, the seven small ships of the Mississippi River Defense Fleet, under the command of Capt. James E. Montgomery, were virtually destroyed by a vastly superior Union squadron in the Battle of Memphis. If Buchanan had been healthy enough to accept his orders, he might have arrived in Memphis just in time to preside over this debacle.[8]

Word of the disaster at Memphis was not the only bad news that week; these were perilous days for the Confederacy everywhere. As Buchanan gradually regained his strength in Greensboro, Union forces on the Virginia peninsula under Maj. Gen. George B. McClellan continued their cautious but seemingly inexorable advance toward Richmond. A Confederate counterattack at Seven Pines stalled them for a day or two, but the battle had a heavy cost. The South lost the services of the southern army commander when Joseph E. Johnston fell badly wounded. The fall of Richmond itself seemed imminent; President Davis sent his family to safety in Raleigh, North Carolina. Anxiety in the capital city was accompanied by an apparent need to allocate blame. As McClellan's army closed in, the Confederate Navy Department ordered a court of inquiry to examine Josiah Tattnall's decision to destroy the *Virginia*. Buchanan assumed that this was merely pro forma; frequently the purpose of such courts was to remove any blame that might otherwise attach itself to the officer in charge. Not this time. In spite of the support of virtually all the officers who were called to testify, the court issued a finding on 11 June that "the destruction of the Virginia was . . . unnecessary at the time and place it was effected." In short, Tattnall had panicked and blown up the ship prematurely.[9]

Most navy officers were appalled. From Greensboro, Buchanan expressed astonishment at the decision. "Can it be so?" he asked Lieutenant Jones incredulously. "I think there must be some mistake." By this time Buchanan was able to move about the house unassisted, although he still needed his crutches—his "sticks" as he called them. Relearning to walk was taking longer than he had expected. His left foot had lost most of its feeling due to the damaged nerve tissue and had to be retrained. "My lameness improves slowly but surely," he wrote to Jones. "Animation is gradually returning to my foot and I feel a daily improvement."[10]

Finally able to travel in late June, Buchanan made his way to Richmond to sit as a member of the court martial that would try Tattnall for his "crime." The court convened on 5 July and got to work two days later. Significantly, in the period between the original finding and the meeting of the court, the strategic situation in Virginia had dramatically reversed. When the initial finding had been issued on 11 June, the Confederacy's days had seemed numbered: McClellan's army was within four miles of Richmond; Joe Johnston lay wounded in a Richmond hospital; and the new army commander, Robert E. Lee, had yet to demonstrate that he was up to the job. But the very next day, "Jeb" Stuart's cavalry departed on a raid around McClellan's army to initiate the campaign that would subsequently be known as the Seven Days. By 7 July, when Buchanan convened the court, Robert E. Lee had driven McClellan's army from the gates of Richmond to the banks of the James River, where it huddled in defensive positions around Harrison's Landing, its offensive potential all but evaporated. Without doubt, these circumstances worked to Tattnall's advantage; it now seemed far less important to find a scapegoat.

The specifications charged Tattnall with "culpable destruction" of the *Virginia*, with "negligence" for failing to ascertain the depth of the James River before attempting to lighten the ship, and with "improvident conduct." The court heard testimony from various officers for ten days. Tattnall was the last witness, and he spoke at length. He cited Buchanan himself as the source for his claim that the *Virginia* could not have survived in the open sea. With the loss of Norfolk, he noted, the only alternative was to take the ship upriver, and that, according to the pilots, could not be done. Indeed, Tattnall pinned most of the blame on the civilian pilots, who, he said, had misled him about the depth of the James River. Even if the *Virginia*'s draft had been reduced enough to allow the ship to make it as far as Hog Island, Tattnall declared, raising it out of the water far enough to achieve that would have exposed the ship's unarmored "knuckle," making it vulnerable in a fight. "A glance at the evidence," he concluded, "will show that the idea of carrying the ship to Hog Island and keeping her there for defense . . . could only have been dismissed as vain and futile."[11]

After Tattnall's testimony, the officers voted. The court declared that the charges were "not proven" and awarded Tattnall "an honorable acquittal." Honorable it may have been, but the taint of the accusation would hang over Tattnall for the rest of the war. He remained on active service and later commanded the Savannah River Squadron, but he would never again be considered for promotion to flag rank.[12]

Just one week later, on 30 July 1862, McClellan's army at Harrison's Landing began to evacuate its camp, with the men marching back to Fort Monroe to embark on transports for the North. For the rest of the summer, as Lee's army moved north, too, and won another victory at the Second Battle of Bull Run, Buchanan remained in Richmond continuing his convalescence and making occasional public appearances. He involved himself in the activities of the Maryland Association, which encouraged Marylanders to fight for the Confederacy in state regiments of their own. He presided over a meeting of the Maryland Association in mid-August and delivered what one witness called "a stirring speech." "More than a year ago," Buchanan told his fellow Free Staters, "you were driven from your homes by the ruthless tyranny of the usurper at Washington, and with a zeal and gallantry worthy of your State, you rushed to arms in defense of Constitutional liberty and Southern independence." Now, he said, Marylanders had the opportunity to liberate their state. No doubt Frederick Douglass would have found an element of irony in Buchanan's plea to his "subjugated brethren" to "break their chains" and "strike for freedom." But as with virtually all southern whites, the irony of such rhetoric eluded Buchanan entirely.[13]

Five days after this speech, Mallory sent to Jefferson Davis the formal request for Buchanan's promotion to admiral. Davis approved the promotion without demur, and within days Admiral Buchanan received orders to go to Mobile, Alabama, to take command of the naval squadron in Mobile Bay and the Naval District of the Gulf. One year, almost to the day, after he had first arrived in Richmond, and two weeks before his sixty-second birthday, Buchanan took the train south to embark on a new chapter in his professional life.[14]

After the bustling frenzy of wartime Richmond, Mobile projected a deceptively placid demeanor. It was certainly as cosmopolitan as Richmond, with its population of thirty thousand and an ethnic mix that included, in the words of visiting Englishman William Howard Russell, "Negroes, mulattoes, quadroons, and mestizos of all sorts, Spanish, Italian, and French, speaking their own tongues, or a quaint *lingua franca,* and dressed in very striking or pretty costumes." Moreover, Mobile was a city of tremendous strategic importance. After the fall of New Orleans in April, it was the only Gulf coast city still under Confederate control that was connected to the interior by railroads: to Mississippi by the Mobile & Ohio, and to Georgia by the newly built Mobile & Great Northern. Even before the war Mobile had boasted a thriving trade. More than three hundred ships carrying more than $3.5 million worth of cotton had left its docks in 1860 alone. Now, blockade runners and commerce raiders were protected within its commodious harbor by both natural and contrived devices.[15]

Across the southern entrance to Mobile Bay, narrow spits of land arched together to provide a natural defensive barrier. On the eastern headland of these promontories was Fort Morgan, named for the Revolutionary War hero of the southern campaigns. Fort Morgan was a substantial masonry structure mounting more than forty guns, mostly rifled thirty-two-pounders and a few ten-inch Columbiads. Fort Gaines, a star-shaped fort on the western headland, was smaller but nevertheless mounted more than twenty guns. In the ship channel between these forts the Confederates had begun to sew mines, or "torpedoes," as they were called then, which forced arriving or departing vessels to sail in a narrow channel under the guns of Fort Morgan.[16]

For the next two years, Buchanan's professional life would be wrapped up in the defense of Mobile Bay. It was a responsibility different in character from anything he had previously attempted. As commander of the naval district, as well as commanding officer of the Confederate squadron in the bay itself, he had to cooperate with army commanders, answer to civil authority, and orchestrate the development of a meaningful naval presence in Mobile Bay. As elsewhere in the Confederacy, his tiny squadron would be significantly overmatched in any confrontation with federal forces. Yet, he had little choice but to do the best he could. "I see very clearly my position here," he wrote to Mallory after he had been in Mobile about a month. "We must meet the enemy as they pass Fort Morgan . . . , and try our strength with him. There is no other alternative."[17]

Ironically, Buchanan's first command crisis concerned the unexpected arrival of a Confederate commerce raider. Only days after Buchanan arrived in Mobile, the css *Florida* limped into port flying the yellow flag that indicated disease onboard. The *Florida* was no ordinary privateer; the Confederacy had staked a lot on this ship. As part of Mallory's *guerre de course* strategy, it had been built secretly in Liverpool as the *Oreto* and taken to British Nassau, where its designated C.S. Navy commander, John H. Maffitt, had come onboard to assume command. Armed secretly at sea and rechristened the *Florida,* it set out with a mostly international crew to conduct a campaign against Yankee merchant ships. Almost at once, however, yellow fever broke out, and the disease ran through the crew with such virulence that it seemed to Maffitt that his entire crew might die before he could reach a friendly port. He made his way first to Cuba, and then, ill himself with the fever, and with only five able-bodied men left onboard, he ran the *Florida* through the gauntlet of Union blockading ships into Mobile Bay on 4 September.[18]

Buchanan ordered Maffitt to anchor the *Florida* in the lower bay, fifteen miles south of the city, where, in spite of the yellow fever, he visited the ship personally on 8 September. It was a sobering experience. Battered by the ships of the blockading fleet during its run into port, and littered with the dead and dying, the *Florida* resembled one of the lower levels of Dante's hell. Buchanan was so moved by Maffitt's circumstances that he not only sent a warm letter of support, but also urged Mallory to do the same, arguing that it "would have a great effect."[19]

Buchanan transferred the crew of the *Florida* to another vessel anchored nearby so that the *Florida* could be cleaned and fumigated. The work went slowly because Buchanan would not allow any men from the shore to help, fearing that the disease would spread. At least some of Maffitt's crew had had enough of danger and death and wanted out, threatening to desert if their resignations were not accepted. Ever the disciplinarian, Buchanan suggested that Mallory place all such men, yellow fever or not, in double irons.[20]

The refit of the *Florida* took months—longer than Buchanan had planned, and much longer than Mallory had expected—and the Confederate navy secretary began to lose patience. How long, he wanted to know, before Maffitt could take the *Florida* to sea? Buchanan assured him that the delay was "unavoidable" because the whole ship had to be repaired as well as cleaned, fumigated, repainted, and refitted. He reported that he visited the ship regularly, and that its crew was doing all that was possible. Even so, it was Christmastime before the ship was finally ready. By then Mallory had lost patience entirely. In part, at least, Mallory's irritation was the result of rumors that Maffitt was spending the time entertaining ladies aboard his ship and hosting dinners and other social events rather than looking to the refitting of his ship. He ordered Maffitt to come to Richmond to explain himself.

Buchanan interceded. For one thing, he was nettled because Mallory had sent the order to Maffitt without first consulting the naval district commander (himself); second, he believed that Mallory misunderstood the circumstances. As it happened, President Davis was in Mobile, returning from a trip to visit the western armies in Tennessee and Mississippi. Throughout that trip, Davis had felt obliged to assuage the delicate feelings of touchy generals; now he found himself cornered by a touchy admiral. Maffitt, Buchanan told him, was being treated unfairly. It was a "grave error" and a "gross act of injustice" to remove Maffitt from command at this juncture. Davis agreed to telegraph Mallory and get the misunderstanding straightened out.[21]

A day later, Buchanan wrote his own letter to Mallory. The *Florida* was indeed ready for sea, he wrote, but escaping Mobile Bay could be done only under certain conditions: it required "hard wind and thick weather" that lasted long enough for a blacked-out vessel to escape through the blockading squadron. He noted that there were never less than seven Yankee ships in the channel, and often there were eight or nine. Maffitt would have to pick his time carefully if he were to have a chance to make it safely to sea. The right conditions had been present only twice since the ship had completed its refit: once when Maffitt was in Mobile on business, and once the day *after* Maffitt received Mallory's letter to go to Richmond. As for the charge that Maffitt had been entertaining onboard the *Florida* rather than attending to his duty, Buchanan wrote that "on two occasions only" Maffitt had invited friends onto the *Florida*. During the first of those, Buchanan had himself been one of the party. He had come onboard to "pay an official farewell visit," and Maffitt had secured his approval to bring a small party of well-wishers onboard as well. "Capt. Maffitt's whole course since he has been under my command has met my approbation," Buchanan asserted.[22]

Thus chided, Mallory restored Maffitt to command. Two weeks later, on 16 January, the *Florida* finally put to sea. Within three days it captured the *Jacob Bell*, a prize valued at $1.5 million—the richest prize ever taken by a Confederate raider. The *Florida* then went on to a long career of commerce raiding, making a total of thirty-seven captures before being taken itself in a controversial action in the neutral harbor of Bahia, Brazil.[23]

Buchanan's involvement with the *Florida* was relatively short-lived. Much more important over the long run was the condition of the little naval squadron in Mobile Bay that fell under his personal command. In his initial visit to the vessels of the squadron, only days after assuming command, he was generally pleased. "I found them in a state of efficiency highly creditable to their officers and the service," he wrote to Mallory. "Their exercises at general quarters I have seldom seen equaled." He promised that in the case of at attack, "our little squadron will do its duty." But he noted, too, that "against ironclad vessels not much can be expected."[24]

Indeed, Buchanan believed that if his "little squadron" were to have any realistic hope of resisting an attack by the enemy fleet, he would first have to accomplish two things: instill a sense of professionalism and discipline, and increase both the number and type of ships under his command. Specifically, he would need some ironclads. During his two-year tenure in command at Mobile, most of Buchanan's efforts were bent toward achieving these twin goals.

As one might expect, discipline came first. Despite his professed pleasure at the relative efficiency of the gunboats in his squadron, Buchanan decided at once that it was essential to establish what he called "proper regular man-of-war discipline" within the command. Here on the periphery of the Confederacy, the navy lacked even the most basic accoutrements of a regular professional service. For one thing, the officers did not even *look* like officers. If they wore uniforms at all, they were the old dark blue uniforms of their previous service in the U.S. Navy. Those without old uniforms made do with what they had. Buchanan was positively appalled when one lieutenant reported to him wearing (as he wrote to a friend), "a *black coat*," the underlining in his letter suggesting the extent of his shocked sensibilities. When Buchanan confronted the officer about his attire, the lieutenant said that it was what he always wore on duty, that he had never been given a regular uniform, and that none of the officers in his previous commands had worn uniforms. Horrified by such "indifference to orders and regulations," Buchanan wrote to Richmond to see if he could not get some gray cloth from which proper uniforms could be made. He urged Mallory to issue "a *positive order* that every officer when on duty should appear in his proper uniform." Soon thereafter, a general order was issued from Richmond declaring that "all officers of the Navy will at all times when on duty wear the prescribed uniform of their grades."[25]

Buchanan sought to impose higher professional standards of conduct as well. As always, he was completely unforgiving when it came to dissipation. Officers found intoxicated, even when off duty, had no place in Buchanan's navy. When Mobile police arrested two navy officers for being "drunk and down" in the public streets, Buchanan sought their dismissal from the service. He asked for additional copies of the navy regulations to ensure that there were "two or three copies" onboard each of his ships. He reported that too many of the officers of the squadron had fallen into habits not appropriate to proper order. "Many appear to think that the Navy was made for their *pleasure & accommodation*," he wrote to Capt. John K. Mitchell in Richmond, "and I take good care to assure them that such is not the case."[26]

Buchanan sought to improve discipline within the ranks as well. Never a particular admirer of "Jack's" moral character, he was especially unimpressed by the sailors he had to depend on in Mobile. A majority of the enlisted men were of foreign birth, with Irishmen making up a plurality, and Buchanan's brand of discipline was a rude awakening for most of them. "There are on board some of these Steamers some of the greatest vagabonds you ever heard of," Buchanan wrote to Mitchell. "One or two hung during these times would have a wonderful effect." If he could not hang them, a dozen lashes laid on the backs of the worst offenders might do nearly as well. But like the U.S. Navy, the Confederate navy forbade the whipping of sailors. As a result, Buchanan could only order that the miscreants be placed in irons or be put to labor on "public works." Alas, he complained to Richmond, there were no public works in Mobile. His own son-in-law, Julius Meiere, now a captain in the Confederate Marine Corps and commanding Mobile's marine contingent, tried to put one culprit to work cleaning weapons in the marines' compound, but the soldier simply refused to work. And without the right to hang or whip the man, there was really nothing Meiere or anyone else could do about it. In frustration, Buchanan wrote to Mitchell: "I am now a stronger advocate than ever for the *lash*."[27]

While metaphorically, if not literally, whipping his new command into a semblance of military order, Buchanan's other preoccupation was to build an ironclad fleet that could be expected to stand up to a Yankee invasion. He did have the *Baltic*, a converted river tug that had been plated over with iron, and which he used as a temporary flagship. But the *Baltic* was slow and unwieldy, and not likely to be of much service in a fight. What he needed was armored ships with heavy guns. Since there was no *Merrimack* to convert, such vessels would have to be built entirely from scratch. The wood for the hulls was still in the forests, the iron still in the ground, and the guns as yet uncast. All of Buchanan's legendary drive and energy would be required to coordinate the efforts of the naval contractors, shipbuilders, iron foundries, gun makers, coal providers, and recruiters to create a naval force out of the elemental raw materials—and to do so before the Yankees offshore decided to try to force their way into the bay. It was a task that called for energy, to be sure, but it would also require discretion, tact, and diplomacy, and it would test Buchanan's inner strength in ways that a battle at sea never could.[28]

The work had begun even before Buchanan arrived in Mobile. In May 1862, while Buchanan was still recovering in Greensboro, Mallory had approved a contract with naval constructor Henry D. Bassett to build two floating batteries at Selma, Alabama, two hundred miles up the Tombigbee River from Mobile. According to the contract, the two vessels were to have been completed by July, but they were still on the stocks at Selma when Buchanan arrived in September. In addition to these two vessels, two much larger ironclad warships were under construction: one at Selma and one at Montgomery. The ship at Montgomery was to be a paddlewheel steamer and was eventually christened the *Nashville*; the vessel being built at Selma, where the two floating batteries were also under construction, was to be a screw propeller ironclad and would become the *Tennessee*. On these four ironclads depended the future security of Mobile Bay.[29]

The same week that Buchanan arrived in Mobile, navy commander

Ebenezer Farrand arrived in Selma with orders from Mallory to superintend completion of the four ironclads. Buchanan wrote him to ask for a progress report on the two floating batteries, which by now should have been virtually finished. The news was not good. Not only were both vessels hopelessly behind schedule, all work was at a complete stop because the builders simply did not have the material needed to finish them. Building the wooden hulls and frames had been easy enough, although the contractors had been forced to use unseasoned wood. The greater problem was that they did not have parts for the engines or iron plate for the armor. Until such scarce items became available, no further work could be done. Then, too, the workforce was crippled by illness in the sickly climate of late-summer Alabama, and the contractors showed little energy in pushing the work.[30]

Energy was exactly what Buchanan could bring to the problem. He sent the best officer he had, Comdr. James D. Johnston, to Selma to compile a comprehensive report of what was needed and to do whatever he could to push the work. Armed with Johnston's report, Buchanan then wrote to Mallory to urge him to pressure the suppliers. Mallory informed him that iron could not be had from the Atlanta ironworks of Schofield & Markham, who had the original contract, but that perhaps some could be found at the Shelby Iron Works in Columbiana, Alabama. Buchanan urged Farrand to explore both sources, and to consider as well using railroad iron to armor the ships. "It is very important that this Battery should be completed at once if possible," he wrote. "Let me hear from you as soon as possible."[31]

By early December, iron plate began to trickle in—some from Atlanta, more from the Shelby Works—but it remained a constant battle to keep the supply flowing. Part of the problem was a shortage of skilled ironworkers, many of whom had been swept up in the army draft. But it wasn't just a scarcity of material or manpower that led to problems; often the difficulties were administrative. In February, Johnston reported from Selma that there was a small mountain of iron plate (four and a half tons of it) simply lying on the wharf, but the army major in command there refused to turn it over to the navy without an order from Richmond. Although Buchanan was probably tempted to order Johnston to simply take the iron, and the army be damned, he followed proper channels and asked Mallory to ask the war secretary to order the army major to deliver the iron to Johnston so that it could be shipped to Mobile.[32]

Another chronic problem was ordnance. When finished, the new ships would need guns. There were many guns in the forts guarding Mobile Bay—more than eighty all told—but they would be needed where they were. Besides, most of them were thirty-two-pounders, which would not have much of an impact on the iron-plated warships Buchanan expected to fight. In any case, the guns of the forts and shore batteries belonged to the army. Buchanan got along quite well with the local army commanders in Mobile. So frequently did he mention his good relations with the army commanders in Mobile that one suspects that it may have pleased his vanity to be accepted by them as an equal. In fact, as a full admiral in the C.S. Navy, he outranked the brigadier and major generals who commanded the forts and garrisons of Mobile Bay. He accompanied them on tours of the fortifications and made suggestions, which they often accepted, about the placement of the guns and the organization of the batteries. He even loaned navy guns to the army with the understanding that they would be returned when the new ships were ready.

What Buchanan really wanted for his new ships were the newer banded Brooke rifles, in the largest caliber he could get. Such weapons were scarce in the Confederacy, and if Buchanan expected to get some of them, he would need to order them from the source. He therefore opened a correspondence with the managers of the Naval Gun Foundry in Selma: first with Colin McRae, the successful businessman who had established the facility, and later with his own former executive officer from the *Virginia*, Catesby Jones, who succeeded to the command of the foundry in June 1863. As early as December 1862, McRae told Buchanan that he could probably get at least one ten-inch gun to him by the end of the year. That would not be enough, of course, but it was a start. Buchanan responded: "We want heavy guns badly to give our Yankee friends a warm reception."[33]

Manpower was a third problem. Indeed, manpower was a problem virtually everywhere in the Confederacy. Given the Union's four-to-one superiority in the number of white males of military age, every commander across the Confederacy was looking for more men. Buchanan was willing to accept untrained landsmen; he was convinced that with the right kind of discipline they could be turned into good sailors. But he could not find men of any description, for by the end of 1862 virtually every man of military age had already been swept up by the draft. Since April, Confederate law had mandated the conscription of all able-bodied white males aged eighteen to thirty-five, and an amendment to that law in September raised the upper age limit to forty-five. Of course, some of those conscripted into the service had—or claimed to have—maritime experience, and if forced to serve the Confederacy, preferred to do it at sea. The law made that possible: according to another amendment passed by Congress in October, any conscript who preferred service in the C.S. Navy was to be granted that option. Buchanan planned to avail himself of this source.[34]

But the law was undercut by the voracious appetite of the undersized Confederate armies for manpower. Almost daily Buchanan received requests from soldiers who desired to transfer from the army to the navy. He dutifully and expectantly sent the list of names to Secretary of War James Seddon and asked that they be transferred. He sent recruiting officers to the conscript camps. He even sent representatives to the armies in the field: to Braxton Bragg's Army of Tennessee and Leonidas Polk's Army of Mississippi. But Seddon did not reply, and the officers came home empty-handed. Not unreasonably, perhaps, most army officials saw requests for transfer to the navy as a way to avoid the obligations of military service. This was an attitude that was shared at the very highest levels of government. Back in the fall of 1861, Mallory had complained to his diary that "the President refuses to permit a man to leave the army to work on the gunboats for the Navy," and that attitude still permeated the War Department. Frustrated by the passive resistance he met everywhere, Buchanan pleaded with Mallory for help. "Unless the Sec of War and the Generals are more liberal towards the Navy in permitting transfers from the Army to the Navy," he wrote, "we cannot man either the gunboats or the floating batteries." Privately, he complained to Mitchell that "*Orders & Laws* are not respected and obeyed by the Army as in the Navy."[35]

Because the Confederacy lacked so many of the traditional elements of naval power, some suggested that the young nation should turn instead to experimental weapons. The *Virginia*, after all, had been an experiment, and it had been wildly successful. Buchanan had always thought of himself as open to new ideas—especially in terms of the application of new technology—but he was dubious about what he saw as gimmick weapons, particularly when the suggestion came from amateurs in naval warfare. He had to be careful in responding to these suggestions lest he offend either a generous spirit or a powerful politician.

He fended off the offer of a ladies' society in Columbus, Mississippi, to sponsor a gunboat; and he carefully explained to Alabama governor John Shorter that the governor's proposal to build fire ships and torpedo rams was unrealistic. Likewise, he had to tell Mallory that the submarine design of James R. McClintock was a failure.[36]

McClintock and his partners had built a submarine in New Orleans, but they had been forced to scuttle it after that city fell to the Yankees in April. Now McClintock was proposing an electrically powered submarine for use in Mobile Bay. Mallory ordered Buchanan to provide him with support, which he did, but the engine could not be made to work. McClintock had to resort to hand cranks for propulsion. In early February 1863, while on a trial run near Fort Morgan, the boat foundered and the members of the crew barely escaped with their lives. Buchanan was not surprised. "I never entertained but one opinion as to the result of this Boat," he confided to Mallory.[37]

In his efforts to obtain iron plate for the armor-clads, to secure guns for the ships and men to man them, all the while staving off the crack-brained proposals of outsiders, Buchanan experienced great frustration. These were not the kind of problems that could be overcome by dint of sheer will or by the application of uncompromising discipline. They required patience, tact, and constant attention to detail. Nevertheless, if the enemy offshore would give him time to complete his preparations, Buchanan was confident that he could win another signal victory. In a letter to his brother-in-law Edward Lloyd back in Maryland, he claimed that the day of final victory was "not far off." "When we thrash the vile vagabonds in [Vicksburg] Mississippi and here," he wrote, "I think they will be tired of trying to subjugate us. *Fight to the death* is now the universal feeling. . . . My preparations to meet them here are still progressing, and if they give us a little more time to complete them, they may *come on* and we will receive them cheerfully."[38]

~13~

THE CSS *TENNESSEE*

I am anxious to have another crack at the vile vagabonds.

Buchanan's plan for the defense of Mobile Bay depended on a collaboration involving the army fortifications onshore, the floating batteries in the bay, and the ironclad vessels that were under construction on the Alabama and Tombigbee Rivers. For six months, as the work at Selma and Montgomery languished, it seemed likely that the forts and the shore batteries would have to bear the brunt of any Yankee attack unassisted. But then, in February 1863, three ships under construction at Selma were successfully launched: the floating batteries *Huntsville* and *Tuscaloosa,* and the ironclad ram *Tennessee.* Of course, at the time of their launching they were merely wooden shells with neither armor nor armament, but at least Buchanan could now begin to hope that he would soon be able to take to sea in command of a formidable squadron of ironclad warships. With such a force he could not only defend Mobile Bay, he could sortie from the bay to attack the Union blockading fleet, and perhaps even steam through Mississippi Sound to New Orleans to reclaim the Crescent City for the Confederacy. Buoyed by such thoughts, he wrote his former executive officer Catesby Jones: "I am anxious to have another crack at the vile vagabonds."[1]

Fulfillment of that vision proved elusive. The two floating batteries were a great disappointment. In early April, Buchanan went onboard the

Tuscaloosa to witness its initial sea trials. Because the Confederates were short on coal (like everything else), he ordered the crew to burn wood during the first run. Alas, even with the engines opened to full throttle, the *Tuscaloosa* barely made headway. Buchanan ordered the captain to stop up the leaks in the boilers and increase the draft of the blowers in the hope of improving the engines' efficiency. A few days later, he came aboard again for another try. Burning coal this time, the engines succeeded in raising steam pressure up to 150 psi, but the *Tuscaloosa* made only about two and a half knots, barely enough, Buchanan reported to Mallory, to stem the current in the harbor. Its sister ship, the *Huntsville*, fared no better; at three knots it "trembled considerably." Resignedly, Buchanan determined that neither vessel could operate as a warship and that they would instead have to serve, as originally designated, as floating batteries.[2]

Buchanan's hope that the gigantic *Nashville*, the enormous paddlewheel steamer being built at Montgomery, would be more of a success lasted a bit longer. It—or at least its unfinished hull—arrived at the Mobile docks in June. The *Nashville* was certainly an imposing vessel; at 270 feet it was as long as the ill-fated *Virginia*, although it appeared even larger because of its paddlewheel design. One officer called it a "tremendous monster." But it was that size that made the *Nashville*'s completion problematical. Its huge superstructure would require an inordinate amount of iron plate if it were to be armored properly—more iron, perhaps, than the Confederacy could afford to invest in a single warship. Throughout the summer of 1863, as Ulysses S. Grant besieged Vicksburg on the Mississippi and Robert E. Lee contemplated an invasion of Pennsylvania, Buchanan wrestled with contractors and suppliers—demanding, pleading, begging, and cajoling—in an effort to obtain iron, guns, and manpower for his ironclad fleet. In the meantime, it became clear that the Confederacy simply could not supply all the material and manpower necessary to make both the *Nashville* and the *Tennessee* operational. Rather than try to complete both vessels simultaneously, therefore, Buchanan decided he would have to concentrate on completing just one ship. His efforts thus focused increasingly, if not quite exclusively, on the *Tennessee*.[3]

Like the *Virginia*, which it so much resembled, the *Tennessee* was a casemate ironclad. Launched in late February from the building ways in

Selma, it shot swiftly into the Alabama River as if eager to begin its naval career. Still without engines, armor, or guns, the *Tennessee* was taken in tow by the river steamer *Southern Republic* and, accompanied by cheers from the workers on the riverbank and with the *Southern Republic*'s calliope tooting out the notes to "Dixie," began its maiden voyage south to Mobile. There, the Confederacy's newest warship was welcomed by an enthusiastic crowd that included Franklin Buchanan.[4]

At 209 feet, the *Tennessee* was some 60 feet shorter than the *Nashville*. More important, its casemate design gave it a low silhouette because the flat deck was supposed to show little or no freeboard once the ship was fully armed and armored. The sloping sides of that casemate were constructed of heavy timbers: more than a foot of yellow pine, covered over again with five and a half more inches of white pine, and then four inches of oak. Buchanan later added two more inches of oak on the inside of the casemate, making the wooden superstructure more than two feet thick altogether. Eventually this would be armored over with five inches of iron plate (six inches on the forward shield). Much of the wood was unseasoned, but the ship's builders simply did not have the luxury of allowing cut timber to season before use. The casemate was cut for ten gun ports, but the three forward and three aft ports were arranged to accommodate a single pivot gun that could fire either directly ahead (or astern) or on either broadside. Thus the *Tennessee* would carry only six guns, but would be able to fire four of them in a broadside at any given time.[5]

Like the *Virginia*, the *Tennessee*'s weak point was its engine plant. Originally, the engines were to have been specially constructed, but like so much else in the Confederacy, they instead had to be jury-rigged, cannibalized from the Yazoo River steamer *Alonzo Child* and transported to Mobile by railroad and barge. Designed for a ship of much less burden, those engines would prove to be sadly underpowered once the *Tennessee* took its guns and iron plating onboard. Although it made eight knots in its initial sea trial, when fully armed and armored the *Tennessee* was unlikely to make any better than the six knots that had been the *Virginia*'s top speed. Mallory wondered if the engines should be replaced, but Buchanan said there was no time. "The *Tennessee* will soon be ready for her iron," he wrote in April. "If the engines and boilers which are now in her are to be replaced by others, it will cause great delay; and she will not be ready for service for several months." In

Buchanan's view, a slow ironclad was better than no ironclad at all.[6]

Throughout the spring and summer, Buchanan worked hard to arm and armor the *Tennessee,* and in all other ways to prepare his new ship for battle. His great fear was that the Union blockading fleet would discover just how weak he was and force its way into the bay before he was ready. Luckily, the Yankees believed that Buchanan's ironclads were *already* operational. Gustavus Fox, who as Welles's assistant acted as a kind of operational chief of staff for the Union navy, warned his commanders in the Gulf to be on the qui vive for Buchanan. "Buchanan has several ironclads in the harbor," he wrote in April at a time when the only operational ironclad in the bay was the *Baltic.* Moreover, Fox thought it likely that Buchanan might attempt a sortie in order to prove his dedication to the rebel cause. "He is a good officer," Fox wrote, "and desperate from his dismissal after begging on his knees to be allowed to withdraw his resignation." Even David Farragut, Buchanan's former messmate from the old 74 *Franklin,* and now the Union commander on the Gulf coast, overestimated Buchanan's force. "Our force was not equal to his," he wrote to a subordinate in late April. But at least Farragut did not fear a confrontation. If Buchanan should sortie, he wrote, "bag him" and "do not let him get back into the bay."[7]

Buchanan had no plans for a sortie—not yet. Granted the respite that his enemy's overestimation of his strength gave him, he focused his energies on getting at least one first-class ironclad ready for battle. By July, the hull of the *Tennessee* was virtually complete except for its armor. The seven-inch-wide plates, rolled at the Shelby Iron Works in Columbiana, were shipped to Selma, where the bolt holes were drilled. Then they were floated downriver on barges to Mobile, where they were affixed by two-and-a-half-inch iron bolts onto the two-foot-thick wooden casemate of the *Tennessee.* Supply never kept up with need. Buchanan wrote to Mallory to explain the delay and to urge him to pressure the suppliers. Meanwhile, he tried to "borrow" iron from the army. He often sought to obtain supplies out of regular channels. "Whenever I can purchase or borrow materials I do so," he wrote to Malloy.[8]

Even after the iron plate arrived, there were other problems to be overcome. The *Tennessee's* armor was to consist of two layers of two-inch plate and one layer of one-inch plate. Occasionally the bolt holes did not line up, and the plate had to be returned to Selma to be redrilled. Unwilling to accept such delays, Buchanan decided that it would be better to have the drilling and cutting done in Mobile to ensure accuracy. Another problem was that the civilian workmen at Mobile could not be bullied into working the long hours that Buchanan thought appropriate to the circumstances. He was disappointed that Joseph Pierce, the civilian contractor in charge, was too easy on the men. "Pearce [sic] is a good man," he wrote privately to a friend, "but too much of an old woman." On at least one occasion, Pierce actually had the workers bolt on "the *wrong* iron," which then had to be removed and replaced, causing more delay. Buchanan would have preferred to put an officer in charge with both the authority to oversee the operations and the willingness to punish workmen who failed to demonstrate proper energy. He could not exercise that kind of personal oversight himself, for he had no flag captain or flag lieutenant to take care of administrative details for him. The various duties of his administrative post generally kept him in his office until after three or so in the afternoon. Only then could he make rounds to the ships of his squadron or to the various work sites. When he did manage a visit, the best he could do was offer short speeches to encourage the men, but even so he had to report to Richmond in midsummer that the work progressed slowly.[9]

One group of workers decided that they worked altogether too hard for the compensation they received, and they called a strike. Here at last was a problem Buchanan knew how to handle. He immediately placed the men under arrest and sent for a conscript officer, who informed them that since they were no longer employed in doing essential work for the government, they would be taken into the army and sent to the front. "Since then," Buchanan reported to Richmond, "I have had no trouble."[10]

Other problems required more creative solutions. Unlike the *Virginia*, which had been converted in a dry dock that allowed the workers relatively easy access to its hull, the *Tennessee* was already afloat, and Mobile had no dry dock. The problem was how to armor the projecting sides of the casemate (known as sponsons), which extended three feet below the waterline. To accomplish this, the workmen ran long, heavy wooden beams from side to side through the vessel's gun ports, then loaded iron plate onto one end of the beams. Eventually the weight careened the hull over onto its side. The workers then clambered into waist-deep water to bolt the iron plate to the sponsons on the exposed side. When one side had been completed, the process was reversed.[11]

There were some problems for which Buchanan did not have answers. The *Tennessee*'s steering chains leading aft to the rudder did not run inside the armored hull, but instead lay in shallow grooves atop the afterdeck, which made them vulnerable to enemy fire. Eventually Buchanan ordered them to be covered over by one-inch iron plate, but that was not a fully satisfactory remedy because one-inch plate was unlikely to stand up to heavy shot at close range. The covers for the *Tennessee*'s ten gun ports presented another difficulty. They had been designed to pivot around a bolt above the gun port: they would be raised by pulleys so that the guns could be fired, then allowed to rotate back into position to cover the gun port while the crew reloaded. But once again, a direct hit on one of these covers was likely to bend it out of shape and make it immovable—and the gun behind it useless. There was no easy solution to either of these design weaknesses, and Buchanan simply had to make do.

Despite these problems, by the end of the summer Buchanan was generally pleased with the progress being made on the *Tennessee*. Pierce departed to supervise work elsewhere, and Buchanan put Commander Farrand in charge. He also ensured that there would be no more trouble with the workforce by having the workers conscripted and assigned to him under orders. After that, he was able to note that "the work has been carried on night and day when it could be done advantageously." With evident satisfaction, he reported to Mallory that while work languished on the *Nashville* for want of materials, work on the *Tennessee* was "progressing very fast."[12]

Buchanan was at least partly sustained in these efforts by the knowledge that his heroism at Hampton Roads had validated him as a southern hero and the Confederate navy's only admiral. Because of that, he no doubt eagerly perused the C.S. Navy's official *Register of Officers* when a copy arrived in Mobile early in 1863. Human nature being what it is, he would almost certainly have turned first to the page listing the admirals. By law, there could be only four admirals in the Confederate navy, and only one had so far been named. And sure enough, there was his name—Franklin Buchanan—listed under the heading of "Admirals." But *above* his name were four dotted lines as if the four admirals senior to him had simply not yet been identified. What could this mean? He wrote to Mallory to find out. "As I am not aware that there are four admirals above me in the Navy," he wrote, "I respectfully ask an explanation of the dotted lines."[13]

Mallory wrote back that the compilation of the register was the responsibility of the Office of Orders and Detail, which Buchanan himself had headed when he first offered his services to the Confederacy, but which was now headed by fellow Marylander French Forrest. It was Forrest, Mallory informed him, who had placed the dotted lines above Buchanan's name. In response to Buchanan's outrage, Secretary Mallory ordered that in each copy of the December 1862 Confederate Navy Register, a small paper patch be glued over the offending dotted lines. (Most extant copies of the Register still bear the patch.)

Buchanan was coldly furious and utterly scornful. Forrest, he decided, was simply jealous: jealous because Buchanan had gotten command of the *Virginia,* jealous because the *Virginia* had won a great victory, and jealous because Buchanan had received a promotion that Forrest had wanted for himself. In his own small (and, as Buchanan saw it, cowardly) fashion, Forrest was attempting to diminish a rival by implying that while Buchanan was indeed an admiral, he was the *least* of admirals, and sure to be surpassed in "conspicuous gallantry" by others.

In a letter to Forrest that was virtually an invitation to a challenge, Buchanan poured ridicule on the man for being so petty. He wrote that he was not surprised by Forrest's *"little act"* because he knew that Forrest had been disappointed not to be made an admiral. "But why you should have expected it, none of your brother officers can tell," he wrote, "for certainly you have never given any evidence, by applying for orders where there was a prospect of *danger,* that you wished to serve your country, or to display gallantry to secure your promotion." This was a stunning charge, for it was virtually an accusation of cowardice, a charge no southern officer could allow to pass unchallenged. Forrest, Buchanan asserted, sought safe jobs at a desk while he sent others into the heat of battle. "I am aware that you have permitted seven of your Juniors to command squadrons when there was a prospect of danger without any dissatisfaction on your part, or application from you for such service." He ended with a final, devastating, gibe: "Your *little act,* in the arrangement of the *dotted lines,* cannot injure me, or interfere with my position in the Navy, nor can they make you an admiral."[14]

Rather than challenge Buchanan to a duel, however, the chief of the Bureau of Orders and Detail tried to explain his way out of what he insisted was a misunderstanding. He claimed that he *had* asked for active service, but that it had been denied to him. Buchanan was unbending and unforgiving. "I am more satisfied than ever," he replied, "of your little act in reference to the dotted lines."[15]

A few weeks later, one of Buchanan's officers showed him a recent copy of the *Richmond Examiner*. A front-page article headed "A Strange Record" included a copy of the letter that Buchanan had written back in May 1861—two years ago—asking Secretary of the Navy Gideon Welles if he could withdraw his resignation from the U.S. Navy. Without saying so, the article managed to imply that Buchanan was less than fully committed to the Confederate cause. It was bad enough that Buchanan had tried to recall his resignation, but the real problem was the last line of his letter to Welles: "I am ready for service." Service against whom, a southern reader might have asked. Did this mean that Buchanan had been ready to accept orders to fight against the South? Buchanan might have been grateful that whoever released this letter to the *Examiner* did not also have access to the private letter he had written to his nephew that same week, in which he had written: "I am as strong a Union man as any in the country." He might also have been grateful that the timing of this exposé was such that it attracted little public attention, for it was printed on 5 May, two days after Lee's astonishing and improbable victory at Chancellorsville and five days before Stonewall Jackson's death, events that drove most other issues out of the public mind. Even so, Buchanan believed that he could not let the implied accusation rest without a response.[16]

In an open letter to the editor of the *Examiner* that was published two weeks later, Buchanan admitted writing the letter to Welles, but claimed that at the time he wrote it, he had reason to believe that "the troubles and difficulties in the country would certainly be arranged when Congress met." Based on that assumption, he had asked Welles to recall his resignation. "This I soon regretted," he wrote, "when it became apparent to all that there could be no reconciliation." His actions in the Confederacy since then, he claimed, "speak for themselves." Privately, he viewed the publication of the letter as a personal attack by his "enemies," and he was fairly sure who was behind it: French Forrest was trying to get even in his own craven and backstairs way for Buchanan's accusation of cowardice. To a friend in Richmond, Buchanan wrote that Forrest was "mean enough to do any thing."[17]

Only days later, Buchanan heard the satisfying news that Forrest was no longer the head of the Office of Orders and Detail. Provoked, perhaps, by Buchanan's gibes, he had requested an active command, and Mallory had made him commodore of the James River Squadron. Forrest's place as head of the bureau was filled by Buchanan's friend John K. Mitchell. "I am glad to see you at the head of the bureau," Buchanan wrote to Mitchell when he heard the news. "We have wanted for some time a man of method and system there. Old Forrest with his selfishness would have ruined the Navy had he been continued there much longer."[18]

As if to prove that every ray of sunlight also casts a shadow, only days later Buchanan received bad news from home. Correspondence with his friends and relatives in Maryland was difficult, but not impossible. He wrote regularly to Nannie and to other members of her family in Talbot County, and letters from home sometimes reached him as well. Some came though the lines—as this one did—but often they had to be mailed to Nassau or Bermuda, then smuggled in through the blockade. This particular letter arrived via a flag of truce, which might have suggested to Buchanan that it was not good news. Federal authorities would not likely have countenanced such intercourse except as a humanitarian gesture. The letter was brief and offered few details, but those were bad enough: the Rest had burned to the ground; little, if anything, had been saved. Indeed, his family had barely escaped with their lives and "the clothes they stood in." It was hard enough being away from his family, but harder still to be able to do nothing to aid them in this crisis. "My separation from all so dear to me is a hard trial," he wrote to Mitchell.[19]

There was bad news of another sort as well. A determined optimist, Buchanan invariably predicted Confederate triumphs in the field, and was often disappointed when news arrived that the South had suffered another reversal. In June and July, as Grant's army besieged Vicksburg, Buchanan was convinced that the rebel armies in Mississippi would crush the invader. On 5 July, ignorant of the fact that Vicksburg had capitulated the day before, surrendering its entire garrison of nearly thirty thousand men, Buchanan wrote to Mitchell that "Grant will be whipped as certain as you are born." A few days later, news arrived of Vicksburg's fall and of Lee's disaster in Pennsylvania. In September, Buchanan celebrated the Confederate victory at Chickamauga, but two months later the papers were filled with news of the ignominious defeat of Braxton Bragg's Army of Tennessee on Missionary Ridge. "We have had a sad reversal in Tennessee," Buchanan wrote. "Bragg is not the man for that army." In spite of all this, Buchanan's inextinguishable optimism was evident in his next sentence: "We are anxiously expecting to hear some good news from Lee."[20]

It was galling not to be able to strike a blow himself, especially because one of the ships parading back and forth on the southern horizon
was his old *Susquehanna.* "It would please me not a little to sink my old
ship," he confided to Lieutenant Jones. But he simply lacked the means
to make the attempt. It was therefore doubly frustrating when eager and
patriotic southerners came to him with what he believed were unrealistic schemes for attacking the enemy offshore. Some of these could be
easily dismissed; others required more tact. A few enterprising individuals came to him having already obtained the backing of political authority for one adventure or another, and expected him to supply them with
matériel. Most of the proposals involved a small body of picked men
stealing offshore in the dark of night to assail a Union warship.
Buchanan was as admiring as anyone of the courage and patriotism that
motivated such requests, and on at least one occasion he was instru-
mental in setting one afoot. But he objected to uncoordinated or unsu-
pervised expeditions by private citizens. "If these private expeditions are
fitted out without being controlled by me," he complained to Mallory,
"their authority will be abused, and those concerned, if captured, will be
treated as pirates."[21]

Other efforts to strike at the enemy warships on the horizon included
the use of underwater explosive devices. Buchanan was certainly an advocate of using torpedoes to block up the harbor channel. When in May
1863 Brig. Gen. Danville Leadbetter advocated a dramatic expansion of
the torpedo program, placing up to 150 torpedoes in the various entrances
to Mobile Bay, Buchanan offered his full support. But he was more skep-
tical of the notion that a small vessel with a spar torpedo extending from
its bow could be propelled out into the Gulf undetected to attack and
destroy an enemy warship. In short, he saw mines as valuable defensive
weapons, but he did not believe that they could be used offensively. For
that reason he declined to equip the *Tennessee* with a spar torpedo. Nevertheless, he was willing to let the experiment be tried. He allowed Midn.
Edward A. Swain to take the CSS *Gunnison,* which *was* armed with a spar
torpedo, into the lower bay to await an opportunity to attack the block-
aders. To Mitchell, he wrote: "I have sent a Torpedo boat down the bay to
operate against the enemy when the weather will permit." But he added:
"I have little faith in those things." In the event, the right conditions
never presented themselves, and the attack never took place.[22]

* * *

Buchanan pinned his hopes not on civilian expeditions or spar torpedoes, but on the successful completion of an iron ship with heavy guns. As summer turned to fall, the *Tennessee* was beginning at last to look like an ironclad warship. Most of its armor was in place, and the next step was to install the guns of the main battery. The ordnance revolution that had been ongoing since mid-century had produced weapons capable of both longer range and greater penetrating power. The old thirty-two-pound smoothbore guns that the *Vincennes* and the *Germantown* had carried would be virtually useless against ironclads. Buchanan knew that the Union monitors carried 11-inch, and even 15-inch, guns that used a sixty-pound charge of black powder to fire a projectile weighing more than four hundred pounds. The Confederacy simply did not have the capability to produce such guns. The best it could do was the Brooke rifle, a cast iron gun reinforced at the breach with wrought iron bands that were heat-shrunk around the gun barrel. Buchanan wanted 9-inch Brooke rifles for the *Tennessee,* but if he could not get them, then 7-inch rifles, or even the 6.4-inch caliber would have to do. To Catesby Jones, who now supervised the gun foundry at Selma, he wrote: "I will take any I can get."[23]

But when it came to industrial productivity, nothing came easy in the Confederacy. Jones worked his men night and day, encouraged, perhaps, by hints from Buchanan that Jones himself might get command of the *Tennessee* when it was ready. But in early December, while workmen were casting a barrel in the gun pit, molten metal escaped the mold and caused an explosion. The foundry building caught fire. The blaze was put out immediately, but it necessarily led to more delay. Not until the day before Christmas 1863 was Jones able to write Buchanan to tell him that he had two 7-inch Brooke rifles ready for the *Tennessee,* and that he hoped to be able to produce some 6.4-inch guns at the rate of one a week.[24]

Buchanan also had to think about how he would man the *Tennessee.* He had every intention of serving onboard himself as the fleet admiral, but he wanted a commanding officer to serve under him, and getting the right man was, in his view, crucial. As always, Buchanan was very judg-mental about the human raw material he had to work with, and on the whole he did not think the officers in the Mobile squadron a particularly impressive lot. He wrote regularly to Mallory or Mitchell to complain about them. One officer was "disposed to be insubordinate"; another was "a disagreeable, quarrelsome person"; another was "unworthy of the position he holds"; and others—many others—were, in his opinion, simply "good for nothing." He urged Mitchell to send him "a clever good officer for the command" of the *Tennessee*.[25]

He had several men in mind for the job. Perhaps just to be politic, he urged Mitchell to give up his job in Richmond and come and take command himself, and he said much the same thing to Jones at Selma. But the most logical candidate for the job was already on the scene. James D. Johnston was a career naval officer who had been serving on the Mobile station since Buchanan had arrived in the fall of 1862. Indeed, Johnston was one of the few officers about whom Buchanan had anything good to say. "He is never idle," Buchanan wrote to Mitchell, "employed with matters connected with the vessels of the Squadron, purchases of all kinds, building the Floating Batteries, procuring the timber, men, and a thousand things which I cannot enumerate." Buchanan was therefore satisfied when Johnston was confirmed as commanding officer of the *Tennessee*.[26]

Obtaining a crew was more difficult. The same manpower problems evident everywhere in the Confederacy were present in Mobile as well. All of Buchanan's ships were short-handed; most had less than half their full complement, though Buchanan asserted melodramatically that this would not prevent them from being fought to the last man. When the *Tennessee* was finally complete, it would need a crew, and the only way Buchanan was likely to get one was to raid the ranks of the Confederate army. As it became increasingly evident that the army was not going to release any of its men, Buchanan pressed harder for Mallory to intercede with Seddon. Finally, in February 1864, the war secretary ordered the local army commander, Dabney Maury, to "detail at once from your command the number of men required by Admiral Buchanan to man his vessel."[27]

Even then, the *Tennessee*'s crew was very much a mixed bag. An undated crew list shows that at one point, at least, only 6 of the 143 crewmen on the *Tennessee* were rated as "seaman," and only 3 as "ordinary seaman." The rest were landsmen, firemen (mostly coal heavers), and boys. Moreover, more than 60 percent (88 of 143) were foreign born, with Irishmen (49) making up more than a third. Perhaps because of that, Buchanan was more than ever resolved to impose his own particular brand of discipline on this ragtag bunch. "I have some hard characters to deal with," he wrote to Mitchell, "and I am determined that they shall not violate orders as they please."[28]

. . .

Even as Buchanan struggled to find a crew for his vessel, he faced a problem even more daunting. By New Year's Day 1864, a virtually completed *Tennessee* floated alongside the dock at Mobile with its iron armor in place and its guns peering from the gun ports. The problem was getting the ship from the Mobile docks into the lower bay, and that was a more significant obstacle than it might seem. For a thousand years and more, the network of rivers that flowed into the upper end of Mobile Bay had deposited silt in a broad fan that extended a dozen miles or more down the bay. Opposite the mouth of the Dog River on the western shore, some six miles below the city, the water shoaled to a depth of only eight feet at high tide. The *Tennessee* drew thirteen feet, and Buchanan estimated that it would have to go nearly twenty miles down the bay before reaching water sufficiently deep to float it. To reach that water, he had to find some way to reduce the ship's draft by at least five feet.[29]

The traditional method for reducing a ship's draft, other than throwing its guns overboard or removing the iron armor—neither of which was acceptable—was to use "camels." This involved lashing heavily laden lighters, or barges, alongside the vessel, then removing the ballast—sand, iron, or even water—from the lighters so that as they rose, they virtually lifted the ship out of the water. Much of the South's resources, both material and psychological, had been invested in this one ship, and it would be a devastating blow to all concerned if the *Tennessee* could not be raised sufficiently to get it over the Dog River Bar and into the lower bay where it could prove its worth as a warship. If the camels proved unsuccessful, all Buchanan's work would have been in vain.

The first effort failed. Long poles run through the *Tennessee*'s gun ports were set atop twin lighters filled nearly to the thwarts with ballast. When the ballast was removed, the ironclad rose a mere twenty-two inches, a good three feet short of what would be necessary. At least one officer in the squadron thought "it was a matter of impossibility to get her over Dog River Bar with any appliances we can command here at present." Buchanan had to rethink his strategy. He considered removing the guns and then replacing them after the *Tennessee* was safely across the bar. But adding the guns had increased the *Tennessee*'s draft by only four inches, and the difficulty of replacing the guns on an ironclad without benefit of dock equipment would be enormous.[30]

Buchanan was not easily discouraged, however. This, perhaps, was his greatest asset as a commanding officer. If conventional camels did not suit, he would contrive new and better ones. He ordered the construction of six specially designed watertight tanks, or what Jones called "sectional docks," which would fit precisely under the hull of the *Tennessee*. These camels would be put in place full of water, then pumped dry. Buchanan's determination and impatience were the driving force of an effort in which few others had much confidence. "I am driving on with the new plan to get the 'Tennessee' over the bar," he wrote to Mitchell. Throughout March and into April, the work crews on shore dedicated themselves to the construction of the new camels. His greatest worry was not that the new camels would fail, but that Farragut might attempt to come into the bay before the *Tennessee* could get over the bar.[31]

As if to test the depth of Buchanan's inner strength and determination, the sectional docks were nearly complete when a fire broke out onshore and two of the six—the two largest—were destroyed. The work had to begin all over again. Undeterred, Buchanan kept up the pace. "I am driving ahead with the camels for the *Tennessee*," he reported to Jones in mid-April. "Four are finished, and the two new ones advancing rapidly." By the first week of May, all six had been safely launched. Once they were filled with water, the workmen began maneuvering them under the hull of the *Tennessee*. It was a slow, painstaking job, but Buchanan was filled with confidence that the new camels would do the trick. "I see no reason why we will not succeed."[32]

And he was right. When pumped dry, the camels lifted the *Tennessee* up to a draft of barely seven feet. Slowly and carefully—"like a giant on stilts," in Johnston's words—the mighty ironclad made its cautious way over the bar, assisted by tugs, on 18 May. Then the camels were flooded again, and the *Tennessee* settled back to its thirteen-foot draft, swimming at last in deep water. Buchanan fairly burst with pride. "I wish you could see the *Tennessee*," he wrote to Jones; "she is a man-of-war."[33]

He had done it. The *Tennessee* was afloat, armed, and manned, and ready to receive the invader. But it was, after all, only one ship. The other vessels in Buchanan's small squadron would count for little in a fight with Union ironclads. Would the *Tennessee* alone be enough to fend off the entire federal fleet? However that question might be answered, Buchanan was ready and willing to put it to the test. He had little choice. "Everybody has taken it into their heads that one ship can whip a dozen," Buchanan wrote privately to Mitchell. "And if the trial is not made, we who are in her, are d——d for life. Consequently the trial must be made."[34]

~14~

THE BATTLE OF
MOBILE BAY

Whip and sink the Yankees, or fight until you sink yourselves,
but do not surrender.

T he *Tennessee* crossed the Dog River Bar on 18 May. Exactly
two weeks earlier, the final and decisive phase of the American Civil War had begun when the Army of the Potomac
crossed the Rapidan River eight hundred miles away in Virginia to begin
a grinding three-month campaign against Robert E. Lee's Army of
Northern Virginia, a campaign that would compel Lee and his outnumbered and undersupplied veterans to fall back to the outskirts of Richmond and Petersburg. On that same day, somewhat closer to home,
Union armies in the West under William Tecumseh Sherman began an
advance in north Georgia that would take them to the outskirts of
Atlanta by the end of the summer. This simultaneous assault was no
coincidence. It was part of a coordinated offensive directed by Ulysses
S. Grant that was designed to pressure the Confederacy from several
points at once. Indeed, in addition to these two major campaigns, other
federal forces were also on the move: the German-born Maj. Gen. Franz
Sigel was advancing up the Shenandoah Valley, Maj. Gen. Benjamin
Butler was moving up the Virginia peninsula, and Nathaniel Banks in
the Mississippi Valley was under orders to coordinate with Rear Adm.
David Farragut in a combined assault on Mobile Bay. After long anticipation, the enemy was finally coming. Or so it seemed.

Grant's commonsense plan to attack the Confederacy simultaneously

from several directions at once was partially undone by the delinquency
of several of his subordinate commanders. Although Sherman in Georgia and Meade in Virginia each advanced as ordered, the other federal
commanders all proved disappointing. Sigel's army met a humiliating
reverse at the Battle of New Market, Butler's Army of the James was
pinned up in the Bermuda Hundred north of Petersburg, and Banks got
sidetracked in a poorly managed cotton-hunting expedition up the Red
River into Texas. As a result of this last misadventure, the federal
assault on Mobile was delayed until late summer. The always impatient
Buchanan was loath to wait for it. He hardly needed the prodding of Jefferson Davis, who wired him the day after the *Tennessee* crossed the bar
"to strike the enemy before he establishes himself on the Bay." With his
ironclad flagship at last under its own power, Buchanan planned to
charge from the bay into the Gulf to attack and destroy the Union
blockading squadron off Mobile.[1]

Back in the spring of 1862, when Buchanan had first assumed command
of the *Virginia,* his initial thought had been to steal out of Gosport Navy
Yard in the dark of night in order to attack an unsuspecting enemy at
first light. He had been foiled on that occasion by the refusal of the
pilots to maneuver his huge ironclad down the Elizabeth River. Now he
hoped that the *Tennessee* could succeed where the *Virginia* had failed.
He would take his new command down the bay in the midnight darkness, then conn his iron monster out into the Gulf to attack the enemy
ships at anchor before they were aware of their peril. The odds would be
against him, but the Confederacy faced long odds everywhere, and
Buchanan hoped to compensate for the odds by stealth, surprise, and
the stout walls of his ironclad casemate.

It took three days after crossing the Dog River Bar for the *Tennessee*'s
crew to clear away the camels, fill the coal bunkers, and stow the ammunition. On 21 May the ironclad was fully stocked and ready for action.
Buchanan came onboard that night, and in a short ceremony the next
morning he raised his blue admiral's pennant and took command.

Characteristically, he delivered a stirring call to battle, and then
announced to the assembled crew that the *Tennessee* would attack the
enemy blockading fleet that very night. He declared dramatically that he
"expected every man to do his duty and stand by his guns until death,
and not Surrender the ship." In words strikingly similar to those he had

uttered on the deck of the *Virginia* two and a half years earlier, he reminded his crew that "the eyes of the people of the Confederacy [are] turned upon us."[2]

He sent the crew to dinner, and afterward put men to work greasing the armor shield. At dusk, he sent all but two of the ship's boats ashore, and the *Tennessee* cleared for action. Similar activity was taking place onboard the other vessels of the squadron: the awkward ironclad *Baltic* and the three wooden steamers—the *Gaines,* the *Morgan,* and the *Selma*. Shortly after dark, with all the preparations complete, Johnston again called the hands to muster and read to them Buchanan's fighting instructions, which were received with three cheers. But as dusk turned to full dark, the wind freshened, and the pilots reported that the seas were now too rough for the *Tennessee* to pass through the channel and into the Gulf. Reluctantly, Buchanan accepted their verdict and ordered Johnston to have the crew stand down.[3]

The next morning was "clear and pleasant," and Buchanan determined to try again. By now, word of the *Tennessee*'s possible sortie had got about, and shortly after breakfast a steamer filled with eager spectators (mostly ladies) from Mobile arrived at the Fort Morgan anchorage to observe the anticipated triumph of this newest Confederate ironclad. From the ramparts of Fort Morgan, Buchanan could see for himself that the federal ships were still in position offshore. Opportunity still beckoned. Lacking another shift in the weather or some other unforeseen disaster, the *Tennessee* and its consorts would sortie that night. After supper the crew topped off the *Tennessee*'s bunkers with coal and Johnston again ordered the ship cleared for action. The hours dragged until finally, at eleven o'clock, the boilers were lit and steam began to build. Just over an hour later, a few minutes past midnight, Buchanan gave Johnston the order to go ahead. The *Tennessee*'s captain passed the order to the engine room, and the reverberation of the engines rose an octave in response, but the ship did not move. Johnston then ordered the engines to reverse. Nothing. The realization soon dawned on all that the great ironclad was fast aground. For the second night in a row, dry-mouthed anticipation turned to instant anticlimax as Buchanan again ordered the crew to stand down.[4]

Buchanan was not willing to wait another day. Just past 4:00 A.M. the rising tide lifted the *Tennessee* off the bottom and Buchanan ordered his little fleet to get under way. As dawn began to color the eastern sky, the

Tennessee, with its small consorts trailing in its wake, eased slowly past the headland crowned by Fort Morgan. By the time the *Tennessee* reached the ship channel, however, it was eight o'clock and full light. As described by an artillery officer in the fort: "The little squadron then steamed slowly down the bay, disdaining longer concealment and heading for the channel as if going out. The Yanks were in line of battle outside the bar and a mile nearer the fort than their usual anchorage and not seeming at all intimidated."[5]

At this critical moment, Buchanan reassessed his position. The element of surprise had been lost and the obvious disparity in numbers was daunting, and that, combined with the uncertainty of the *Tennessee*'s stability in the relatively open waters of the Gulf of Mexico, made a successful sortie in broad daylight little more than a forlorn hope. Buchanan concluded that despite the high expectations in Richmond, as well as those of his immediate audience both afloat and ashore, and despite his own eagerness to engage the enemy, discretion was in this case by far the better part of valor. It may have been the most uncharacteristic decision of his professional career. With feelings that can only be imagined, he ordered Johnston to anchor. The watching artilleryman in the fort recorded that "our fleet getting almost opposite the fort, [it] came to anchor in the most harmless and pacific way."[6]

Embarrassed, no doubt, by his inability to fulfill the high expectations of the observers in the fort (and the ladies who had come down the bay to watch), Buchanan sought to explain himself to the only judges that mattered, his superiors in Richmond. He telegraphed Mallory to explain that he had been unable to surprise the enemy, that the odds against him were overwhelming, and that the pilots were concerned about the stability of the *Tennessee* in the Gulf of Mexico. Despite all that, he avowed that he was prepared to disregard all these risks if Mallory thought he should do so. Of course, Mallory had little choice but to wire back telling Buchanan to use his best judgment. Thus released from any immediate obligation to risk everything on a single throw of the dice, Buchanan resolved to keep the *Tennessee* in the relatively calm waters of Mobile Bay and await Farragut's attack. Very likely, he anticipated that he would not have long to wait. In fact, he waited nine weeks.[7]

Not everyone was as understanding of Buchanan's dilemma as Mallory, or as forgiving. The civilian population of Mobile, which had waited two years for the completion of the much-vaunted *Tennessee,* was eager for the wonderful ship to drive off their Yankee tormentors. Catesby Jones's uncle, Robert Page, a former navy captain who was serving as a brigadier general in the Provisional Army of the Confederacy and commanding the garrison of Fort Morgan, attributed Buchanan's decision to a failure of nerve. Page asserted that Buchanan should have taken the *Tennessee* out into the Gulf the moment it was launched. He believed that Buchanan had surrendered both surprise and the initiative by failing to act at once. Timorousness was a fault that few had ever ascribed to Old Buck. Nevertheless, Buchanan sensed that despite Mallory's official support for his decision, public opinion had turned against him. "Buchanan looks humbled and thoughtful," Page wrote to his nephew at Selma, "the Secretary has let B. off easier than I expected."[8]

Despite the widespread disappointment ashore, Buchanan's decision to call off the daylight sortie into the Gulf was unquestionably a wise one. Indeed, that he would even consider such a high-risk mission was a measure of his impetuosity. Such a scheme might have been successful on a dark night in calm waters; under such circumstances, Buchanan might have found one or more of the blockading vessels at anchor, a motionless and unsuspecting target. But with the enemy alerted and under way, the *Tennessee* had little chance of achieving success, and every chance of foundering in the Gulf chop. Too much of the South's precious resources had been invested in the *Tennessee* to risk losing everything in a desperate sortie. Buchanan knew that. But it did not keep him from chaffing at his awkward situation. At last he had a warship worthy of the name, and he still could not come to grips with the enemy.

The rest of the summer passed quietly. While Lee in Virginia and Johnston in Georgia commanded the headlines as they attempted to parry the nearly continuous assaults of Grant and Sherman, the federal fleet offshore continued to grow. Indeed, the number of ships in the blockading squadron increased almost weekly: from eleven to thirteen to seventeen. To Buchanan it was evident that Farragut was building up his forces for an assault. Meanwhile, Buchanan's own force grew not at all. In fact, he had to send the cranky *Baltic* back to Mobile as "unseaworthy." That left him with only the three wooden gunboats to accompany the *Tennessee*: the *Morgan* (six guns), the *Gaines* (six guns), and the *Selma* (four guns). It was a far cry from the fleet of half a dozen ironclads he had envisioned when he first accepted command in the fall of 1862.[9]

In late July an ironclad monitor joined the blockading fleet for the first time, and a week later two more arrived. Buchanan studied them from the ramparts of Fort Morgan. From that vantage point they were barely perceptible on the southern horizon. Only "the continuous volume of thick smoke issuing from their low smokestacks" betrayed their presence. So low was their profile that one Confederate officer wrote that the smoke seemed to be issuing from "the ocean itself."[10]

For much of the summer, Buchanan did not sleep onboard the *Tennessee*. The interior of the ironclad during the Gulf coast summer was excruciatingly uncomfortable; the surgeon on the *Tennessee*, Dr. Daniel Conrad, later wrote that it was "impossible" to sleep onboard. Most nights the crew slept topside under the stars, but frequent heavy rain often drove them belowdecks, where Conrad compared the environment to "the terrible moist, hot atmosphere simulating the oppressiveness which precedes a tornado." Although back in January Buchanan had declared to Mitchell that he wanted only those officers who "prefer the *discomfort* of an *iron clad* to the comforts *on shore*," the sixty-three-year-old admiral spent most of his evenings ashore. Page gossiped to his nephew that Buchanan not only slept ashore, he also spent much of his time in Mobile rather than with the squadron. Disapprovingly, Page suggested that it was because "he has some taste of the discomforts of an ironclad."[11]

Others criticized Buchanan publicly. The Mobile newspapers continued to express confidence that the Confederate squadron would surely triumph if and when the Union fleet finally attacked, but underneath their boastful assertions was a hint of reproach that more was not being done to raise the blockade. Was there nothing the Confederate navy could do but await the inevitable enemy attack? In all likelihood, there was not. By late July, observers in Fort Morgan counted no fewer than twenty-three vessels waiting outside the bay, including three monitors and several mortar boats. On 1 August those enemy ships began to send down their upper yards, stripping away nonessential impedimenta for imminent action. It was clear to all that an attack was only hours away, and Buchanan moved back aboard the *Tennessee* determined to be at hand when the storm broke.[12]

At a few minutes past 6:00 A.M. on 5 August, Buchanan was awakened by the ship's quartermaster, who presented him with the compliments of the officer of the deck and informed him that the enemy fleet was getting under way. Instantly awake, Buchanan made his way as quickly as he could to the deck atop the ironclad's casemate. From there he could see for himself that the enemy's ships were on the move, black smoke pouring from their stacks as they steamed purposefully toward the ship channel off Fort Morgan. "Get under way, Captain Johnston," he ordered. Johnston ordered the deck crew to buoy the anchor chain and slip the cable, then he allowed the hands a quick cup of ersatz coffee before they assumed their action stations. At seven o'clock Buchanan signaled the gunboats of his squadron to conform to the movements of the flagship, and his little fleet got under way, moving slowly in a rough line abreast toward the narrow ship channel. Already the guns of Fort Morgan were trying the range against the approaching enemy fleet.[13]

As was his custom when action was imminent, Buchanan formally addressed the crew. "Now men," he said, "the enemy is coming, and I want you to do your duty; and you shall not have it to say when you leave this vessel that you were not near enough to the enemy, for I will meet them, and then you can fight them alongside side of their own ships; and if I fall, lay me on one side and go on with the fight, and never mind me—but whip and sink the Yankees, or fight until you sink yourselves, but do not surrender."[14]

Buchanan's plan was to position the *Tennessee* across the northern exit from the ship channel, "capping the T" of the advancing federal squadron and putting his ships in position to fire their broadside guns down the length of the enemy column. Then, when the range closed sufficiently, he would ram the lead ship, sinking it in the ship channel, and attack the rest of the federal fleet with his guns. The *Tennessee*'s great strength, he knew, was its ram. It was the *Virginia*'s ram that had doomed the *Cumberland*; now he would use a similar device to sink Farragut's flagship—or whatever federal vessel was first through the channel.

As the *Tennessee* rounded the headland and took position at the northern end of the ship channel, Buchanan got a better look at the approaching enemy. The morning was bright and clear with a gentle haze that turned the sky a milky white, and the sea was as smooth as glass. The light breeze from the west would work to the federals' advantage once the firing started, for it would blow the smoke of the broadsides into the faces of the gunners at Fort Morgan. As Buchanan peered from the slit in the *Tennessee*'s armored pilothouse, he could see the federal ships advancing not in a single column, but in two. The column to his left—the one nearest the fort—was led by a monitor, with other monitors in line behind it. Although Buchanan could not have known it, the lead monitor was the USS *Tecumseh,* which Farragut had placed at the head of the column because he believed it to be his most powerful ship. It carried two gigantic fifteen-inch guns in its armored turret, each capable of firing a 440-pound bolt, and its specific mission was to engage and sink the *Tennessee.* Beyond and slightly behind the line of monitors was a second column of federal warships composed of wooden-hulled steam frigates, including, presumably, Farragut's flagship, the *Hartford.* Each of the frigates had a smaller gunboat lashed alongside its port side.[15]

The gunners in Fort Morgan were firing slowly and deliberately at the approaching enemy. Shell splashes erupted around the federal ships, which were returning fire, the white smoke from their broadsides beginning to obscure their formation. For his part, Buchanan was determined to hold his fire until the last possible minute to ensure maximum impact. As he watched the steady approach of the enemy fleet, the bow of the lead monitor turned slightly to port, aiming its prow directly at the *Tennessee* with the evident intention of ramming it. The gunners on the *Tennessee* adjusted their sights as the monitor approached. "Do not fire," Johnston cautioned the gunners, "until the vessels are in actual contact." The range slowly closed as those few on the *Tennessee* who had a vantage point watched. Then, suddenly and unexpectedly, the bow of the *Tecumseh* heaved up out of the water. The thump of an underwater explosion reached the watchers on the *Tennessee* a moment later. The Union monitor turned onto its port side; its bow plunged downward and its stern rose from the sea, exposing its brass propeller, which was still turning. Then it shot downward like an arrow and vanished. The whole incident lasted barely twenty-five seconds, and only a handful of survivors flailed in the roiling water where the *Tecumseh* had been. At least one torpedo had proved its value.[16]

Viewers of this spectacle were temporarily stunned. Dr. Conrad, the ship's surgeon, recalled that "there was a dead silence on board the *Tennessee*; the men peered through the port holes at the awful catastrophe, and spoke to each other only in low whispers." Ironically, there was cheering from some of the federal ships, where it was believed that the *Tennessee* had exploded. Even as the federals belatedly appreciated what had happened to the *Tecumseh,* they faced another crisis that threatened their entire operation. In its eagerness to close the *Tennessee,* the *Tecum-*

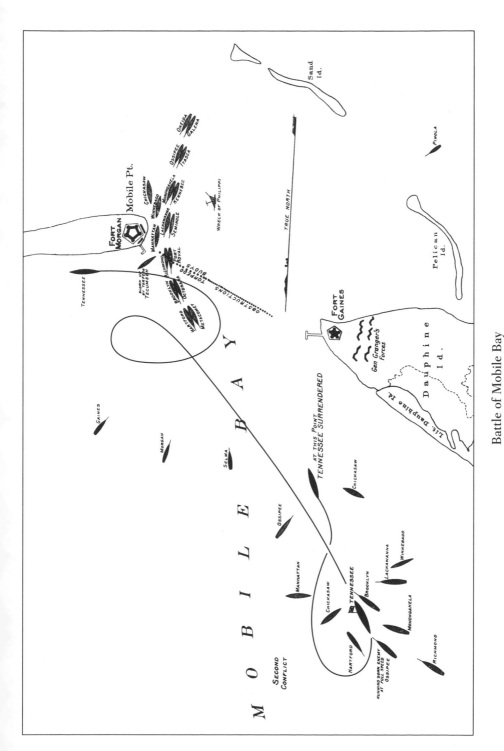

Battle of Mobile Bay

From Official Records of the Union and Confederate Navies in the War of the Rebellion, *series 1.*

seh had veered to port, and in so doing had forced the lead ship of the second column, the USS *Brooklyn,* to give way to port also. The *Brooklyn*'s commanding officer, Capt. James Alden, was alarmed to discover that he was being pinched in toward the deadly minefield. Then the *Tecumseh* blew up, proving that the mine threat was very real. At about the same moment, Alden spotted "a row of suspicious-looking buoys" directly under his bow. He ordered all stop, then half astern. The *Brooklyn* began backing down on the *Hartford,* which was second in line. As the ships of the federal column bunched together, the guns from Fort Morgan redoubled their fire. The federal attack stalled.[17]

Although Buchanan, whose vision was obscured by the smoke of the gunfire, could not have known it, this was when Farragut took matters in hand. He ordered the *Hartford* to steam past the *Brooklyn* to port, through the minefield, in order to avoid having his entire column of ships collide into one another like a collapsing accordion. The rest of his ships followed him. In part because some of the torpedoes had faulty primers, and in part due to luck, Farragut's wooden fleet made it through the minefield without suffering further damage.[18]

Now it was Buchanan's turn. He ordered Johnston to get up a full head of steam and aim the *Tennessee* directly for the *Hartford,* which was now leading the federal squadron out of the minefield. Alas, the *Tennessee*'s plodding speed made such an attack an exercise in frustration. Two and a half years earlier, when Buchanan had commanded the *Virginia,* he had rammed and sunk the *Cumberland* with relative ease largely because his target had waited passively at anchor to receive the *Virginia*'s charge. The circumstances in Mobile Bay were quite different. A ship under way had little to fear from a ram whose top speed was only six knots. As the *Tennessee* closed the range to the *Hartford,* Farragut's vessel shot ahead— Johnston later wrote that it "seemed to fly up the bay." As the *Hartford* passed well in front of the *Tennessee,* gunners on both ships fired at one another. A shell from the *Tennessee*'s bow gun smashed into the *Hartford* and inflicted a number of casualties, but it could not do the kind of fatal damage below the waterline that a ram might. Meanwhile, the *Hartford*'s nine-inch shells glanced harmlessly off the *Tennessee*'s armored casemate. However gratifying it was that the enemy's shells did no damage, the inability of the *Tennessee* to ram the federal flagship must have alarmed Buchanan. He saw now that his lumbering ironclad was unlikely to inflict a decisive blow unless somehow he could catch the enemy at anchor.[19]

Nevertheless, he had little option at the moment but to try again. Having missed his chance at the *Hartford,* he ordered the *Tennessee* to execute a turn to starboard to try again. The wide turning radius of the *Tennessee* made such a maneuver awkward and time-consuming. The big ironclad had to swing out in a wide circle before steadying back on a collision course with the next ship in line, Alden's *Brooklyn.* Having learned from his inability to catch up to the *Hartford,* Buchanan recalculated his angle of approach. Once again, however, although the *Tennessee's* engines strained at full throttle, the *Brooklyn* easily eluded his charge, passing a good twenty feet ahead of him. Again the federals fired, and again the shot bounced off the *Tennessee's* armored casemate, a sailor on the *Brooklyn* noting that they "didn't seem to have any more effect on her than a bullet on the hide of an Alligator."[20]

One by one, the federal frigates passed the lumbering *Tennessee* and headed north into the bay. Buchanan made a run at two more of them, the *Richmond* and the *Lackawanna,* but failed each time to make contact, though he did punish them with his 6.4- and 7-inch guns. The *Oneida* got the worst of the *Tennessee's* attack, suffering thirty-eight casualties, including its captain, J. R. Madison Mullany, whose arm had to be amputated. But despite inflicting significant damage, none of the *Tennessee's* shots came close to sinking any of the enemy ships. The federal fleet—all save the ill-fated *Tecumseh* and the side-wheel steamer *Phillipi,* which ran aground—had managed to get safely into the bay. Buchanan broke off the action and ordered Johnston to take the *Tennessee* back to its anchorage off Fort Morgan.[21]

While Buchanan and the *Tennessee* battled the enemy's main battle line, the other ships of his squadron attempted to do their part as well. They had begun by concentrating fire on the *Hartford,* and Farragut later reported that their fire was more damaging than that of the *Tennessee.* But soon they had their hands full fighting off an assault by the Union gunboats. The six-gun *Gaines* and the four-gun *Selma* acquitted themselves well. Indeed, the *Gaines* was hit seventeen times and was literally sinking before its commander beached it near the fort. The *Selma,* too, carried on an unequal battle with three federal warships until forced to strike its flag. Only the *Morgan* proved a disappointment. Its captain, Lt. Comdr. George W. Harrison, broke off the fight and retreated to the relative safety of the shoal waters near Fort Morgan.[22]

Although he would later criticize Harrison in his report, Buchanan had no time for recriminations now. As the *Tennessee* steamed slowly back to Fort Morgan, Buchanan ordered a damage inspection. The news was gratifying. Although the exterior accouterments such as the smokestack, boat davits, and handrails had all been blasted away by the fire from the enemy fleet, the armored casemate was undamaged, the engines were sound, and there had been no serious casualties.[23]

Because the *Tennessee* had gone into battle before the hands could be fed, Johnston ordered the crew to go to breakfast. While they ate, Buchanan assessed his circumstances, "stumping up and down the deck" deep in thought. A number of factors assailed his mind. He could see the enemy fleet, consisting of three ironclad monitors and fourteen armed steamers, dropping anchor four miles away, well beyond the range of the guns of Fort Morgan. Clearly, the Confederate wooden gunboats were used up: captured, sunk, or too damaged to return to the fight. Only Buchanan's *Tennessee* was still in a position to renew the contest. Should it? He had failed to prevent the enemy's entry into Mobile Bay. What was his responsibility now? Much later, he would tell a fellow officer that during those critical moments he was recalling the fate of the *Virginia*. After its fight with the *Monitor*, the *Virginia* had remained inactively in port until it had to be destroyed by its own crew—an event that had led to a court martial. Unwilling for the *Tennessee* to suffer the same fate—to be trapped "like a rat in a hole"—he decided to renew the action. In his subsequent report he wrote that he "renewed the attack with the hope of sinking some of them [the enemy vessels] with our prow"—that is, by ramming. If so, he might have been better advised to wait until nightfall in order to attack an anchored enemy in the dark. That, after all, had been his original concept back in May. But another factor at work here was his recollection of the long and frustrating summer when the local papers had been filled with questions about why Buchanan's mighty ironclad remained inactive day after day. What would the public say now if he remained anchored under the guns of Fort Morgan with the enemy squadron in plain sight on a clear day? Very likely, in his mind, there was no excuse that an honorable gentleman would accept for not renewing the action at once.[24]

He turned to Johnston and ordered him to get the *Tennessee* under way again. "Follow them up, Johnston," one officer recalled him saying, "we can't let them off that way." As the *Tennessee* moved up the bay, his intentions became obvious to every man onboard, and a murmur ran along the deck. One crewman muttered: "The old admiral has not had his fight out yet; he is heading for that big fleet; he will get his fill of it up there." Another wrote later: "It looked to me that we were going into the jaws of death." Dr. Conrad could hardly believe it. "Are you going into that fleet, Admiral?" he asked. "I am, sir," was Buchanan's terse reply. Turning away, Conrad incautiously ventured the opinion that "we'll never come out of there whole." Overhearing the remark, Buchanan instantly rounded on him: "That's my lookout, sir!"[25]

Out in the federal anchorage, lookouts reported that the *Tennessee* was moving in their direction. Farragut was surprised that Buchanan would renew the fight so soon, but he did not hesitate to order his own vessels to clear for action. He directed them to concentrate on trying to ram the ironclad since their guns seemed to have little effect. He ordered his own flag captain to aim the *Hartford* directly at the approaching vessel. Buchanan, too, sought out the opposing flagship. Like two jousters in a medieval tournament, the *Hartford* (at ten knots) and the *Tennessee* (at four knots) steamed directly at one another. At their combined speed of fourteen knots, it took fifteen minutes for the two ships to cover the four miles that separated them. Meanwhile other federal ships were also racing to get in on the fight.

The Union monitor *Monongahela* was the first to close the *Tennessee*. Johnston saw it coming and passed the word along the deck: "Steady yourselves. . . . Stand by." At the last moment, he put the helm over so that the monitor would strike them at an angle. The prow of the 1,378-ton monitor smashed into the side of the *Tennessee*. Most of the men onboard were sent sprawling by the impact, and the *Tennessee* was thrown off course, spinning around, one officer recalled, "as upon a pivot." But it sustained no serious damage, the armored sponsons taking the blow without yielding. Johnston was jubilant. "We are all right!" he cried out, as if surprised that it should be so. "They can never run us under now."[26]

If so, it was not for lack of trying. The ships of the federal squadron circled the *Tennessee* like a pack of dogs that had cornered a fox, and took turns trying to run it down. Farragut's orders to his captains were to try to drive their ships up and over the *Tennessee*'s flat decks, literally mounting the ship and forcing it underwater. As they did so, they also fired their guns at near point-blank range into the *Tennessee*'s casemate.

The range was so close that several men on the *Tennessee* were burned by bits of wadding and chunks of black powder that blasted through the open gun ports. Others were wounded by small arms fire as men on the federal ships aimed their rifles and pistols at those narrow openings. Meanwhile, the *Tennessee's* guns were firing as well. Buchanan left the maneuvering to Johnston while he exercised personal supervision over the guns. The sound of the guns resonating inside the small casemate, the sulfuric smell of the white smoke, and the heat of the engines on an August morning, which raised the temperature in the *Tennessee* to over 140 degrees, combined to produce a nautical version of hell itself.[27]

The *Lackawanna* was the next to strike the *Tennessee*. The wooden steam frigate hit the *Tennessee* squarely on its port side just abaft the beam, and the blow heeled the ram over heavily to starboard, driving the stern temporarily below the waterline. But the impact did more damage to the assailant than to the victim. The *Lackawanna's* stem was crushed, broken by the heavily armored knuckle of the *Tennessee's* protruding sponsons. After the initial collision, the *Lackawanna's* bow scraped along the side of the ram to a point opposite its stern. The force of the blow had turned the *Tennessee's* head to port, so the two ships lay parallel to one another. The gunners on both ships fired as fast as they could load from a range of only about twelve feet. Men on both ships screamed insults at one another as they worked. Swept up in the fight, they used any weapon at hand: sailors on the *Lackawanna* threw a spittoon and a holystone at the *Tennessee*; a sailor on the *Tennessee* leaned out a gun port and stabbed a federal sailor with his bayonet. Much more seriously, one of the nine-inch shells from the *Lackawanna* hit squarely on one of the *Tennessee's* gun port covers and jammed it half open so that it would neither open nor close. The *Tennessee* was down from six guns to five. The two vessels gradually slipped apart, but that merely created the opportunity for yet another federal ship to attack.[28]

All this time, Johnston had been attempting to conn his ship toward Farragut's *Hartford*. Twice thrown off his course by the attacks of other federal ships, he returned each time to steady on the *Hartford*, which was now within close range. The two ships closed on one another bow to bow, but once again Johnston put the helm over at the last moment to avoid a head-on collision, and the two ships struck obliquely. They scraped past one another, the muzzles of their guns almost touching. The *Hartford* carried twelve guns in each broadside, and at this range they could hardly miss. All twelve shells, however, glanced off the armored casemate. For its part, the *Tennessee* had only five operational guns—and only three that would fire to port. The primers failed on two of the three, so the Confederate gunners got off only a single shot against the *Hartford*, though that one shell exploded on the *Hartford*'s berth deck, killing five men and wounding eight. Farragut's flag captain, Percival Drayton, later claimed that as the two ships slid past one another, he spotted Buchanan through an open gun port and, overcome by fury, threw his binoculars at him, screaming: "You infernal traitor."[29]

Once the *Hartford* slipped past, one of the federal monitors crept up the port side of the *Tennessee*. Very likely it was the *Manhattan*, sister ship of the *Tecumseh*, which also carried fifteen-inch guns in its armored turret. Peering from one of the *Tennessee*'s gun ports, Lt. Arthur D. Wharton watched in mingled awe and terror as a "slowly revolving turret revealed the cavernous depth of a mammoth gun" only yards away. "Stand clear the port side!" he hollered, and a moment later a huge concussion struck the casemate as a 440-pound bolt crashed against the five inches of armor and nearly two feet of wood that made up the *Tennessee*'s casemate. Unlike earlier shells from federal nine- and eleven-inch guns, this one opened a hole in the *Tennessee*. Buchanan had ordered nets to be affixed to the interior sides of the casemate so splinters would not be sent flying across the gun deck. That precaution no doubt saved many lives, but the daylight now visible through the side of the *Tennessee* proved that it was not invulnerable to shot.[30]

In addition to the *Manhattan*, the double-turreted *Chickasaw* also pounded the *Tennessee*'s casemate at close range. In less than an hour, the *Chickasaw* fired fifty-two shells into the *Tennessee* from a distance its commander estimated to be ten to fifty yards. Buchanan could not return fire, for with one gun port jammed and the primers regularly misfiring on his other five guns, he could bring few working weapons to bear on the enemy, even though he was literally surrounded by targets. He called for a party of workmen to try to unjam the stuck gun port. Two men stood with their backs to the casemate holding a metal bolt over the pivot rod, while two more struck it with sledgehammers. Buchanan was personally supervising their labor when a shell smashed into the casemate directly opposite where they were working. The men holding the bolt died instantly, "split in pieces." Buchanan was struck by flying debris and fell to the deck. His left leg—his good leg—was broken in a compound fracture and bent out at an impossible angle. Immediately the cry went up that the admiral was hit. He was placed near the side wall of the casemate just under the angled roof, and soon Dr. Conrad came running up to him. "Admiral, are you badly hurt?" he asked. "Don't know," was the terse reply.[31]

Conrad concluded at once that he could not treat Buchanan on the gun deck of the *Tennessee* in the midst of a raging fight, and determined to move him to the surgical cockpit below. He lifted up the sixty-three-year-old admiral and hoisted him onto his back. With Buchanan hanging on, Conrad carried him "down the ladder to the cock-pit, his broken leg slapping against me as I moved slowly along." Once below, Conrad applied a temporary splint, and Buchanan evinced his characteristic stoicism by propping himself up against the bulkhead and asking for reports of the battle. Soon, Captain Johnston· arrived in person. "Well, Johnston," Buchanan said lightly, "they have got me again." Johnston expressed his condolences, but Buchanan was all business. "You'll have to look out for her now; it is your fight." "All right," Johnston replied. "I'll do the best I know how."[32]

Johnston left, and the fight continued; but before long he was back. The fusillade of enemy shells had severed the steering chains on the afterdeck, and the *Tennessee*'s rudder no longer answered the wheel. Without its steering mechanism, the *Tennessee* was no longer maneuverable. Moreover, with the ship's funnel shot away, Johnston could not raise steam in the boilers. The gun port that Buchanan had tried to clear remained jammed, and the primers on the other guns were unreliable. The *Tennessee* could not fight back effectively, and it could not run for safety. Johnston asked Buchanan if he did not think they should surrender. It had come to this. But Buchanan had few qualms; the situation spoke for itself. "Do the best you can, sir," he told Johnston. "And when all is done, surrender."[33]

Johnston wasted little time. As he wrote later in his report, it was clear that "the ship was now nothing more than a target for the heavy guns of the enemy." He resolved to surrender at once. From the pilothouse, he took down the Confederate flag. But in the fury of battle that gesture was ambiguous. He realized what had to be done. He tied a white handkerchief to a boarding pike and raised it above the ship, and at last the firing stopped.[34]

* * *

From the cockpit belowdeck, Buchanan noted the cessation of noise. He also noted the jolt of yet another collision as the federal monitor *Ossipee* came alongside with more vigor than intended. Soon, down the ladder came two men dressed in blue, petty officers or common sailors, who demanded Buchanan's sword. The old admiral refused. He would surrender his sword to no one save Farragut or his appointed deputy. The two men moved forward as if determined to take it anyway, and Master's Mate W. S. Forrest, who was acting as Buchanan's aide, stepped in front of them. When it appeared that the two men intended to have their way at any cost, Forrest knocked one of them down. The situation might have descended into chaos had several federal officers not arrived just then. The captain of the *Ossipee*, William S. LeRoy, ordered the arrest of the two men who had tried to claim Buchanan's sword, and Buchanan formally surrendered it instead to Lt. Pierre Giraud, who took it to Farragut.[35]

Ordinarily, Buchanan would have gone aboard the *Hartford* to present his sword personally—Old Buck was a stickler for the conventions of sea warfare—but his condition made that impossible. With the adrenalin of battle now wearing off, the pain hit him in great waves; Conrad thought it likely that Buchanan's leg would have to be amputated. That thought may have influenced his mood by the time Farragut's surgeon, Dr. Jacob Palmer, arrived onboard with Farragut's compliments. When Dr. Palmer asked him what he could do to ease his pain, Buck replied, "I only wish to be treated kindly as a prisoner of war." Palmer, who sensed hostility in Buchanan's tone, responded: "Admiral Buchanan, you know perfectly well you will be treated kindly." Buchanan merely replied: "I am a Southern man, an enemy, and a rebel," as if to suggest that such credentials were certain to provoke cruelty from Yankees. When Palmer asked him if he would like to be taken aboard the *Hartford* so that he could talk with Farragut, Buchanan replied that he did not pretend to be a particular friend of Farragut's, and that he would be satisfied with any disposition the federals might make of him. The only request he made was that his aide and his surgeon be allowed to accompany him to whatever destination Farragut had in mind.[36]

At sixty-three and badly wounded, with his ship battered into submission and the Confederacy itself in its twilight days, Franklin Buchanan remained characteristically defiant.

⁓⋇15⋇⁓

HOME FROM THE SEA

My conscience assures me that I strove to do my duty,
and I must rest content under my present misfortune.

*T*he wound Buchanan received in the Battle of Mobile Bay was
more severe than the one he had received during the fight in
Hampton Roads more than two years earlier. On that occasion, the bullet had passed through his right thigh without hitting bone.
This time, the flying metal inside the *Tennessee's* casemate had shattered
the bones of his left leg. Dr. Conrad was convinced that the leg would
have to be amputated. But whatever treatment was indicated, it could
not take place onboard a ship of war. Buchanan needed to be moved to a
hospital.

Commander Johnston surrendered the *Tennessee* at just past 9:00 A.M.
on 5 August 1864. That same afternoon, Farragut obtained permission
from General Page at Fort Morgan, where the Confederate flag still flew,
to send the wounded of both sides to the U.S. naval hospital at Pensacola. Page agreed, and Buchanan was carried from the hot, damp, and
sulfuric confines of the *Tennessee's* casemate to the deck of the USS
Metacomet, which left the harbor the next morning under a flag of truce.
That afternoon, Buchanan was safely settled in the hospital at the Pensacola Navy Yard.[1]

Buchanan was a celebrity prisoner, and he received red carpet treatment from his captors. In part this was because of Farragut's determination to honor his defeated foe. The Union admiral wrote Gideon Welles

that while Buchanan was "a rebel and a traitor to the Government that had raised and educated him," he had also been "one of [the navy's] ablest officers." And Farragut insisted that "no one knew him better or appreciated his capacity more highly" than he. Accordingly, Farragut readily acceded to Buchanan's request that Dr. Conrad be allowed to accompany him into captivity, and he also allowed Buchanan's two aides, Lts. R. M. Carter and W. S. Forrest, to travel with him.[2]

At Pensacola, Buchanan received particular attention from the Union fleet surgeon, Dr. Jacob Palmer, who made it his personal mission to save Buchanan's leg. And, indeed, within a few days it was evident that the leg would *not* have to be amputated. Buchanan sent messages to friends and family assuring them that he was in reasonable health and doing well. He wrote to Major General Maury in Mobile to let him know that the doctors had saved his leg, and he insisted that his mind was at ease as well. "As my conscience assures me that I strove to do my duty," he wrote, "I must rest content under my present misfortune."[3]

Buchanan remained in the Pensacola hospital for two months. His health improved daily as his leg mended and the weather cooled. He drafted his formal report to Mallory on the Battle of Mobile Bay, which he was allowed to forward to Richmond. He received mail and even packages; Nannie sent him several boxes of "good things to eat." Dr. Palmer acted as a go-between for the Buchanans, keeping Nannie informed about her husband's health, and maintaining a friendly correspondence with her even after Buchanan left his care. He, at least, was ready to call an end to this uncivil war: "Enough, dear madam, that we should have public strife: the people who exchange blows do not initiate the wounds they make."[4]

Buchanan left Pensacola on 18 November onboard the steamer *Fort Morgan* bound for Key West, the first stop on his journey to a New York prison. He had his own private apartment on the upper deck, and both of his loyal aides, as well as yet another federal surgeon, traveled with him. He was comfortable enough and assured one and all that he was improving steadily. After a short stop at Key West, the *Fort Morgan* continued north to Hampton Roads, the scene of Buchanan's one great naval triumph, and then finally to Fort Lafayette in New York Harbor, which was to be his home for the next three months.

Located on a small island in the Verrazano Narrows, Fort Lafayette was no ordinary prisoner-of-war camp. It was reserved for the dangerous and the notorious, among them newspapermen who expressed public sympathy for the Confederacy, minor politicians whose loyalty was uncertain, and officers who had resigned their commissions in the U.S. Army or Navy to fight for the Confederacy. The octagonal stone-and-brick fort had thirty-foot walls, and the several score prisoners were housed in its lower casemates, which had been bricked off to form individual cells. The only light in those cells came through the empty gun ports, which were covered by iron gratings. The inmates were allowed to exercise in the central parade ground twice a day. By the time Buchanan arrived there in December 1864, they had formed a kind of prison society that included discussion groups and even a handwritten newspaper, which they circulated among themselves.

Like the other celebrity prisoners, Buchanan had a cell to himself and was allowed to receive visitors. Nannie made her way north from Maryland's Eastern Shore, and it was a poignant moment when husband and wife were reunited after a separation of three years and five months. Their reunion was subdued, however, because of the requirement that a Union officer remain in the room with them at all times. "We were under great restraint," Buchanan later wrote to their daughter Elizabeth, "and could not converse freely as we wished. . . . We both had much to say to each other which had to be omitted." Later, he received visits from his daughter Alice and from his brother McKean, a survivor of the frigate *Congress*, which had been destroyed by Buchanan's *Virginia* in the Battle of Hampton Roads.[5]

His leg continued to mend, and his remarkable constitution was evidenced by the fact that his overall health actually improved. Soon he could take advantage of the regular exercise periods, though he had to use two canes to support himself as he hobbled about the parade ground. Emotionally, too, he seemed at ease with his circumstances. "I have made up my mind that I am to remain here during my captivity," he wrote to Elizabeth in January, "and I shall be as happy and as cheerful under the circumstances as possible." As if to assure her of his state of mind, he wrote, "I have much to live for, and will do all in my power to retain my health and spirits. . . . I look forward with perfect confidence and certainty that I will be again with you all and our dear Ma at a happy home somewhere, if not at our old once happy one of the Eastern Shore."[6]

Determined that he should not remain indefinitely in the dreary confines of Fort Lafayette, Nannie went to Washington to lobby for his release, or at least his exchange. Lincoln met with her and listened to her pleas for mercy, but then gently explained that if he released Buchanan, he would have to do the same for every other wounded officer who fell into Union hands. Moreover, an exchange would be difficult because the Confederates did not hold a prisoner of an equally exalted rank to trade for him. Back in August, Farragut had suggested that Buchanan might be exchanged for several U.S. Navy officers and seamen who were being held in Texas, and perhaps out of sympathy for his wounded foe, he urged a quick repatriation. But Welles had vetoed that suggestion and instead issued the orders that had sent Buchanan north.[7]

Whether or not it was because Lincoln spoke to him after Nannie's visit, by December Welles had changed his mind. Government approval for an exchange was secured in January, although the administrative machinery delayed the fulfillment of the agreement for nearly two months. It was Grant who broke the logjam. He asked Secretary of War Edwin Stanton to send Buchanan to City Point, in Virginia, so that he could be swapped for "some of our sailors from Southern prisons."[8]

When Buchanan learned that he was to be exchanged in mid-February, it must have seemed something of a mixed blessing. Certainly he was anxious to be released from imprisonment, and he would have considered it his duty to return to his command. But he would once again be separated from Nannie and the rest of his family, some of whom had been able to visit him at Fort Lafayette. Then, too, if he was being exchanged, it was presumably with the understanding that he could still make some contribution to the Confederate war effort. But at age sixty-four, and unable to walk without the support of two canes, what contribution would be expected of him? With such thoughts, he boarded a navy steamship on 18 February and journeyed from New York back to Hampton Roads. From there, he was transported up the James River to City Point, the federal supply base for Grant's army outside Petersburg. On 4 March (the date of Lincoln's second inaugural), he was turned over to Confederate authorities. That same afternoon, he made his way to Richmond.[9]

He could take little solace in what he saw in the Confederate capital. The Confederacy was reduced to a fortified island of resistance, held together by an unbroken line of entrenchments stretching from Petersburg to Richmond, and manned by Lee's small, ragged, and underfed army. What a contrast it was to what he had seen at City Point, where the huge federal army stored its mountains of ordnance and foodstuffs. With the imminent return of spring weather, Grant's army would once again begin to pressure the thin defensive lines of Lee's army. Only a miracle would save the Confederacy then.

Buchanan's stay in Richmond was brief. Crippled as he was, duty called. He headed south for Mobile: first on the Confederacy's dilapidated railroad system, then by steamboat, arriving in the Gulf city in early April just as the Confederacy was falling apart. Indeed, he could be no more than a witness as federal forces closed in on Mobile from land and sea. On 12 April, as the last Confederate troops marched out of the city, abandoning it to the enemy, news arrived of Lee's surrender at Appomattox three days earlier.[10]

In Buchanan's absence, Comdr. Ebenezer Farrand had succeeded to command of the Confederate naval squadron at Mobile. At first he tried to flee upriver with three of the surviving vessels, but on 4 May he opened negotiations with the federals, and a week later he surrendered his ships, accepting a parole on behalf of himself, his officers, and his men. Buchanan was not included. Unwilling to be made a prisoner a second time, he continued northward hoping somehow to reach Demopolis, Alabama, some 150 miles up the Tombigbee River.

En route, he stopped briefly at the home of Joseph Davis, the Confederate president's older brother, who welcomed him as a friend. Davis's granddaughter, Lise Mitchell, recorded in her journal that night that Buchanan was "a noble looking officer. Clean shaven and bald, what hair he has is perfectly white. His grayish blue eyes have such an expression of intelligence and benevolence that they are very attractive." She noted, too, that he was "still quite lame, and walks with two sticks." Despite that, he was also unconquered and not yet ready to admit final defeat. When Lise expressed concern that her uncle the president might be caught by Yankee cavalry, Buchanan assured her that Davis was certain to escape across the Mississippi and carry on the fight from the West, or even from Mexico. Neither of them knew that Davis was already in federal custody, having been captured three days before at Irwinville, Georgia. As for himself, Buchanan told Lise that he had not yet accepted a parole from the Yankees, but confessed that he might have to do so soon, "since there [was] no longer a navy, and consequently no work" for him to do.[11]

Three days later Buchanan did accept a parole, and made his second trip from Mobile to Hampton Roads on a Union warship, this time as a paroled prisoner. When the ship put into Hampton Roads, news of the final end of the war led to his release, and he returned by public conveyance to Maryland—to the Eastern Shore and the Rest, or what there was of it. It was a poignant moment: A sixty-five-year-old man, his thin hair completely white, and so crippled that he could not walk without the support of two canes, returned at last to his prewar residence after an absence of nearly four years. Although he knew that his beloved home had been destroyed by fire, it must still have been a blow to find its charred remains abandoned, and his family living off the charity of friends.

Lacking a home of their own, the Buchanans lived for more than a year at the neighboring estate of Fairview, whose owner, Harry Oliver, was temporarily in Europe. When the Olivers returned, the Buchanans moved to Knightly, the home of the Winders (who were also Lloyd in-laws), while a new house was built at the Rest. The new building was more modest than the old; it was Victorian rather than Georgian, and resembled a town home more than it did a plantation. But the view of the Miles River was unchanged, and the new house boasted a number of shaded verandahs where Franklin and Nannie could enjoy summer afternoons. Although it was less grand than the building it replaced, Buchanan loved it nearly as much.[12]

If they were at last in their own home again, there was still the problem of supporting themselves. Having foresworn his U.S. Navy commission to fight for the Confederacy, Buchanan had lost his pension. He and Nannie would have to live off the yield of the hundred or so acres of land they owned around the Rest. Money had been a problem for the Buchanans throughout their married life, but the circumstances they faced in the postwar years were the most difficult of all. They were never in danger of starving, for unlike lands in other parts of the South, the Eastern Shore had not been worn out by season after season of cotton cultivation. As one wag suggested, Talbot County lands were only "discouraged" rather than "exhausted." Corn replaced wheat as the dominant crop, and it found a ready market in Baltimore and elsewhere. But farming a hundred acres of corn would never yield enough to support the Buchanans in the relatively grand style they had enjoyed in the antebellum years.[13]

The scar tissue of war was less visible on the Eastern Shore than elsewhere. No armies had crossed its flat fields or fought among its stands of pine. For the most part, Talbot County remained physically unchanged. Although the Rest had burned, it had been a victim of accident rather than war. The one great difference, of course, was that the slaves were now free. Lincoln's 1863 proclamation had not affected slaves in Maryland, for it had applied only to those parts of the country in rebellion. A new state constitution in Maryland had abolished slavery within the state in November 1864. Although this did not significantly affect Buchanan's financial circumstances, his brother-in-law Edward Lloyd lost nearly eight hundred slaves valued at more than a million dollars, a vast fortune at the time.

Neither Edward Lloyd nor Buchanan was pleased by the fact of black emancipation, but the impact of this political and legal revolution was muted by the geographical isolation of the Eastern Shore. For the most part, blacks stayed on the land they had always worked and accepted small wages or, more often, a share of the crop they produced, so that old relationships remained in place. In many cases, young blacks were bound over to white families as their "wards," though the practical distinction between wards and slaves was often unclear.[14]

Besides the elimination of slavery, there were a number of other changes in Maryland that Buchanan found unwelcome. The new state constitution had weakened the representation of the countryside (and particularly the Eastern Shore) and had established, for the first time, free public schools. Buchanan found himself required to pay ten cents on each hundred dollars of the assessed value of his property so that the state could pay for these schools. He was pleased to know that blacks were not eligible for this handout. Although it was no longer illegal to teach blacks to read and write, the state was not going to pay for them to learn. The relatively few blacks who did go to school did so under the auspices of one or another of several charitable institutions. Most shocking of all, there was talk of disenfranchising ex-Confederates (such as Buchanan) and at the same time giving the vote to blacks. Such an upside-down world was disorienting. Buchanan was alarmed and a little disgusted to learn that President Andrew Johnson's amnesty declaration on Christmas Day of 1868 did not extend to those—like Buchanan and Semmes—who had left loyal states to fight for the Confederacy.[15]

But if Maryland's social revolution came quickly, it also ended early. Conservative Democrats soon regained control of the government, and in 1867, even before the Buchanans moved into their new home at the

Rest, another new state constitution was in place that repealed most of the progressive legislation passed during the war. The free schools stayed, but the representation of the Eastern Shore and southern Maryland was reestablished in the legislature. Maryland's conservatives also passed a series of "black codes," which defined the social role of free blacks. To ensure white control, these laws required all adult black males to be employed by a white person. Any who were unemployed were declared vagrant and subject to arrest. Blacks arrested for vagrancy were turned over to a white employer who put them to work, paying no wages but supplying room and board. Blacks could not travel on the public roads or assemble in groups, except at church services. A black woman was not to be considered a competent witness against a white man accused of rape. In effect, the post–Civil War black codes replaced the prewar slave codes.[16]

A conservative himself, Buchanan approved of the effort by Maryland conservatives to limit the social revolution triggered by the Civil War. In the same spirit, he thoroughly disapproved of the effort by Republican Radicals in Congress to interfere with this system of race control. He was outraged by their proposals, and he shared his outrage with his friends. He wrote to John Randolph Tucker, who had commanded the *Patrick Henry* in the Battle of Hampton Roads, to suggest that he was ready to take up arms again. "From present prospects at Washington," he wrote, "many of us may yet be found under arms in sustaining the Constitution of the U.S. *or some other* which will embrace the whole South." Not long afterward, he told a reporter from the local newspaper that although his legs were both weakened from war wounds, "they are ready and able to carry me against the only revolutionists in the country, the Radicals, who are doing all in their power to destroy the government." He would have found ridiculous the suggestion that he had spent four years under arms in an attempt to "destroy the government" himself.[17]

Of course, there were happy events, too. In the fall of 1866, Sallie Lloyd, Buchanan's oldest daughter, married Thomas F. Screven, the brother of her sister Ellen's husband, George Screven. And a few months later the Buchanans were honored by a visit from Jefferson Davis. After two years in captivity while the government tried to decide what to do with him, the Confederate ex-president had been released on bond, and he spent several months visiting friends in the Chesapeake Bay area. On a wintry, snowy night in mid-December, the Buchanans bundled up in a sleigh and made their way to Wye House for a reception in his honor. Several hundred attended, and Davis held court, signing autographs and discussing the history he was planning to write. If the Buchanans were only faces in the crowd that night, a few days later Davis paid them the signal honor of returning their visit, traveling to the Rest for a luncheon with the old admiral and his wife on 18 December 1867.[18]

Throughout this difficult period, the Buchanans' money problems remained unresolved. Then, in the fall of 1868, only days before his sixty-eighth birthday, Buchanan launched himself into a new career when he accepted an offer to become president of the Agricultural College of Maryland, the forerunner of the present University of Maryland. Buchanan's reasons for accepting are self-evident: in addition to the honor it bestowed, the position paid a salary. For the college trustees who tendered him the offer, this was only the latest chapter in a battle of wills with the state legislature. During the war, the college had earned a reputation as a bastion of southern sympathy. It deliberately refused to fly the national flag at commencement each year, and no less than five of its trustees had been arrested at one time or another on suspicion of treason.[19]

When the war ended, the college was struggling to survive. Seeking to energize their conservative client base, the trustees offered the vacant college presidency to George Washington Custis Lee, the son of Robert E. Lee, and himself a former Confederate general. The legislature responded with a resolution that in making such an appointment, the college had proved itself "an unsafe place for the education of our young men, and wholly unworthy of either State or Federal patronage." More sensitive to the public mood than the trustees, General Lee declined the job, later succeeding his father as president of Washington College, soon to become Washington and Lee. The Maryland Agricultural College thereupon turned to Charles L. C. Minor, and he was the president when the college reopened its doors in October 1867. But Minor could not attract students. And when the state assembly, disgusted by the taint of treason that continued to linger around the school, cut back its support, the college was threatened with extinction. Planters' sons, the school's target audience, were too cash poor to pay the increased tuition.[20]

Unwilling to give in altogether, the trustees turned to another ex-Confederate hero to head the school: Admiral Franklin Buchanan. To their delight, Old Buck took up the duties with his usual energy. But he also undertook them with an admiral's sense of order and hierarchy. He told his friends that his goal was "to restore the College to the confidence of the state and make it useful to her sons." To do that, he first needed to increase the number of students. There were fewer than a dozen students enrolled at the school when Buchanan took the reins. To attract more, he slashed tuition. It worked; enrollment soared from a handful to nearly a hundred. But in the process Buchanan committed the college to six thousand dollars worth of debts, and did not bother to inform the trustees about it. Neither did he bother to file the required annual report. It may well be, as one authority speculates, that Buchanan "viewed himself as an honored hero in retirement" and did not think he needed to bother with the details of paperwork. But it was unwise, and it left him open to criticism.[21]

The entire faculty of the college consisted of only four professors, and almost at once two of them fell afoul of Buchanan's notions of proper order and personal responsibility: Prof. James Higgins, a medical doctor who taught practical science, and Prof. Baptista Lorino, who taught languages. Higgins's sin was that he failed to meet his classes regularly. Buchanan expostulated to a friend that "during the last three months, not a lesson was taught in Dr. H's department, and this is only part of his improper conduct." As for Lorino, according to a story told in hushed tones within the Buchanan family, Buchanan suspected him of homosexuality. If so, he never voiced such charges publicly, saying only that Lorino was guilty of "immoral and dishonorable conduct." Without first consulting with the Board of Trustees, Buchanan dismissed both men.[22]

In doing so, he exceeded his authority. The college bylaws required him to report to the trustees any professor who was unfit. Instead, Buchanan fired the professors, then informed the trustees that he had done so. Since these two professors constituted exactly half the total faculty of the school, the event was major news. The trustees were divided, and the two professors lobbied hard against Buchanan, insisting that they had been fired largely because Buchanan was opposed to a classical curriculum. As far as Buchanan was concerned, such behavior only proved their unworthiness and validated his decision. He learned from one of the trustees that Higgins actually offered a bribe to one trustee if he would conveniently misplace a number of proxy votes that would sustain the firings.[23]

In the end, the board sustained the firing of Higgins but retained Lorino. As always with Buchanan, half a loaf was not enough. He insisted that when "political influence" became a factor in an institution of learning, "its usefulness [was] destroyed." He resigned. It was more than a noble gesture, for the loss of the job would mean continued financial hardship. But as he expressed it to a friend: "We Confederates are *poor,* but thank God *poverty cannot make us sacrifice principle or reputation."* Ironically, one of Buchanan's successors in this job was William H. Parker, who had commanded the *Beaufort* in the Battle of Hampton Roads and whom Buchanan had described as "delinquent in his duty" and not "fit to command."[24]

Buchanan returned to the Rest, where, in his own words, he took up his "hoe, spade and rake" to tend his farm. His reference was metaphorical rather than descriptive, for he did not labor in the fields. Nevertheless, his reduced circumstances meant that he had to continue to look for some means by which he could secure the financial well-being of his family. Like many other ex-Confederates, he found an opportunity in the insurance business. In the postbellum years, insurance companies discovered that placing the name of a revered Confederate general (or admiral) on the letterhead of their company was worth thousands in advertising dollars. Southerners who worried about the financial future of their own families saw a gleam of hope in life insurance policies, and were willing to part with a few of their hard-earned dollars if the policy was vetted by one of their former leaders. Buchanan succumbed to the offers of the Life Association of America and accepted a job as the company's secretary and Alabama state manager.[25]

Leaving Nannie behind once again, the sixty-nine-year-old ex-admiral moved back to Mobile in January 1870. It was unpleasant work in a lonely environment, and he left after a year and a half in June 1871. On his resignation, the board members passed a resolution praising his service. In it they declared that Buchanan "discharged all the offices of Secretary and State manager with great zeal, the most marked fidelity, and with the utmost promptitude. . . . We deem his departure for his Maryland home a great loss to our Association, to our Board and our city." The city had apparently forgiven him for his defeat in 1864, for the local newspaper mourned his decision to leave as well: "Language is inade-

quate to express how high he stands in the respect and admiration of a
city in which both his civic and military virtues have been illustrated."[26]

Buchanan returned to the Rest for the last time in the fall of 1871. There
would be no more adventures for him, and he accepted that fact with his
usual pragmatism. Although he now needed his cane only for long walks,
he took fewer of them. Now that he was past seventy, his active past was
catching up with him. While he continued to shake his head at news of
the latest Radical proclamation (the Fifteenth Amendment, giving blacks
the right to vote, was ratified that summer), he was no longer filled with
a desire to take up arms in opposition. A visitor to Talbot County in the
summer of 1871 reported that "the old prejudices" of Eastern Shore society were "beginning to yield." Then, too, more and more of the southern
states were returning conservatives to power, and the revolutionary fer-
vor of the Radicals seemed to be waning.[27]

Buchanan seldom left the Rest, and his health was a daily concern.
In the summers he watched the Miles River from his porch; in winter,
he watched the fire. He was courteous to his neighbors and kind to his
grandchildren, and unfailingly polite in his social discourse. As one local
authority phrased it: He "beguiled the time . . . with the peaceful pursuits of husbandry and the pleasing duties of a generous hospitality." In
April 1874, in what may have been the last letter he ever wrote, he
declined an invitation to dinner. "I regret exceedingly I cannot be with
you," he wrote in his own hand, his script still characterized by the bold,
swift strokes he had employed since his youth, "for I am too feeble to
venture out [in] such dismal weather as this."[28]

Only days later, he caught a cold that turned into pneumonia. His
condition steadily worsened, and he died quietly at home, attended by
two doctors and several friends, as well as his beloved Nannie. He was
interred the following Thursday (14 May 1874) at Wye House in the
Lloyd family cemetery behind the orangery. At his feet were placed the
two iron cannonballs he had brought back with him from the Mexican
War as souvenirs and then rescued from the Yankee militia in the secession spring of 1861. He wouldn't let them be taken then . . . and he has
them still.

~❧ Epilogue ✦~

RETROSPECTIVE

*Thus I am forever separated from a service in which I have felt such
pride, and in which I have spent so many happy years of my life
in the faithful performance of my duty.*

B uchanan's naval career spanned a half century of revolutionary change. The grog-drinking, lash-wielding, sail-driven navy
of wooden ships and iron men that he had joined in 1815 had
yielded grudgingly but inexorably to a less tradition-bound and more technically sophisticated navy of steam plants, rifled guns, and iron armor. While
he embraced the new technology, Buchanan was a stout defender of tradition when it came to issues of personal behavior and shipboard discipline.
Indeed, throughout the navy's fifty-year metamorphosis, Buchanan deliberately and consciously cast himself as a champion of high standards, stern
discipline, and personal responsibility. His was a universe of moral absolutes,
and he was as demanding of himself as he was unforgiving of others.

As he rose from midshipman to lieutenant to commander to captain,
Buchanan compiled an impressive list of firsts both individually and on
behalf of the U.S. Navy. He was the first superintendent of the Naval
Academy, the first to charge ashore at Tuxpan to capture the Mexican
fort there, the first American official to set foot on Japanese soil, and the
first naval officer to conn a U.S. warship up the Yangtze River. By 1860
he was at the peak of his profession.

When the nation broke apart in 1861, Buchanan relied on the pole star
of duty to guide him as he made the most fateful decision of his life. Alas,
it failed to provide the kind of pure and unfractured light that he wanted

233

and needed. His decision to resign, almost instantly regretted, led him to make his way south to Richmond and offer his services to the Confederacy. He threw himself into his Confederate duties with the same enthusiasm and commitment that he demonstrated in all his professional assignments. He willingly, even eagerly, risked his life despite his advanced age, and suffered two serious combat wounds for his trouble. Until the day he died, he professed pride in his Confederate service and insisted that the defeat of the South was a great historical tragedy. Yet it is hard to avoid the conclusion that on a personal level, the greatest tragedy of his life was his severance from the navy he had loved for forty years.

Buchanan always felt that the U.S. Navy had rejected him. When Gideon Welles refused to allow him to withdraw his resignation, he was distraught. "I am made an unhappy man," he wailed to a nephew. Then he became angry. Spurned by the service to which he had given two-thirds of his life, he sought an opportunity to achieve rank and status in the navy of the Confederacy, which in time made him an admiral. He was grateful for the opportunity, and proud of his achievements, even in defeat.

Although Gideon Welles rejected him, the U.S. Navy itself did not forget him. Thirty years after his death, when the Naval Academy underwent a dramatic transformation during the administration of Theodore Roosevelt, the new quarters of the superintendent were christened Buchanan House; and forty years after that, during World War II, the navy named a destroyer for him (DD-484).

On 11 May 1961, almost exactly one hundred years after Buchanan submitted his resignation to Gideon Welles at Main Navy, the U.S. Navy held a ceremony at Todd Shipyard in Seattle to commission a guided missile destroyer, the newest USS *Buchanan* (DDG-14). A huge fifty-star American flag adorned the bow of the new ship, and below it, in mute testimony to the vessel's namesake, hung a smaller Confederate battle flag. Mrs. Nancy Hardcastle Fisher, Buchanan's great-granddaughter, smashed a bottle of champagne against the vessel's bow; the Thirteenth Naval District Band struck up *Maryland My Maryland,* itself inspired by the same Pratt Street massacre that had triggered Buchanan's resignation from the navy; and the *Buchanan* slid into the waters of Elliott Bay. The principal speaker that day was a U.S. Navy admiral named Ulysses S. Grant Sharp.

The irony that assails the modern reader in considering this tableau suggests the dissonance inherent in the life of a man who devoted himself wholeheartedly to his duty, and yet ended his career fighting against the navy he had so dearly loved.

~≺ Notes ≻~

ABBREVIATIONS USED IN THE NOTES

B&L   *Battles and Leaders of the Civil War*
FB   Franklin Buchanan
Hagley Hagley Museum and Library, Wilmington, Delaware
HSP   Historical Society of Pennsylvania, Philadelphia
MHS   Maryland Historical Society, Baltimore
MOC   Eleanor S. Brokenbrough Library, The Museum of the Confederacy,
        Richmond, Virginia
NA   National Archives, Washington, D.C.
NRC   Naval Records Collection (National Archives)
OR   *Official Records of the Union and Confederate Armies in the War of the
        Rebellion,* series 2
ORN   *Official Records of the Union and Confederate Navies in the War of the
        Rebellion,* series 1
RG   Record Group (National Archives)
Rutgers Rutgers University Libraries (State University of New Jersey)
SHC   Southern Historical Collection (Wilson Library, UNC)
UNC   University of North Carolina, Chapel Hill
USNA   United States Naval Academy
VHS   Virginia Historical Society, Richmond
Yale   Yale University Library, New Haven, Connecticut

PROLOGUE

1. FB's physical description, written in his own hand, is dated 1852 and is in the Simon Gratz Collection, HSP.

2. All subsequent quotations in the Prologue are from FB to Du Pont, 20 May 1861 (W9-10862), Du Pont Letters, Hagley.

CHAPTER 1. A MID IN THE MED

1. Roberdeau Buchanan, *Genealogy of the McKean Family of Pennsylvania,* 128; the obituary is quoted in Charles Lee Lewis, *Admiral Franklin Buchanan, Fearless Man of Action,* 4.

2. Laetitia Buchanan to Secretary of the Navy, 5 August 1815, Miscellaneous Letters, NRC, RG 45, reel 73. Although he always considered himself a Marylander, Buchanan's appointment was from the state of Pennsylvania.

3. Christopher McKee, *A Gentlemanly and Honorable Profession: The Creation of the Naval Officer Corps, 1794–1815*, 59–118.

4. Daniel Ammen, *The Old Navy and the New: Memoirs of Rear Admiral Daniel Ammen, U.S.N.*, 35; Alexander Slidell Mackenzie, *The Life of Commodore Oliver Hazard Perry*, 141.

5. Buchanan's *Java* Journal (USNA no. 5), 28 January, 1–4 and 10 February 1817.

6. Gardner Allen, *Our Navy and the Barbary Corsairs*.

7. Mackenzie, *Oliver Hazard Perry*, 106–9.

8. Ibid., 111–12.

9. Ibid., 112–13.

10. Buchanan's *Java* Journal (USNA no. 5), 7 March 1817.

11. Mackenzie, *Oliver Hazard Perry*, 119.

12. Ibid., 133.

13. Ibid., 134.

14. Lewis, *Admiral Franklin Buchanan*, 31.

15. Buchanan's *Franklin* Journal (USNA no. 2), 29 January, 1 February 1818.

16. Ibid., 18 and 26 May 1819; Lewis, *Admiral Franklin Buchanan*, 35.

17. Receipt dated August 1820, Buchanan Papers, MHS.

CHAPTER 2. CHASING PIRATES AND OTHER ADVENTURES

1. McKee, *A Gentlemanly and Honorable Profession*, chap. 1.

2. Buchanan's *Dorothea* Journal (USNA no. 5), 13 April 1821.

3. Ibid., entries for February–June 1822.

4. Navy Register for 1822 and 1823; Buchanan's *Weasel* Journal (USNA no. 31).

5. *Debates and Proceedings in the Congress*, 17th Cong., 2d sess., 371. The language of the bill was duplicated in Porter's orders: Smith Thompson to David Porter, 1 February 1823, in David D. Porter, *Memoir of Commodore Porter of the United States Navy*, 278–81. A collateral duty of this squadron was to make at least a gesture toward enforcing the laws against the slave trade, declared illegal in 1807 and underscored by new legislation passed in 1818.

6. Porter, *Memoir*, chapter 17.

7. Buchanan's *Weasel* Journal (USNA no. 31), 25 February 1823.

8. Ibid., 28 February 1823.

9. Buchanan's *Hornet* Journal (USNA no. 31), entries of January 1825. The authority is McKee, *A Gentlemanly and Honorable Profession*, 229.

10. Buchanan's *Baltimore* Journal (USNA no. 6), 30 October 1826.

11. Ibid., 8 November 1826.

12. Ibid., 9 November 1826.

13. Ibid., 12 November 1826.

14. Ibid., 13 November 1826.
15. Ibid., 19–20 and 25 November 1826.
16. Ibid., 14 December 1826.
17. Ibid., 17 December 1826.
18. Ibid., 2–5 January 1827.
19. Buchanan's *Ruth* Journal (USNA no. 6), 28 February 1827.
20. Buchanan's *Natchez* Journal (USNA no. 6), 26 July 1827.
21. Ibid., 17–20 August 1827.
22. Ibid., 15 September, 14 October, and 6 November 1827, 5 and 10 January 1828.
23. Ibid., 10, 15, and 16 October 1827.
24. Ibid., 23 March 1828.
25. Ibid., 31 March 1828.
26. Ibid., 2 and 22 April 1828.
27. Ibid., 25 July 1828.
28. Ibid., 22 August and 22 November 1828.

Chapter 3. Nannie Lloyd

1. Charles Lowndes and Sarah Lloyd were married on 4 May 1826. Register of Marriages (1823–1847), Talbot County, CR 11932 (reel 1228), 37, St. Michael's Parish Collection, Maryland Hall of Records.
2. Buchanan's *Constellation* Journal, 12 and 26 July 1830, 2 June 1831, SHC, UNC.
3. *Richmond Dispatch*, 13 May 1883. The author of the newspaper story told it as a kind of parable and concluded with the assertion that by the end of the journey Buchanan had won the sailors' respect.
4. Oswald Tilghman, *History of Talbot County, Maryland, 1661–1861*, 1:204; Alicia Lloyd to Edward Lloyd, 12 November 1836, Lloyd Papers, MHS, reel 17.
5. Tilghman, *History of Talbot County*, 1:184–210.
6. Ibid., 1:189; Frederick Douglass, *Life and Times of Frederick Douglass*, 37.
7. Douglass, *Life and Times of Frederick Douglass*, 62.
8. FB to Du Pont, 27 June 1833 (W93661), Du Pont Papers, Hagley.
9. Ibid.
10. Buchanan's *Delaware* Journal, entries for July–September, SHC, UNC.
11. Ibid., 15 September 1834.
12. Buchanan's *United States* Journal, 1 and 4 May 1834, SHC, UNC.
13. Ibid., 14 August 1834.
14. Sallie Scott Lloyd to Anne Lloyd Lowndes, 8 August 1834, Lloyd Family Papers (privately held); Marriage Records (1810–1845), Anne Arundel County, CR 49 1582 (reel 1228), 104, Maryland Hall of Records.
15. The description of the house is in the *Baltimore American and Daily Commercial Advertiser*, 14 March 1844. The couple's difficulties with money are evident in Nannie Buchanan to Sallie Lloyd, 6 November and 23 December 1845, both in Lloyd Papers, MHS, reel 18. See chapter 5 below.

16. Alicia Lloyd to Edward Lloyd, 17 October 1836, Lloyd Papers, MHS, reel 17.

17. Register of Baptism, Marriages, and Funerals (1836–53), St. Michael's Parish (M1158), Christ Church, St. Michael's Parish Collection, Maryland Hall of Records; Nannie Buchanan to Sallie Lloyd, 15 October [1845?], 21 February 1845, and 9 December 1845, all in Lloyd Papers, MHS, reel 18.

18. Nannie Buchanan to Sallie Lloyd, 21 February 1845, Lloyd Papers, MHS, reel 18.

19. Ibid.; Virginia Tayloe Lewis, "Washington Society before the War," typescript in the possession of Nancy Reeder, Towson, Md.

20. FB to Paulding, 7 March 1839, Officer's Letters, NRC, RG 45, reel 121.

21. Buchanan, *Genealogy of the McKean Family*, 155.

22. [Henry James Mercier], *Life in a Man-of-War, or Scenes in "Old Ironsides" during Her Cruise in the Pacific*, 20.

23. Ibid., 75.

24. Ibid., 131.

Chapter 4. Command: The USS *Vincennes*

1. "Blue Jacket" to J. G. Bennett, 27 November 1842, clipping in K. R. Owen Collection, MHS.

2. Salter to Navy Department, 6 August 1842, quoted in Lewis, *Admiral Franklin Buchanan*, 83.

3. FB to James Espy, 10 December 1842, *Vincennes* Letter Book (USNA no. 30).

4. FB to David Conner, 14 December 1842, *Vincennes* Letter Book (USNA no. 30).

5. FB to Secretary of the Navy, 19 December 1842, *Vincennes* Letter Book (USNA no. 30).

6. FB to Secretary of the Navy, 27 December 1842, and 10, 17, 22, and 24 January 1843; and FB to Stewart, 21 January 1843, all in *Vincennes* Letter Book (USNA no. 30); FB to Du Pont, January 1843, Du Pont Papers, box 16, Hagley.

7. FB to Du Pont, 29 September 1845 (W9-4495), Du Pont Papers, Hagley.

8. FB to J. O. Smith, 11 July 1844; and FB to Henshaw, 8 December 1843, both in *Vincennes* Letter Book (USNA no. 30).

9. FB to Upshur, 13 December 1842 and 3 January 1843, both in *Vincennes* Letter Book (USNA no. 30).

10. FB to Hooe, 30 November 1843, *Vincennes* Letter Book (USNA no. 30).

11. FB to Conner, 9 July 1844, *Vincennes* Letter Book (USNA no. 30). Hooe was suspended from the service but was later pardoned and reinstated. See *Army and Navy Chronicle* 12 (26 March 1842): 153.

12. FB to Montgomery, Armstrong, and Graham, 9 April 1844, *Vincennes* Letter Book (USNA no. 30). Italics in original.

13. FB to U.S. Consul at St. Iago, n.d., *Vincennes* Letter Book (USNA no. 30).

14. FB to Mitchell, Wainwright, and Bryan, 13 February 1843, *Vincennes* Letter Book (USNA no. 30).

15. Sequence of events derived from Buchanan's *Vincennes* Journal, 21 February 1843 (USNA no. 31).

16. FB to Stewart, 21 February 1843; FB to Hastings, 22 February 1843; and FB to Secretary of the Navy, 24 February 1843, all in *Vincennes* Letter Book (USNA no. 30).

17. FB to Thompson, 6 April 1843, *Vincennes* Letter Book (USNA no. 30).

18. FB to Hargous, 6 April 1843, *Vincennes* Letter Book (USNA no. 30).

19. FB to Upshur, 18 April 1843, *Vincennes* Letter Book (USNA no. 30).

20. FB to Dimond [U.S. consul at Vera Cruz], 19 June 1843; and FB to Hargous, 19 June 1843, both in *Vincennes* Letter Book (USNA no. 30).

21. FB to Henshaw, 27 July 1843, *Vincennes* Letter Book (USNA no. 30).

22. FB to Thompson, 28 July 1843, *Vincennes* Letter Book (USNA no. 30).

23. FB to Johnson, 29 August 1843, *Vincennes* Letter Book (USNA no. 30).

24. FB to Thompson, 28 August and 9 September 1843, both in *Vincennes* Letter Book (USNA no. 30).

25. FB to Stewart, 23 September 1843, *Vincennes* Letter Book (USNA no. 30).

26. FB to Editors, 9 December 1843, *Vincennes* Letter Book (USNA no. 30).

27. FB to Chase, 23 December 1843; FB to Mattison, and FB to Cmdr, Home Squadron, both 9 January 1844, all in *Vincennes* Letter Book (USNA no. 30).

28. Buchanan's *Vincennes* Journal (USNA no. 31), 13 January 1844.

29. FB to Murphy, 21 May 1844; FB to Semmes, 8 June 1844; and FB to Conner, 22 June 1844, all in *Vincennes* Letter Book (USNA no. 30).

30. FB to Secretary of the Navy, 4 July 1844, *Vincennes* Letter Book (USNA no. 30). Also in Commander's Letters, NRC, RG 45, reel 32.

CHAPTER 5. THE NAVAL SCHOOL

1. Read et al. to Bancroft, 25 June 1845, in James R. Soley, *Historical Sketch of the United States Naval Academy*, 49.

2. Ibid.

3. Samuel E. Morison, *"Old Bruin,"* 132.

4. Reprinted in *Army and Navy Chronicle* 12 (19 February 1842): 78.

5. Henry F. Sturdy, "The Founding of the Naval Academy by Bancroft and Buchanan," 1369; Sturdy, "The Establishment of the Naval School at Annapolis," 1–17.

6. Bancroft to Read et al., 25 June 1845, in Soley, *Historical Sketch*, 49.

7. Bancroft to FB, 7 August 1845, Secretary's Letters, NRC, RG 45, reel 40; FB to Du Pont, misdated 4 August 1843 [1845] (W9-4218), Du Pont Papers, Hagley.

8. FB to Du Pont, misdated 4 August 1843 [1845] (W9-4218), Du Pont Papers, Hagley (italics in original); Bancroft to FB, 7 August 1845, Secretary's Letters, NRC, RG 45, reel 40.

9. Read et al. to Bancroft, 25 June 1845, in Soley, *Historical Sketch,* 48; Bancroft to FB, 7 August 1845, Secretary's Letters, NRC, RG 45, reel 40.
10. FB to Bancroft, 14 August 1845, Commander's Letters, NRC, RG 45, reel 33; Bancroft to FB, 7 August 1845, Secretary's Letters, NRC, RG 45, reel 40.
11. Language professors were paid only $624 per year.
12. FB to Du Pont, 29 September 1845 (W9-4495), Du Pont Papers, Hagley.
13. Sturdy, "The Founding of the Naval Academy," 1370; FB to Bancroft, September 1845, Commander's Letters, NRC, RG 45, reel 33; Nannie to her mother, 6 November 1845, Lloyd Papers, MHS, reel 18.
14. FB to Yancey, 8 October 1845, Commander's Letters, NRC, RG 45, reel 33; Thomas G. Ford, "History of the Naval Academy," chap. 9.
15. Nannie to her mother, undated latter: "Friday morning" [1845?], Lloyd Papers, MHS, reel 18.
16. Nannie to her mother, 6 November 1845, Lloyd Papers, MHS, reel 18.
17. The "Rules and Regulations" are reproduced in Soley, *Historical Sketch,* 241–45; Buchanan's speech is on pp. 63–66. The quotation is from Ford, "History of the Naval Academy," chap. 9, 32.
18. Ford, "History of the Naval Academy," chap. 9, 48.
19. Girault to FB, 24 November 1845, Commander's Letters, NRC, RG 45, reel 33.
20. Ochiltree to FB, 25 November 1845, Commander's Letters, NRC, RG 45, reel 33.
21. FB to Bancroft, 26 November 1845, Commander's Letters, NRC, RG 45, reel 33.
22. Bancroft to FB, 28 November 1845, Secretary's Letters, NRC, RG 45, reel 40.
23. FB to Bancroft, 12 December 1845; clipping in FB to Bancroft, 27 January 1846, both in Commander's Letters, NRC, RG 45, reel 33.
24. Bancroft to FB, 19 February 1846, Secretary's Letters, NRC, RG 45, reel 41. For other examples, see Bancroft to FB, 28 February and 2 March 1846, both in ibid.
25. Bancroft to FB, 20 February 1846, Secretary's Letters, NRC, RG 45, reel 41.
26. Nannie to her mother, 6 November and 9 December [1845?], and an undated letter (Tuesday), all in Lloyd Papers, MHS, reel 18.
27. Two letters, both Bancroft to FB, both dated 4 May 1846, Secretary's Letters, NRC, RG 45, reel 41.
28. Nannie to her mother, 14 December [1845?], Lloyd Papers, MHS, reel 18.
29. Ibid.
30. House Executive Documents, 29th Cong., 1st sess., no. 2, p. 647; *Niles Weekly Register,* 31 January 1846.
31. Ford, "History of the Naval Academy," chap. 9.
32. FB to Bancroft, 16 July 1846, Commander's Letters, NRC, RG 45, reel 35.
33. FB to Buchanan, 14 May 1846, Commander's Letters, NRC, RG 45, reel 34; Bancroft to FB, 15 May 1846, Secretary's Letters, NRC, RG 45, reel 41.

Chapter 6. War and Diplomacy

1. K. Jack Bauer, *The War with Mexico, 1846–1848*, 1–80; John S. D. Eisenhower, *So Far from God: The U.S. War with Mexico, 1846–1848*, 3–68.
2. K. Jack Bauer, *Surfboats and Horse Marines: U.S. Naval Operations in the Mexican War, 1846–48*, 15–36.
3. Craig L. Symonds, *The Naval Institute's Historical Atlas of the U.S. Navy*, 72.
4. *Dictionary of American Naval Fighting Ships*, 4:91.
5. FB to James R. Harrison, 22 June 1847, quoted in Lewis, *Admiral Franklin Buchanan*, 121.
6. Perry to Mason [Secretary of the Navy], 24 April 1847, Home Squadron Letters, NRC, RG 45, reel 5.
7. Logbook of the *Germantown*, 11, 14, and 17 April 1847, NRC, RG 45, NA.
8. Ibid., 18 April 1847; Bauer, *Surfboats and Horse Marines*, 102–9.
9. Perry to Mason, 24 April 1847, Home Squadron Letters, NRC, RG 45, reel 5; Bauer, *The War with Mexico*, 103–5; Charles C. Jones Jr., *The Life and Services of Commodore Josiah Tattnall*, 64.
10. Arthur Winslow, *Francis Winslow, His Forebears and Life, Based upon Family Records and Correspondence during XXX Years*, 171.
11. Ibid., 171–72.
12. FB to James R. Harrison, 22 June 1847, quoted in Lewis, *Admiral Franklin Buchanan*, 119–20.
13. Winslow, *Francis Winslow*, 174.
14. Perry to Mason, 24 June 1847, Home Squadron Letters, NRC, RG 45, reel 5.
15. William Harwar Parker, *Recollections of a Naval Officer*, 122.
16. Ibid., 123.
17. FB to James R. Harrison, 22 June 1847, quoted in Lewis, *Admiral Franklin Buchanan*, 121.
18. Parker, *Recollections of a Naval Officer*, 124–25.
19. Logbook of the *Germantown*, 28 June and 2 August 1847, NRC, RG 45, NA.
20. Perry flew his flag in the *Germantown* from 9 August to 10 November 1847. Logbook of the *Germantown*, NRC, RG 45, NA; Perry to Mason, 11 January 1848, William Elliot Griffis Collection, Rutgers.
21. FB to Du Pont, 20 September 1849 (W9-5517), Du Pont Papers, Hagley.
22. FB to Du Pont, 20 September 1849 (W9-5517), 27 January 1851 (W9-6018), and 5 February 1851 (W9-6026), all in Du Pont Papers, Hagley.
23. FB to Du Pont, 8 November 1849 (W9-5563), Du Pont Papers, Hagley.
24. FB to Graham, 27 January 1852, Commander's Letters, NRC, RG 45, reel 43; Logbook of the *Susquehanna*, 10 November 1852 (USNA no. 18).
25. Aulick to Graham [Secretary of the Navy], 9 August 1851, *Susquehanna* Letter Book (no. 17), John H. Aulick Papers, USNA; Aulick to Dobbin, 4 August and 8 December 1853, Captain's Letters, NRC, RG 45, reel 351.
26. Graham to Aulick, 4 October and 18 November 1851, Confidential Letters,

NRC, RG 45, reel 2; FB to Graham, 27 January and 3 April 1852, Commander's Letters, NRC, RG 45, reel 43; Aulick to Marshall, 5 February 1853, *Susquehanna* Letter Book (no. 17), John H. Aulick Papers, USNA.

27. FB to Graham, 22 April and 24 July 1852, Commander's Letters, NRC, RG 45, reels 43 and 44; FB to Du Pont, 5 April 1852 (W9-6318), Du Pont Papers, Hagley.

28. FB to Du Pont, 10 March 1853 (W9-6661), Du Pont Papers, Hagley.

29. Aulick to Graham, 18 February 1852; and Aulick to Kennedy, 16 November 1852, both in *Susquehanna* Letter Book (no. 18), John H. Aulick Papers, USNA; FB to Du Pont, 10 March 1853 (W9-6661), Du Pont Papers, Hagley. Aulick was accused of impropriety for shipping as passengers both his own son and the chevalier de Macedo onboard the *Susquehanna*. For details of these accusations, see Aulick to Graham, 17 February 1852, *Susquehanna* Letter Book (no. 18), John H. Aulick Papers, USNA.

30. FB to Du Pont, 10 March 1853 (W9-6661), Du Pont Papers, Hagley; FB to Kennedy, 16 December 1852, Commander's Letters, NRC, RG 45, reel 44.

31. Aulick to Kennedy, 7 February 1853, *Susquehanna* Letter Book (USNA no. 18), John H. Aulick Papers, USNA; Logbook of the *Susquehanna*, 11 March 1853 (USNA no. 18); Aulick to Dobbin, 1 June 1853, Captain's Letters, NRC, RG 45, reel 351.

32. Curtis T. Henson, *Commissioners and Commodores: The East India Squadron and American Diplomacy in China*, 90; Morison, *"Old Bruin,"* 293–96. Perry blamed Kelley, not Buchanan, for giving in to Marshall's demands. See Perry to Kennedy, 9 April 1853, East India Squadron Letters, NRC, RG 45, reel 7.

33. Logbook of the *Susquehanna*, 23 May 1853 (USNA no. 18).

CHAPTER 7. THE MYSTERIOUS ORIENT

1. Perry's biographer suggests that Perry probably had a hand in drafting his own orders. See Morison, *"Old Bruin,"* 284. The text of the letter is printed in its entirety in Francis L. Hawks, *Narrative of the Expedition of an American Squadron to the China Seas and Japan*, 256–57.

2. Hawks, *Narrative*, 153.

3. Ibid., 155; Logbook of the *Susquehanna*, 28 May 1853 (USNA no. 18).

4. Logbook of the *Susquehanna*, 6 June 1853 (USNA no. 18).

5. Hawks, *Narrative*, 216.

6. Ibid., 217–18.

7. The storeship *Supply* was left behind at Naha. Logbook of the *Susquehanna*, 1 July 1853 (USNA no. 18).

8. Morison, *"Old Bruin,"* 377.

9. Hawks, *Narrative*, 234.

10. Ibid., 237. Morison attributes the American responses in this negotiation to Perry in his biography (*"Old Bruin,"* 326); but while Perry was unquestion

ably the overall commander and final decision maker, it is evident from the transcript that it was Buchanan who conducted the negotiations, and that he checked with Perry only when forced to yield on a point. See "Notes of a Conversation aboard the Susquehanna, Saturday, July 9, 1853," in FB to Dobbin, 3 March 1855, Commander's Letters, NRC, RG 25, reel 48. Throughout Buchanan's report, Kayama Eizaemon is referred to as "Yezaimon."

11. "Notes of a Conversation aboard the Susquehanna, Saturday, July 9, 1853," in FB to Dobbin, 3 March 1855, Commander's Letters, NRC, RG 45, reel 48.
12. Ibid.
13. Ibid., 11 July 1853.
14. Ibid., 12 July 1853 (afternoon).
15. Hawks, *Narrative,* 249.
16. "Report of Conversation between Capt. Buchanan, Capt. Adams, Captain of the Fleet, Lieut. Contee, Flag Lieutenant, and Yezaimon, Governor of Uraga, on Wednesday afternoon July 13th 1853," in FB to Dobbin, 3 March 1855, Commander's Letters, NRC, RG 45, reel 48.
17. Hawks, *Narrative,* 253–54.
18. Ibid., 255; "Report of the Conversation on Thursday morning, July 14th, after the Official Interview at Heori-kamma," in FB to Dobbin, 3 March 1855, Commander's Letters, NRC, RG 45, reel 48. This conversation is also printed in Hawks, *Narrative,* 263–64.
19. Morison, *"Old Bruin,"* 339–41.
20. Perry to Secretary of the Navy, 14 January 1854, East India Squadron Letters, NRC, RG 45, reel 8.
21. A description of the landing is in Perry to Dobbin, 20 March 1854, East India Squadron Letters, NRC, RG 45, reel 8. See also, Hawks, *Narrative,* 343–46.
22. The text of the Japanese response is printed in Hawks, *Narrative,* 349–50. A commercial treaty between the United States and Japan was secured four years later in 1858.
23. A list of the gifts brought by the Americans is provided in Hawks, *Narrative,* 356–57n.
24. Perry to FB, 20 March 1854, East India Squadron Letters, NRC, RG 45, reel 8.
25. Details of the *Susquehanna's* movements up the Yangtze are in Harris to FB, 5 June 1854, part of a packet of letters from FB to Dobbin, 3 March 1855, Commander's Letters, NRC, RG 45, reel 48. See also Henson, *Commissioners and Commodores,* 109–10.
26. FB to Commander of the Forces, 25 May 1854, and reply, 26 May 1854, both in Commander's Letters, NRC, RG 45, reel 48.
27. "A Mandatory Dispatch," 30 May 1854, Commander's Letters, NRC, RG 45, reel 48.

28. FB to Ministers of State at Nanking, 30 May 1854, Commander's Letters, NRC, RG 45, reel 48.

29. FB to Perry, 14 August 1854, Commander's Letters, NRC, RG 45, reel 48.

30. McLane to Perry, 2 September 1854, Commander's Letters, NRC, RG 45, reel 48.

31. FB to Dobbin, 8 January 1855, Commander's Letters, NRC, RG 45, reel 48.

32. Perry to FB, 2 February 1852, William Elliot Griffis Collection, Rutgers.

33. Christopher Adams, "Reform in Action: Discipline and the Perry Expedition."

34. Logbook of the *Susquehanna,* 4 October 1853, NRC, RG 24, NA.

35. Ibid., 3 September 1854.

36. Ibid., 5 September 1854.

37. Ibid.

38. The authority is Adams, "Reform in Action," 24. McLane's advice is in Bent to Perry, 1 September 1854, East India Squadron Letters, NRC, RG 45, reel 8.

39. Document dated 4 September 1854, contained in FB to Dobbin, 10 March 1855, Commander's Letters, NRC, RG 45, reel 48. Perry's letter is dated 5 September 1854 and is in East India Squadron Letters, NRC, RG 45, reel 8.

40. Document dated 4 September 1854, contained in FB to Dobbin, 10 March 1855, Commander's Letters, NRC, RG 45, reel 48.

Chapter 8. The Immortal Fifteen

1. FB to Du Pont, 7 March 1850 (W95690), and 11 March 1858 (W98841), both in Du Pont Papers, Hagley.

2. Joseph T. Durkin, *Stephen R. Mallory: Confederate Navy Chief,* 77. The statistics are taken from an address by Mallory to Congress on 15 May 1856: *Congressional Globe,* 34th Cong., 1st sess., 573.

3. FB to Du Pont, 8 September 1850 (W95888), and 15 September 1850 (W95896), both in Du Pont Papers, Hagley.

4. "An Act to Promote the Efficiency of the Navy," U.S. *Statutes at Large,* 28 February 1828, 32d–33d Cong., 1851–55, 10:616–17.

5. James Merrill, *Du Pont: The Making of an Admiral,* 218–19; Frances L. Williams, *Matthew Fontaine Maury, Scientist of the Sea,* 276.

6. *Congressional Globe,* 13 February 1856, 34th Cong., 1st sess., 399.

7. FB to Du Pont, 23 September 1855 (W9-7519), Du Pont Papers, Hagley.

8. Merrill, *Du Pont,* 220.

9. FB to Du Pont, 23 September 1855 (W9-7519), Du Pont Papers, Hagley.

10. Maury to Otey, 20 September 1855, in Jacquelin Ambler Caskie, *Life and Letters of Matthew Fontaine Maury,* 69–71.

11. Caskie, *Life and Letters of Matthew Fontaine Maury,* 62.

12. FB to Du Pont, 23 September 1855 (W9-7519), Du Pont Papers, Hagley.

13. Caskie, *Life and Letters of Matthew Fontaine Maury,* 62–63; Williams, *Matthew Fontaine Maury,* 280, 283.
14. FB to Du Pont, 24 December 1855 (W9-7627), Du Pont Papers, Hagley.
15. Ibid.
16. FB to Du Pont, 15 February 1856 (W9-7723), Du Pont Papers, Hagley.
17. *Congressional Globe,* 4 February 1856, 34th Cong., 1st sess., 346.
18. *Congressional Globe,* 13 March 1856, appendix, 242, 345. Houston sought to initiate an investigation of several members of the board, all of them Buchanan's allies, but not of Buchanan himself. See ibid., 502, 617–18.
19. FB to Du Pont, 30 March 1856 (W9-7813), Du Pont Papers, Hagley.
20. FB to Du Pont, 11 March 1858 (W9-8841), Du Pont Papers, Hagley.
21. FB to Du Pont, 14 September 1856 (W9-8032), and 18 January 1857 (W9-8157), both in Du Pont Papers, Hagley.
22. *Congressional Globe,* 12 January 1857, 34th Cong., 3d sess., 301–2; FB to Du Pont, 18 January 1857 (W9-8157), Du Pont Papers, Hagley.
23. FB to Du Pont, 22 February 1857 (W9-8196), Du Pont Papers, Hagley.
24. FB to Du Pont, 3 April 1857 (W9-8246), Du Pont Papers, Hagley.
25. The characterization of the Retirement Board as a Star Chamber seems to have originated with Maury (Maury to Otey, 21 September 55) and was picked up in the Senate debate by John J. Crittenden: *Congressional Globe,* 15 May 1856, 34th Cong., 1st sess., 585.
26. FB to Du Pont, 15 February 1856 (W9-7723), 3 April 1857 (W9-8246), both in Du Pont Papers, Hagley.
27. FB to Du Pont, 20 May 1857 (W9-8409), Du Pont Papers, Hagley.
28. Williams, *Matthew Fontaine Maury,* 308; FB to Du Pont, 11 March 1858 (W9-8841), Du Pont Papers, Hagley.
29. FB to Du Pont, 15 February 1856 (W9-7723), Du Pont Papers, Hagley.

CHAPTER 9. WAR CLOUDS

1. FB to Du Pont, 14 September 1856 (W9-8032), 4 August 1856 (W9-7992) both in Du Pont Papers, Hagley.
2. FB to Du Pont, 11 August 1852 (W9-6425), Du Pont Papers, Hagley.
3. Tilghman, *History of Talbot County,* 2:218.
4. FB to Du Pont, 9 July 1861 (W9-11002) (first passage), 14 September 1856 (W9-8032), both in Du Pont Papers, Hagley.
5. FB to Du Pont, 4 August 1856 (W9-7992), Du Pont Papers, Hagley.
6. Pierce's State of the Union message (2 December 1856) is in James D. Richardson, *A Compilation of the Messages and Papers of the Presidents,* 5:397–417. The quotation is from p. 409. Buchanan's reaction is in FB to Du Pont, 8 December 1856 (W9-8104), Du Pont Papers, Hagley.
7. Barbara Jeanne Fields, *Slavery and Freedom on the Middle Ground: Maryland during the Nineteenth Century.*

8. Tilghman, *History of Talbot County,* 1:213–17; David D. Porter, *The Naval History of the Civil War,* 27.

9. Fields, *Slavery and Freedom on the Middle Ground,* xi.

10. Ibid., 69.

11. FB to Du Pont, 11 March 1858 (W9-8841), Du Pont Papers, Hagley.

12. FB to Du Pont, 6 June 1859 (W9-9362), 9 July 1859 (W9-9438), both in Du Pont Papers, Hagley.

13. The 1860 vote in Talbot County is tabulated in Charles B. Clark, *The Eastern Shore of Maryland and Virginia,* 1:541.

14. FB to Du Pont, 26 December 1860 (W9-10583), Du Pont Papers, Hagley.

15. FB to Dahlgren, 8 January 1861, Navy Yard Letters, NRC, RG 45, NA; Buchanan's general order is dated 1 February 1861 and is in *ORN,* 4:413.

16. Lincoln's inaugural address is in *The Collected Works of Abraham Lincoln,* 4:265; Welles to FB, 30 March 1861; and FB to Welles, 6 April 1861, both in *ORN,* 4:228, 240.

17. Lewis, *Admiral Franklin Buchanan,* 163n; Robert Schneller, *A Quest for Glory: A Biography of Rear Admiral John A. Dahlgren,* 180.

18. The proclamation is dated 15 April 1861 and is in Lincoln, *Collected Works,* 4:332.

19. J. W. Forney to Welles, 20 April 1861; Welles to FB, 19 April 1861; Welles to Dahlgren, 19 April 1861, all in *ORN,* 4:416, 284.

20. FB to George Buchanan Coale (nephew), 29 May 1861, quoted in Lewis, *Admiral Franklin Buchanan,* 165.

21. FB to Welles, 4 May 1861, in Lewis, *Admiral Franklin Buchanan,* 164n; FB to Engle, 4 May 1861, published along with Engle's reply in the *New York Courier and Enquirer,* 21 May 1861.

22. FB to George Buchanan Coale, 29 May 1861, in Lewis, *Admiral Franklin Buchanan,* 167.

23. This scenario and the quotations on the next several pages are all from FB to Du Pont, 9 and 11 July 1861 (W9-11002), Du Pont Papers, Hagley.

CHAPTER 10. THE CONFEDERATE NAVY

1. FB to Du Pont, 11 July 1861 (W9-11002), Du Pont Letters, Hagley.

2. J. Thomas Scharf, *History of the Confederate States Navy,* 1:32–33; William S. Dudley, *Going South: U.S. Navy Officer Resignations & Dismissals on the Eve of the Civil War,* 12–19; William C. Davis, *"A Government of Our Own": The Making of the Confederacy,* 146.

3. Raphael Semmes, *Memoirs of Service Afloat,* 76.

4. See the table of officer resignations in Dudley, *Going South,* 34–55. Mayo's letter to Welles is quoted in ibid., 22.

5. FB to Welles, 4 May 1861, in the *Richmond Examiner,* 5 May 1863; FB to Du Pont, 11 July 1861 (W9-11002), Du Pont Letters, Hagley.

6. FB to Du Pont, 26 December 1860 (W9-10583), Du Pont Letters, Hagley; FB to Coale [his nephew], 29 May 1861, quoted in Lewis, *Admiral Franklin Buchanan*, 167. The evidence that Buchanan opened correspondence with Richmond authorities in August is circumstantial. He wrote Du Pont in July that he had *not* been in contact with Confederate authorities, but a month later Mary Chesnut recorded in her diary that she had "heard from Captain Buchanan." Since there is no evidence that she and Buchanan were friends, or even acquaintances, it is likely that the letter came not to Mary but to her husband, James Chesnut, who was an aide to Jefferson Davis. See Mary Chesnut, *Mary Chesnut's Civil War*, 146 (entry of 15 August 1861).

7. Lewis, *Admiral Franklin Buchanan*, 172n.

8. *Richmond Examiner*, 24 January 1862, quoted in Emory Thomas, *The Confederate State of Richmond: A Biography of the Capital*, 69.

9. Durkin, *Stephen R. Mallory*, 137.

10. Ibid., 136–39; Raimondo Luraghi, *A History of the Confederate Navy*, 1:13; William N. Still Jr., *Iron Afloat: The Story of the Confederate Ironclads*, 8.

11. Confederate Navy Regulations, quoted in Durkin, *Stephen R. Mallory*, 138.

12. James R. Soley, "The Union and Confederate Navies," *B&L*, 1:624; H. Ashton Ramsay, "Narrative," Subject File of the Confederate Navy, 1861–1865, NRC, RG 45, NA, reel 13.

13. Act of 21 April 1862, quoted in Scharf, *History of the Confederate States Navy*, 1:33–34; Dudley, *Going South*, 16–17; Ramsay, "Narrative," Subject File of the Confederate Navy, 1861–1865, NRC, RG 45, NA, reel 13.

14. Scharf, *History of the Confederate States Navy*, 1:33, 2:534–55; Soley, "The Union and Confederate Navies," *B&L*, 1:624.

15. FB to Tucker, 8 February 1862; Barney to FB, 16 December 1861; and FB to Tucker, 18 February 1862, all in *ORN*, 6:765, 752, 771–72.

16. The legislation authorizing letters of marque is printed in Scharf, *History of the Confederate States Navy*, 1:54–55.

17. Stephen R. Mallory Diary (4 September 1861), SHC, UNC.

18. Lee to Samuel Cooper, 21 November 1861, in Robert E. Lee, *The Wartime Papers of Robert E. Lee*, 87–88.

19. Mallory to his wife, 31 August 1862, Stephen Mallory Letters, P. K. Yonge Collection, University of Florida Library.

20. Scharf, *History of the Confederate States Navy*, 1:94–110.

21. Report of the [Confederate] Secretary of the Navy, 29 March 1862, Subject File of the C.S. Navy, 1861–1865, NRC, RG 45, NA, reel 8.

22. Scharf, *History of the Confederate States Navy*, 1:146–56; Luraghi, *History of the Confederate Navy*, 113–17; Still, *Iron Afloat*, 18–23.

23. Scharf, *History of the Confederate States Navy*, 1:152; Gene A. Smith, *Iron and Heavy Guns: Duel between the "Monitor" and "Merrimac,"* 31–32; Still, *Iron Afloat*, 20.

24. William R. Cline, "The Ironclad Ram *Virginia*," 244.

25. Luraghi, *History of the Confederate Navy,* 117; Mallory to Tucker, 2 March 1862, *ORN,* 6:779.

26. William C. Davis, *Jefferson Davis: The Man and His Hour,* 394; Thomas, *Confederate State of Richmond,* 77–79.

27. Mallory to FB, 24 February 1862, *ORN,* 6:776–77.

Chapter 11. Iron against Wood: The Battle of Hampton Roads

1. The quotation is from Eugenious Alexander Jack, *Memoirs of E. A. Jack, Steam Engineer,* css "Virginia," 14; the engineering characteristics are from Ramsay, "Narrative," Subject File of the Confederate Navy, 1861–1865, NRC, RG 45, NA, reel 13.

2. Mallory to FB, 24 February 1862, *ORN,* 6:776–77.

3. Ramsay, "Narrative," Subject File of the Confederate Navy, 1861–1865, NRC, RG 45, NA, reel 13; Wood, "First Fight of Ironclads," *B&L,* 1:694; John R. Eggleston, "Narrative of the Battle of the *Merrimac,*" 168.

4. The noted historian is William N. Still Jr. in *Iron Afloat,* p. 23.

5. Mallory to FB, 2 and 7 March 1862, *ORN,* 6:779, 780–81.

6. Catesby ap Roger Jones, "Services of the *Virginia,*" 67.

7. Parker, *Recollections,* 271; H. Ashton Ramsay, "Wonderful Career of the *Merrimac,*" 310.

8. Ramsay, "Wonderful Career," 311.

9. William Norris, "The Story of the Confederate States Ship 'Virginia,'" 205.

10. Parker, *Recollections,* 271–72; Richard Curtis, *History of the Famous Battle between the Iron-clad "Merrimac," C.S.N., and the Iron-clad "Monitor" and the "Cumberland" and "Congress" of the U.S. Navy,* 5.

11. Virginius Newton, "The *Merrimac* or *Virginia,*" 7; Parker, *Recollections,* 273; Eggleston, "Narrative," 169.

12. This text is an amalgam of the recollections of two witnesses to the event: Ramsay, "Wonderful Career," 310; and Cline, "The Ironclad Ram," 244. See also Eggleston, "Narrative," 170. One witness remembered it quite differently. Eugenius A. Jack, the third assistant engineer, recalled it this way: "I heard when I came to the command of this vessel aspersions upon my loyalty and doubts of my courage and zeal. I promise you that when this day's work is over, there will be no cause for suspicions" (*Memoirs of E. A. Jack,* 14). Very likely Jack confused Buchanan's address when he took command on 4 March with the one he gave while going into battle.

13. E. V. White, *The First IronClad Naval Engagement in the World,* 3; Curtis, *History of the Famous Battle,* 6.

14. Curtis, *History of the Famous Battle,* 6.

15. FB report, 27 March 1862, *ORN,* 7:44; Jones, "Services of the *Virginia,*" 68; Eggleston, "Narrative," 171.

16. Ramsay, "Wonderful Career," 310.

17. White, *First IronClad*, 3.

18. FB to Mallory, 27 March 1862, *ORN*, 7:44.

19. Parker claimed that the *Cumberland* went down "at 2:40 pm precisely" (*Recollections*, 275). See also Eggleston, "Narrative," 172.

20. FB to Mallory, 27 March 1862, *ORN*, 7:44.

21. Ibid.

22. Ramsay, "Wonderful Career," 311.

23. Curtis, *History of the Famous Battle*, 7.

24. Parker, *Recollections*, 276; Newton, "The *Merrimac*," 9.

25. Parker, *Recollections*, 276.

26. FB to Mallory, 27 March 1862, *ORN*, 7:45.

27. Lieutenant Eggleston rendered this passage as "Destroy that —— ship" ("Narrative," 173). Almost certainly the expletive deleted was the one offered here.

28. Jack, *Memoirs of E. A. Jack*, 14; Eggleston, "Narrative," 173.

29. Jones, "Services of the *Virginia*," 70; Phillips to Jones, 8 March 1862, *ORN*, 7:42; Curtis, *History of the Famous Battle*, 8.

30. FB to Mallory, 27 March 1862, *ORN*, 7:44.

31. Ramsay, "Wonderful Career," 311.

32. Pendergrast to Marston, 9 March 1862, *ORN*, 7:24. Losses on the *Congress* were almost exactly the same as those on the *Cumberland*: 120.

33. Jack, *Memoirs of E. A. Jack*, 16; FB to Mallory, 27 March 1862, *ORN*, 7:45–46; Eggleston, "Narrative," 173.

34. Jones, "Services of the *Virginia*," 71; FB to Mallory, 27 March 1862, *ORN*, 7:46.

35. R. Thomas Campbell, *Gray Thunder: Exploits of the Confederate States Navy*, 41–57; William C. Davis, *Duel between the First Ironclads*, 116–137; Smith, *Iron and Heavy Guns*, 74–91.

Chapter 12. Confederate Admiral

1. FB to Tucker, 14 March 1862; and FB to Mallory, 25 March 1862, both in *ORN*, 7:56–57. The congressional resolution is dated 12 March 1862, and is in *ORN*, 7:62.

2. Tattnall to Buchanan, 12 March 1862, *ORN*, 7:57–58.

3. FB to Mallory, 27 March 1862, *ORN*, 7:44–49.

4. FB to Mallory, 27 March 1862, Buchanan Letter Book, SHC, UNC.

5. Mallory to Davis, 7 April 1862, *ORN*, 7:43; FB to Mallory, 21 and 28 April 1862, both in Buchanan Letter Book, SHC, UNC.

6. George Minor to Robert Minor, 18 March 1862, Minor Family Papers, VHS; John T. Wood to his wife, 13 April 1862, John Taylor Wood Papers, SHC, UNC; FB to J. S. B. Dorsey, 21 April 1862, Buchanan Letter Book, SHC, UNC.

7. Mallory to Smith Lee, 3 May 1862, *ORN*, 11:783; FB to Mallory, 10 and 26 May 1862, both in Buchanan Letter Book, SHC, UNC.

8. FB to Forrest, 3 June 1862, Buchanan Letter Book, SHC, UNC.

9. Court finding, 11 June 1862, *ORN*, 7:787–88.

10. FB to Jones, 19 June 1862, *ORN*, 7:788–89.

11. The charges against Tattnall are in *ORN*, 7:791; Tattnall's testimony is on pp. 791–98.

12. Ibid.

13. Wood to his wife, 21 August 1862, John Taylor Wood Papers, SHC, UNC; *Richmond Examiner*, 22 August 1862.

14. Mallory to Davis, 19 August 1862, *ORN*, 7:62.

15. Arthur Bergeron, *Confederate Mobile*, 4. The quotation is from William Howard Russell, *My Diary North and South*, 108.

16. Bergeron, *Confederate Mobile*, 4–5; Earl W. Fornell, "Mobile during the Blockade," 29–43.

17. Bergeron, *Confederate Mobile*, 31–33; FB to Mallory, 26 September 1862, Buchanan Letter Book, SHC, UNC.

18. Emma M. Maffitt, "The Confederate Navy," 264–67.

19. FB to Mallory, 8 September 1862, Buchanan Letter Book, SHC, UNC.

20. FB to Maffitt, 13 September 1862, Buchanan Letter Book, SHC, UNC.

21. Journal of J. N. Maffitt, 30 December 1862, *ORN*, 1:769.

22. Bergeron, *Confederate Mobile*, 69–70; FB to Mallory, 1 January 1863, Buchanan Letter Book, SHC, UNC.

23. Frank Owsley Jr., *The C.S.S "Florida": Her Building and Operations*; Maffitt, "The Confederate Navy," 315–16.

24. Luraghi, *History of the Confederate Navy*, 280; FB to Mallory, 12 September 1862, Buchanan Letter Book, SHC, UNC.

25. FB to Mitchell, 2 and 5 April 1863, Buchanan Letters, VHS; General Order, 17 April 1863, Buchanan Letter Book, SHC, UNC.

26. FB to Forrest, 27 October 1862; and FB to Mallory, 7 January 1863, both in Buchanan Letter Book; FB to Mitchell, 5 April 1863, Buchanan Letters, VHS (italics in original).

27. FB to Mitchell, 2 April and 22 June 1863, Buchanan Letters, VHS.

28. Scharf, *History of the Confederate States Navy*, 2:550; Luraghi, *History of the Confederate Navy*, 38–39; William N. Still Jr., *Confederate Shipbuilding*, 47.

29. Luraghi, *History of the Confederate Navy*, 280–83; William N. Still Jr., "Selma and the C.S. Navy," 19–37.

30. FB to Farrand, 15 October 1862, Buchanan Letter Book, SHC, UNC.

31. FB to Johnston, 24 October 1862; and FB to Farrand, 26 November 1862, both in Buchanan Letter Book, SHC, UNC. There were only three iron-rolling mills in the Confederacy capable of producing the kind of armor plate that Buchanan needed: the Tredegar Works in Richmond, the Atlanta Rolling Mill (formerly Schofield & Markham), and the Shelby Works in Columbiana, Alabama.

32. FB to Mallory, 26 February 1863, Buchanan Letter Book, SHC, UNC; Still, "Selma and the C.S. Navy," 27–28; Luraghi, *History of the Confederate Navy,* 42–43.

33. FB to Colin McRae, 3 December 1862, Buchanan Letter Book, SHC, UNC; Luraghi, *History of the Confederate Navy,* 44–45.

34. Luraghi, *History of the Confederate Navy,* 26.

35. FB to Seddon, 15 December 1862; FB to Forrest, 19 December 1862; and FB to Mallory, 6 April 1863, all in Buchanan Letter Book, SHC, UNC; FB to Mitchell, 2 April 1863, Buchanan Letters, VHS (italics in original); Stephen Mallory Diary, 1 August 1861, SHC, UNC.

36. FB to Mrs. J. W. Harris, 10 and 25 October 1862, Papers of Mrs. J. W. Harris, MOC; FB to Shorter, 3 December 1862; and FB to Mallory, 14 February 1863, both in Buchanan Letter Book, SHC, UNC.

37. Luraghi, *History of the Confederate Navy,* 252–54; FB to Mallory, 14 February 1863, Buchanan Letter Book, SHC, UNC.

38. FB to Edward Lloyd, 25 December 1862, Lloyd Papers, reel 18, MHS.

Chapter 13. The CSS *Tennessee*

1. FB to Jones, 14 May 1863, *ORN,* 7:63.

2. FB to Mallory, 6 April and 13 May 1863, both in Buchanan Letter Book, SHC, UNC.

3. Still, *Iron Afloat,* 195.

4. Still, "Selma and the Confederate Navy," 19–37; Still, *Iron Afloat,* 192–93; Luraghi, *History of the Confederate Navy,* 282–83.

5. Scharf, *History of the Confederate States Navy,* 2:553–55; Still, *Confederate Shipbuilding,* 59.

6. Scharf, *History of the Confederate States Navy,* 2:553–55; FB to Mallory, 6 April 1863, Buchanan Letter Book, SHC, UNC.

7. Fox to Rowan, 6 April 1863; Farragut to Bailey, 22 April 1863; and Farragut to Goldsborough, 21 May 1863, all in *ORN,* 20:123, 157, 206.

8. FB to Mallory, 20 September 1863, Buchanan Letter Book, SHC, UNC.

9. FB to Mallory, 8 June 1863, Buchanan Letter Book, SHC, UNC; FB to Jones, 7 May 1863, *ORN,* 21:896–97; FB to Mitchell, 5 and 22 June, and 5 July 1863, all in Buchanan Letters, VHS.

10. FB to Mitchell, 22 June 1863, Buchanan Letters, VHS.

11. FB to Mallory, 20 September 1863, Buchanan Letter Book, SHC, UNC.

12. FB to Mitchell, 5 July 1863, Buchanan Letters, VHS; FB to Mallory, 31 August and 20 September 1863, Buchanan Letter Book, SHC, UNC.

13. FB to Mallory, 22 January 1863, Buchanan Letter Book, SHC, UNC.

14. FB to Forrest, 3 February 1863, Buchanan Letter Book, SHC, UNC (italics in original).

15. FB to Forrest, 24 February 1863, Buchanan Letter Book, SHC, UNC.

16. FB to Welles, 4 May 1861, in *Richmond Examiner*, 5 May 1863; FB to Coale, 29 May 1861, in Lewis, *Admiral Franklin Buchanan*, 166.

17. *Richmond Examiner*, 18 May 1863; FB to Mitchell, 5 June 1863, Buchanan Letters, VHS.

18. FB to Mitchell, 2 April 1863, Buchanan Letters, VHS. The James River Squadron saw no action during Forrest's tenure of command.

19. FB to Mitchell, 5 June 1863, Buchanan Letters, VHS.

20. FB to Mitchell, 5 July and 2 December 1863, Buchanan Letters, VHS.

21. FB to Jones, 14 May 1863, *ORN*, 7:63; FB to Mallory, 6 November 1863, Buchanan Letter Book, SHC, UNC.

22. FB to Mallory, 6 November 1863; and FB to Swain, 9 November 1863, both in Buchanan Letter Book, SHC, UNC; FB to Mitchell, 17 October 1863, Buchanan Letters, VHS.

23. FB to Jones, 15 December 1863, *ORN*, 20:856.

24. FB to Jones, 21 December 1863; Jones to FB, 24 December 1863, both in *ORN*, 20:858.

25. FB to Mallory, various letters in May and June 1863, all in Buchanan Letter Book, SHC, UNC; FB to Mitchell, 5 April 1863, Buchanan Letters, VHS.

26. FB to Mitchell, 5 June 1863, Buchanan Letters, VHS.

27. FB to Mallory, 16 July, 28 September, and 23 October 1863, all in Buchanan Letter Book, SHC, UNC; Seddon to Maury, 23 February 1864, *ORN*, 21:879.

28. "Descriptive List of the Crew of the Confederate States Steamer *Tennessee*," no date, MOC; FB to Mitchell, 17 October 1863, Buchanan Letters, VHS.

29. FB to Mitchell, 11 March 1863, Buchanan Letters, VHS.

30. Simms to Jones, 5 March 1864, *ORN*, 21:881; FB to Mitchell, 11 March 1864, Buchanan Letters, VHS.

31. Eggleston to Jones, 7 March 1864; FB to Jones, 24 March 1864, both in *ORN*, 21:883, 885; FB to Mitchell, 11 March 1864, Buchanan Letters, VHS.

32. FB to Jones, 14 April and 7 May 1864, both in *ORN*, 21:892, 896.

33. "Journal of Mr. John C. O'Connell, CSN," in *Two Naval Journals: 1864*, ed. C. Carter Smith Jr., 2 [hereafter cited as O'Connell diary]; FB to Jones, 14 April 1864, *ORN*, 21:892.

34. FB to Mitchell, 13 March 1864, Buchanan Letters, VHS.

Chapter 14. The Battle of Mobile Bay

1. Davis to FB, 19 February 1864, in Jefferson Davis, *Jefferson Davis, Constitutionalist: His Letters, Papers and Speeches*, 6:181–82.

2. O'Connell diary, 22 May 1864, 2.

3. Ibid., 23 May 1864, 2.

4. Ibid., 23 and 24 May 1864, 2–3.

5. Ibid., 24 and 25 May 1864, 2–3; abstract log of the *Tennessee*, *ORN*, 21:934–35; Robert Tarleton to Sallie Lightfoot, 27 May 1864, Tarleton Papers, Yale.

6. Tarleton to Lightfoot, 27 May 1864, Tarleton Papers, Yale.

7. This telegram has not been found, but its content is evident in several contemporary sources, including Tarleton to Lightfoot, 27 May 1864, Tarleton Papers, Yale; and the O'Connell diary, 24 May 1864, 3.

8. Page to Jones, 26 June 1864, *ORN*, 21:903–4.

9. Maury to Cooper, 5 July 1864; and FB to Johnston, 20 July 1864, both in *ORN*, 21:904, 907.

10. Daniel B. Conrad, "Capture of the C.S. Ram *Tennessee* in Mobile Bay, August, 1864," 72.

11. Ibid.; FB to Mitchell, 26 January 64, Buchanan Letters, VHS (italics in original); Page to Jones, 26 June 1864, *ORN*, 21:903–4.

12. Tarleton to Lightfoot, 4 August 1864, Tarleton Papers, Yale.

13. Scharf, *History of the Confederate States Navy*, 2:560n; R. Thomas Campbell, *Southern Thunder: Exploits of the Confederate States Navy*, 134–58; Chester Hearn, *Mobile Bay and the Mobile Campaign: The Last Great Battles of the Civil War*, 100–20.

14. James D. Johnston, "The Ram *Tennessee* at Mobile Bay," *B&L*, 4:402; Conrad, "Capture of the Ram *Tennessee*," 72–73.

15. Conrad, "Capture of the Ram *Tennessee*," 73; Farragut to Welles, 12 August 1864, *ORN*, 21:416.

16. Johnston, "The Ram *Tennessee*," *B&L*, 4:402; Foxhall A. Parker, "The Battle of Mobile Bay," 227–28; Hearn, *Mobile Bay and the Mobile Campaign*, 87–89; Scharf, *History of the Confederate States Navy*, 2:560n. Raimondo Luraghi argues that the *Tecumseh* was driven off course and into the minefield by gunfire from Fort Morgan. See Luraghi, *History of the Confederate Navy*, 452 (67n).

17. Alden to Farragut, 6 August 1864, *ORN*, 21:445.

18. As the *Hartford* passed the *Brooklyn*, Alden supposedly warned Farragut about the torpedoes in the water ahead, to which Farragut is supposed to have replied: "Damn the torpedoes." See the discussion of this incident in Charles Lee Lewis, *David Glasgow Farragut*, 469–70 (n. 40).

19. Johnston, "The Ram *Tennessee*," *B&L*, 4:402.

20. "Hav" to his mother; 6 August 1864, Collection of Nancy Lloyd (private).

21. Mullany to Farragut, 15 December 1864, *ORN*, 21:485–87. At least some of the damage to the *Oneida* was the result of gunfire from the *Morgan*.

22. FB to Mallory, 25 August 1864, *ORN*, 21:576–77.

23. Conrad, "Capture of the Ram *Tennessee*," 74.

24. Ibid., 80; FB to Mallory, 25 August 1864, *ORN*, 21:577.

25. Conrad, "Capture of the Ram *Tennessee*," 75; O'Connell diary, 5.

26. Hearn, *Mobile Bay and the Mobile Campaign*, 103; Conrad, "Capture of the Ram *Tennessee*," 75–76.

27. Conrad, "Capture of the Ram *Tennessee*," 76.

28. Marchand to Farragut, 5 August 1864, *ORN*, 21:466; Conrad, "Capture of the Ram *Tennessee*," 77; Hearn, *Mobile Bay and the Mobile Campaign*, 103–5.

29. Drayton to Farragut, 6 August 1864, *ORN*, 21:426; Hearn, *Mobile Bay and the Mobile Campaign*, 105; Clarence E. McCartney, *Mr. Lincoln's Admirals*, 72.

30. Parker, "The Battle of Mobile Bay," 35.

31. Perkins to Farragut, 13 October 1864, *ORN*, 21:681; Conrad, "Capture of the Ram *Tennessee*," 77.

32. Conrad, "Capture of the Ram *Tennessee*," 77–78.

33. Johnston to Buchanan, 13 August 1864, *ORN*, 21:580; O'Connell diary, 6.

34. Ibid.

35. Conrad, "Capture of the Ram *Tennessee*," 78–79.

36. Ibid.; Scharf, *History of the Confederate States Navy*, 2:571–72.

CHAPTER 15. HOME FROM THE SEA

1. Journal of John B. Marchand, *ORN*, 21:820; Farragut to Granger, 6 August 1864 (7:30 A.M.), *ORN*, 21:515.

2. Farragut to Welles, 4 September 1864, *ORN*, 21:544.

3. FB to Maury, 10 August 1864, quoted in Lewis, *Admiral Franklin Buchanan*, 247.

4. Jacob Palmer to Nannie Buchanan, 8 December 1864, Buchanan Family Papers, SHC, UNC.

5. FB to Elizabeth Buchanan, 8 January 1865, quoted in Lewis, *Admiral Franklin Buchanan*, 249.

6. Ibid.

7. Welles to Farragut, 6 September 1864, *ORN*, 21:627.

8. Grant to Stanton, 15 February 1865, *OR*, 8:226.

9. Hoffman to Canby, 14 March 1865, and Dwight to S. P. Lee, 7 March 1865, both in *OR*, 8:342, 365.

10. Bergeron, *Confederate Mobile*, 190.

11. Scharf, *History of the Confederate States Navy*, 2:595; Lise Mitchell Journal, 13 May 1865, Tulane.

12. Lewis, *Admiral Franklin Buchanan*, 251–52.

13. "Down the Eastern Shore," *Harper's* 43 (October 1871): 706; Charles Wagandt, "Redemption or Reaction? Maryland in the Post–Civil War Years," 146.

14. Wagandt, "Redemption or Reaction?" 155n.

15. Robert J. Brugger, *Maryland: A Middle Temperament*, 307–8; W. E. B. Du Bois, *Black Reconstruction in America*, 564.

16. Wagandt, "Redemption or Reaction?" 187.

17. FB to Tucker, 20 February 1868, Tucker Family Papers, SHC, UNC; *Easton Journal*, 19 November 1868, quoted in Lewis, *Admiral Franklin Buchanan*, 254.

18. Lewis, *Admiral Franklin Buchanan*, 252.
19. George H. Callcott, *A History of the University of Maryland*, 163.
20. Resolution quoted in ibid., 176.
21. FB to George Hughes, 8 August 1869, Simon Gratz Collection, HSP; Callcott, *History of the University of Maryland*, 178.
22. FB to Hughes, 8 August 1869, Simon Gratz Collection, HSP; Tilghman, *History of Talbot County*, 1:592.
23. FB to Hughes, 8 August 1869, Simon Gratz Collection, HSP.
24. Ibid.
25. Ibid.
26. Resolution signed by Robert W. Smith, M. G. Hudson, and W. L. Baker: clipping in the Buchanan Family Papers, SHC, UNC.
27. "Down the Eastern Shore," 706.
28. Tilghman, *History of Talbot County*, 1:592; FB to J. W. C. Powell, 29 April 1874, Simon Gratz Collection, HSP.

~➤ Bibliography ~➤

MANUSCRIPTS
Eleanor S. Brokenbrough Library, The Museum of the Confederacy, Richmond,
Virginia
  Papers of Mrs. J. W. Harris
  Descriptive List, Crew of CSS *Tennessee*
  Miscellaneous Navy Collection
Hagley Museum and Library, Wilmington, Delaware
  Logbook of the USS *Franklin*
  Samuel Francis Du Pont Papers
Historical Society of Pennsylvania, Philadelphia
  Dreer Collection, American Navy
  Elting Papers, Navy
  Simon Gratz Collection
  McKean Family Papers
Lloyd Family Collection (privately held), Wye House, Maryland
  Lloyd Family Letters
Maryland Historical Society, Baltimore
  Album of clippings kept by K. R. Owen
  Lloyd Family Collection
  Regulations for the Government of U.S.S. *Susquehanna*, 1853
Maryland State Archives, Annapolis
  Land Records, Talbot County, Maryland
National Archives, Washington, D.C.
  Record Group 24:
    Logbook of the USS *Susquehanna*, 1853–54
  Record Group 45:
    Letters Received by the Secretary of the Navy from Captains, 1805–61 and
      1866–85 (Captain's Letters)
    Letters Received by the Secretary of the Navy from Commanders, 1804–86
      (Commander's Letters)
    Letters Received by the Secretary of the Navy from Commanding Officers,
      East India Squadron, 1841–61 (East India Squadron Letters)

Letters Received by the Secretary of the Navy from Commanding Officers, Home Squadron, 1842–61 (Home Squadron Letters)

Letters Received by the Secretary of the Navy from Officers, 1802–86 (Officer's Letters)

Letters Sent by the Commandant, Washington Navy Yard: Naval Shore Establishment, 1814–1911 (Navy Yard Letters)

Logbook of the USS *Germantown*, 1847–48

Miscellaneous Letters Received by the Secretary of the Navy, 1801–84 (Miscellaneous Letters)

Miscellaneous Letters Sent by the Secretary of the Navy, 1798–1886 (Secretary's Letters)

Subject File of the Confederate States Navy, 1861–65

Rutgers University Libraries (State University of New Jersey)

William Elliot Griffis Collection (Perry-Buchanan Letters)

Southern Historical Collection, University of North Carolina, Chapel Hill

Buchanan Family Papers, 1801–1913

Franklin Buchanan Letter Book, 1862–63

Franklin Buchanan Log Book, 1829–34

Stephen R. Mallory Diary

William Porcher Miles Papers, 1860

Tucker Family Papers, 1868

John Taylor Wood Diary

John Taylor Wood Papers, 1861–65

Talbot County Library, Easton, Maryland

Samuel A. Harrison Collection

James C. Mulliken Collection

Tulane University, New Orleans, Louisiana

Lise Mitchell Journal

United States Naval Academy Special Collections, Nimitz Library, Annapolis, Maryland

John H. Aulick Papers

Susquehanna Letter Book (vols. 17 and 18)

Cruise journals kept by Buchanan (in chronological order):

Java (USNA no. 5) 26 January–3 March 1817

Franklin (USNA no. 2) 23 August 1818–21 April 1820

Dorothea (USNA no. 5) 7 April 1821–10 June 1922

Weasel (USNA no. 31) 15–28 February 1823

Hornet (USNA no. 31) 30 July 1824–22 February 1825

Baltimore (USNA no. 6) 30 October 1826–5 January 1827

Ruth (USNA no.6) 9 February 1827–2 April 1827

Natchez (USNA nos. 5 and 31) 2 July 1827–24 November 1828 (The rough log in no. 5 is copied in a fair hand in no. 31.)

Vincennes (USNA no. 31) 17 December 1842–15 August 1844

Cruise journals kept by others:
 Susquehanna (USNA no. 18) 25 December 1850–24 September 1852 (kept by
  Passed Midn. Frederick A. Boardman)
 Letter books kept by Buchanan
  Vincennes (USNA no. 30) 12 December 1842–13 August 1844
 Other Buchanan notebooks
  Rigging Tables (USNA no. 47) 1834
  Instructions Regarding Salutes (USNA no. 71) 1838
Virginia Historical Society, Richmond
 John Yates Beall Papers
 Franklin Buchanan Letters
 Elizabeth Byrd Nicholas Papers
 Minor Family Papers
 John Kirkwood Mitchell Papers
Yale University Library
 Tarleton Papers
P. K. Yonge Collection, University of Florida Library, Gainesville
 Stephen R. Mallory Letters

NEWSPAPERS
American and Daily Commercial Advertiser (Baltimore)
Easton Star, Easton, Maryland
Evening Capital, Annapolis, Maryland
Gazette, Annapolis, Maryland
Gazette, Easton, Maryland
New York Herald
New York Journal
Richmond Examiner

PUBLISHED AND UNPUBLISHED WORKS
Adams, Christopher. "Reform in Action: Discipline and the Perry Expedition."
 Undergraduate honors thesis, U.S. Naval Academy, 1996.
Allen, Gardner. *Our Navy and the Barbary Corsairs.* Hamden, Conn.: Archon
 Books, 1905, 1965.
*American State Papers, Documents, Legislative and Executive of the Congress of
 the United States.* Class VI: *Naval Affairs.* 4 vols. Washington, D.C.: Gales
 & Seaton, 1832.
Ammen, Daniel. *The Old Navy and the New: Memoirs of Rear Admiral Daniel
 Ammen, U.S.N.* Philadelphia: J. B. Lippincott, 1898.
Anderson, Bern. *By Sea and by River: The Naval History of the Civil War.* New
 York: Knopf, 1962.
Battles and Leaders of the Civil War. 4 vols. New York: Century Magazine, 1888.

Bauer, K. Jack. *Surfboats and Horse Marines: U.S. Naval Operations in the Mexican War, 1846–48*. Annapolis: Naval Institute Press, 1969.

———. *The War with Mexico, 1846–1848*. New York: Macmillan, 1974.

Bergeron, Arthur. *Confederate Mobile*. Jackson: University Press of Mississippi, 1991.

Brugger, Robert J. *Maryland: A Middle Temperament, 1634–1980*. Baltimore: Johns Hopkins University Press, 1988.

Buchanan, Roberdeau. *Genealogy of the McKean Family of Pennsylvania*. Lancaster, Pa.: Inquirer Printing, 1890.

Callcott, George H. *A History of the University of Maryland*. Baltimore: Maryland Historical Society, 1966.

Campbell, R. Thomas. *Gray Thunder: Exploits of the Confederate States Navy*. Shippensburg, Pa.: Burd Street Press, 1996.

———. *Southern Thunder: Exploits of the Confederate States Navy*. Shippensburg, Pa.: Burd Street Press, 1996.

Caskie, Jaquelin Ambler. *Life and Letters of Matthew Fontaine Maury*. Richmond, Va.: Richmond Press, Inc., 1928.

Chesnut, Mary. *Mary Chesnut's Civil War*. Edited by C. Vann Woodward. New Haven: Yale University Press, 1982.

Clark, Charles B. *The Eastern Shore of Maryland and Virginia*. New York: Lewis Historical Publishing Company, 1950.

Cline, William R. "The Ironclad Ram *Virginia*." *Southern Historical Society Proceedings* 32 (1904): 243–49.

Conrad, Daniel B. "Capture of the C.S. Ram *Tennessee* in Mobile Bay, August, 1864." *Southern Historical Society Papers* 19 (1891): 72–82.

Coski, John M. *Capital Navy: The Men, Ships, and Operations of the James River Squadron*. Campbell, Calif.: Savas Woodbury, 1996.

Curtis, Richard. *History of the Famous Battle between the Iron-clad "Merrimac," C.S.N., and the Iron-clad "Monitor" and the "Cumberland" and "Congress" of the U.S. Navy*. Norfolk: S. B. Turner & Son, 1907.

Dahlgren, Madeleine V. *Memoir of John A. Dahlgren*. New York: Charles L. Webster, 1891.

Davis, Jefferson. *Jefferson Davis, Constitutionalist: His Letters, Papers and Speeches*. 8 vols. Edited by Dunbar Rowland. Jackson: Mississippi Department of Archives and History, 1923.

Davis, William C. *Duel between the First Ironclads*. Baton Rouge: Louisiana State University Press, 1975.

———. *"A Government of Our Own": The Making of the Confederacy*. New York: Free Press, 1994.

———. *Jefferson Davis: The Man and His Hour*. New York: Harper Collins, 1991.

Dictionary of American Naval Fighting Ships. Washington, D.C.: Naval History Division, 1968.

Douglass, Frederick. *Life and Times of Frederick Douglass.* 1892. Reprint, New York: Macmillan, 1962.

"Down the Eastern Shore." *Harper's* 43 (October 1871): 702–8.

Du Bois, W. E. B. *Black Reconstruction in America.* 1935. Reprint, New York: Russell & Russell, 1966.

Dudley, William S. *Going South: U.S. Navy Officer Resignations & Dismissals on the Eve of the Civil War.* Washington, D.C.: Naval Historical Foundation, 1981.

Durkin, Joseph T. *Stephen R. Mallory: Confederate Navy Chief.* Chapel Hill: University of North Carolina Press, 1954.

Eggleston, John R. "Narrative of the Battle of the *Merrimac.*" *Southern Historical Society Proceedings* 41 (1916): 166–78.

Eisenhower, John S. D. *So Far from God: The U.S. War with Mexico, 1846–1848.* New York: Random House, 1989.

Fields, Barbara Jeanne. *Slavery and Freedom on the Middle Ground: Maryland during the Nineteenth Century.* New Haven: Yale University Press, 1985.

Ford, Thomas G. "History of the Naval Academy." Unpublished manuscript in Special Collections of Nimitz Library, USNA (1887).

Fornell, Earl W. "Mobile during the Blockade." *Alabama Historical Quarterly* 23 (Spring 1961): 29–43.

Gardner, Robert, ed. *Conway's History of the Ship: Steam, Steel, & Shellfire, the Steam Warship, 1815–1905.* Annapolis: Naval Institute Press, 1992.

Guy, Anita A. *Maryland's Persistant Pursuit to End Slavery, 1850–1864.* New York: Garland, 1997.

Hawks, Francis L. *Narrative of the Expedition of an American Squadron to the China Seas and Japan.* Washington, D.C.: Congress of the United States, 1856.

Hearn, Chester. *Mobile Bay and the Mobile Campaign: The Last Great Battles of the Civil War.* Jefferson, N.C.: McFarland, 1993.

Henson, Curtis T. *Commissioners and Commodores: The East India Squadron and American Diplomacy in China.* University: University of Alabama Press, 1982.

——. "The United States Navy and China, 1839–1861." Ph.D. diss., Tulane University, 1965.

Hoehling, A. A. *Thunder at Hampton Roads: The U.S.S. "Monitor"—Its Battle with the "Merrimack" and Its Recent Discovery.* New York: Da Capo Press, 1976, 1993.

Jack, Eugenius A. *Memoirs of E. A. Jack, Steam Engineer, CSS "Virginia."* White Stone, Va.: Brandywine, 1998.

Jones, Catesby ap Roger. "The Iron-Clad Virginia." *Virginia Magazine of History and Biography* 49 (October 1941): 297–303.

——. "Services of the *Virginia.*" *Southern Historical Society Proceedings* 11 (1883): 65–75.

Jones, Charles C. Jr. *The Life and Services of Commodore Josiah Tattnall.* Savannah: Morning News Steam Printing Office, 1878.

Lee, Robert E. *The Wartime Papers of Robert E. Lee.* Edited by Clifford Dowdy. New York: Da Capo Press, 1961.

Lewis, Charles Lee. "Admiral Franklin Buchanan." *Confederate Veteran* 37 (1929): 414–19.

——. *Admiral Franklin Buchanan, Fearless Man of Action.* Baltimore: Norman Remington, 1929.

——. *David Glasgow Farragut.* Annapolis: Naval Institute Press, 1943.

Lincoln, Abraham. *The Collected Works of Abraham Lincoln.* 8 vols. Edited by Roy S. Basler. New Brunswick: Rutgers University Press, 1953–68.

Luraghi, Raimondo. *A History of the Confederate Navy.* Annapolis: Naval Institute Press, 1996.

Mackenzie, Alexander Slidell. *The Life of Commodore Oliver Hazard Perry.* New York: Harper & Brothers, 1840.

Maffitt, Emma M. "The Confederate Navy." *Confederate Veteran* 25 (1917): 315–17.

Magruder, P. H. "A Walk through the Naval Academy in Bygone Days and Today." *U.S. Naval Institute Proceedings* 58 (May 1932): 673–84.

McCartney, Clarence E. *Mr. Lincoln's Admirals.* New York: Funk & Wagnalls, 1956.

McKean, Cornelius. *McKean Genealogies for the Early Settlement of McKeens or McKeans in America to the Present Time.* Perry, Iowa: Kenyon Printing, 1902.

McKee, Christopher. *A Gentlemanly and Honorable Profession: The Creation of the Naval Officer Corps, 1794–1815.* Annapolis: Naval Institute Press, 1991.

[Mercier, Henry James]. *Life in a Man-of-War, or Scenes in "Old Ironsides" during Her Cruise in the Pacific.* Boston: Houghton Mifflin, 1927.

Merrill, James M. *Du Pont: The Making of an Admiral.* New York: Dodd Mead, 1986.

Morison, Samuel E. *"Old Bruin": Commodore Matthew Calbraith Perry.* Boston: Little, Brown, 1967.

Newton, Virginius. "The *Merrimac* or *Virginia.*" *Southern Historical Society Proceedings* 20 (1892): 1–26.

Norris, William. "The Story of the Confederate States Ship 'Virginia' (Once Merrimac)." *Southern Historical Society Proceedings* 42 (1917): 204–33.

Owsley, Frank Jr. *The C.S.S. "Florida": Her Building and Operations.* Philadelphia: University of Pennsylvania Press, 1965.

Parker, Foxhall A. "The Battle of Mobile Bay." *Papers of the Military Historical Society of Massachusetts* 12 (1902): 211–43.

Parker, William Harwar. *Recollections of a Naval Officer* [1883]. Edited by Craig L. Symonds. Annapolis: Naval Institute Press, 1985.

Paul, A. B. *Despot's Heel on Talbot.* Easton, Md.: A. B. Paul, 1966.

Paullin, Charles O. "Beginnings of the United States Naval Academy." *U.S. Naval Institute Proceedings* 50 (February 1924): 173–94.

Porter, David D. *Memoir of Commodore Porter of the United States Navy.* Albany: J. Munsell, 1875.

———. *The Naval History of the Civil War.* New York: Scribner's, 1886.

Ramsay, H. Aston [*sic*]. "Wonderful Career of the *Merrimac.*" *Confederate Veteran* 15 (1907): 310–13.

Richardson, James D. *A Compilation of the Messages and Papers of the Presidents, 1789–1897.* 10 vols. Washington, D.C.: U.S. Government Printing Office, 1897.

Rix, William. *Life in a Southern City during the War.* Royalton, Vt.: privately printed, n.d. [ca. 1880].

Russell, William Howard. *My Diary North and South.* 1863. Reprint, New York: Harper & Row, 1961.

Scharf, J. Thomas. *History of the Confederate States Navy.* 2 vols. 1887. Reprint, Salem, N.H.: Ayer Company, 1988.

Schneller, Robert. *A Quest for Glory: A Biography of Rear Admiral John A. Dahlgren.* Annapolis: Naval Institute Press, 1996.

Semmes, Raphael. *Memoirs of Service Afloat.* 1869. Reprint, Secaucus N.J.: Blue & Gray Press, 1987.

Shipp, J. F. "The Famous Battle of Hampton Roads." *Confederate Veteran* 24 (1916): 305–7.

Smith, C. Carter Jr., ed. *Two Naval Journals: 1864.* Mobile: Graphic Inc., 1964.

Smith, Gene A. *Iron and Heavy Guns: Duel between the "Monitor" and "Merrimac."* Fort Worth: Ryan Place Publishers, 1996.

Soley, James R. *Historical Sketch of the United States Naval Academy.* Washington, D.C.: Government Printing Office, 1876.

Still, William N. Jr. "Confederate Naval Strategy: The Ironclad." *Journal of Southern History* 27 (August 1961): 330–43.

———. *Confederate Shipbuilding.* Athens: University of Georgia Press, 1969.

———. "The Confederate States Navy at Mobile, 1861 to August 1864." *Alabama Historical Quarterly* 30 (Fall–Winter 1968): 127–39.

———. *Iron Afloat: The Story of the Confederate Ironclads.* Columbia: University of South Carolina Press, 1971.

———. "Selma and the C.S. Navy." *Alabama Review* 15 (January 1962): 19–37.

———. "Technology Afloat." *Civil War Times Illustrated* 14 (November 1975): 4–9, 40–47.

Sturdy, Henry Francis. "The Establishment of the Naval School at Annapolis." *U.S. Naval Institute Proceedings* (April 1946), suppl., 1–17.

———. "The Founding of the Naval Academy by Bancroft and Buchanan." *U.S. Naval Institute Proceedings* 61 (October 1935): 1367–1403.

Sweetman, Jack. *The U.S. Naval Academy: An Illustrated History.* Annapolis: Naval Institute Press, 1979.

Symonds, Craig L. *The Naval Institute's Historical Atlas of the U.S. Navy.* Annapolis: Naval Institute Press, 1995.

Taylor, Fitch W. *The Broad Pennant, or A Cruise in the United States Flag Ship of the Gulf Squadron during the Mexican Difficulties.* New York: Leavitt, Trow & Company, 1848.

Thomas, Emory. *The Confederate State of Richmond: A Biography of the Capital.* Austin: University of Texas Press, 1971.

Tilghman, Oswald. *History of Talbot County, Maryland, 1661–1861.* 2 vols. Baltimore: Regional Publishing Company, 1967.

Tindall, William. "True Story of the *Virginia.*" *Virginia Magazine of History and Biography* 31 (1923): 1–38, 89–145.

Todorich, Charles. *The Spirited Years: A History of the Antebellum Naval Academy.* Annapolis: Naval Institute Press, 1984.

U.S. Congress. *Annals of the Congress of the United States.* 42 vols. Washington, D.C.: Gales & Seaton, 1834–1856.

U.S. Statutes at Large. Boston: Little, Brown, 1859–.

Wagandt, Charles. "Redemption or Reaction? Maryland in the Post–Civil War Years." In *Radicalism, Racism, and Party Realignment: The Border States during Reconstruction,* ed. Richard O. Curry. Baltimore: Johns Hopkins University Press, 1969.

War of the Rebellion: Official Records of the Union and Confederate Armies in the War of the Rebellion. 4 series, 128 vols. Washington, D.C.: Government Printing Office, 1894–1922.

War of the Rebellion: Official Records of the Union and Confederate Navies in the War of the Rebellion. 2 series, 28 vols. Washington, D.C.: Government Printing Office, 1894–1922.

Wheeler, Richard. *In Pirate Waters: Captain David Porter, USN, and America's War on Piracy in the West Indies.* New York: Thomas Y. Crowell, 1969.

White, E. V. *The First IronClad Naval Engagement in the World.* Portsmouth, Va.: E. V. White, 1906.

Williams, Frances L. *Matthew Fontaine Maury, Scientist of the Sea.* New Brunswick: Rutgers University Press, 1963.

Wilstach, Paul. *Tidewater Maryland.* Indianapolis: Bobbs-Merrill, 1931.

Winslow, Arthur. *Francis Winslow, His Forebears and Life, Based upon Family Records and Correspondence during XXX Years.* Norwood: Plimpton Press, 1935.

⤚ゝ *Further Reading* ⤚ゝ

Surprisingly, Buchanan has attracted only one other biographer. Seventy years ago, Charles Lee Lewis (also a professor at the Naval Academy) published *Admiral Franklin Buchanan, Fearless Man of Action* (Baltimore: Norman Remington). The subtitle suggests a great deal about the thrust of the book. Lewis is uncritical of his subject, and at times his narrative has the feel of a boy's adventure story, designed more to inspire than to inform. It does not have the same thoughtful assessment or clear style of Lewis's subsequent biography of *David Glasgow Farragut* published fourteen years later (Annapolis: Naval Institute Press, 1943).

Buchanan was little help to his biographers. He kept no diary, wrote no memoir. Very likely many of his private papers were burned in the fire that destroyed the Rest in 1863. Sadly, no letters between Buchanan and his wife, Nannie, have survived. There are, however, a number of scattered collections of Buchanan letters. In particular, two excellent and essential collections contain a number of private letters that Buchanan wrote to close friends. Between 1820 and 1860, Buchanan wrote some three score gossipy letters to Samuel F. Du Pont. Those letters, housed at the Hagley Museum and Library in Wilmington, Delaware, provide an invaluable window into Buchanan's private thoughts. After the Civil War began, the Buchanan–Du Pont relationship was severed, and Buchanan's closest epistolary confidant became John K. Mitchell, to whom he wrote some two dozen letters from Mobile in 1863–64. These are housed at the Virginia Historical Society in Richmond. Beyond these collections, the best sources for studying Buchanan are his cruise journals and letter books. Most of the former are in the Special Collections of the Nimitz Library at the U.S. Naval Academy; his wartime letter book is in the Southern Historical Collection at the Wilson Library of the University of North Carolina, Chapel Hill. The official letters of the Navy Department from Record Group 45 of the National Archives (available on microfilm) are essential for Buchanan's naval service up to 1860; and the printed *Official Records of the Union and Confederate Navies in the War of the Rebellion,* 28 vols. (Washington, D.C.: Government Printing Office, 1894–1922) are just as essential for his service after 1861.

Other valuable contemporary sources for the study of Franklin Buchanan are the published works of his contemporaries. These include Alexander Slidell Mackenzie's *The Life of Commodore Oliver Hazard Perry* (New York: Harper & Brothers, 1840), which is based partly on Mackenzie's recollections as one of Buchanan's messmates aboard the *Java*; Henry James Mercier's *Life in a Man-of-War* (Boston: Houghton Mifflin, 1927), which recounts the cruise of the *Constellation* in the Pacific in 1839–40; and Arthur Winslow's account of Francis Winslow (*Francis Winslow, His Forebears and Life* [Norwood: Plimpton Press, 1935]), which covers the naval war against Mexico. Contemporary accounts of the Battle of Hampton Roads include William Harwar Parker's *Recollections of a Naval Officer,* first published in 1883 and available in a modern edition (Annapolis: Naval Institute Press, 1985), and a recently published memoir by Eugenius A. Jack, who was an engineer on the *Virginia* (*Memoirs of E. A. Jack, Steam Engineer, CSS "Virginia"* [White Stone, Va.: Brandywine Publishers, 1998]). Useful contemporary accounts of the fighting in Mobile Bay include Foxhall A. Parker's "The Battle of Mobile Bay," which has been reprinted in a number of places, including the *Papers of the Military Historical Society of Massachusetts* (Boston: Griffith-Stillings Press, 1902); and the description Buchanan's flag captain, James D. Johnston, wrote for *Century* magazine, available in *Battles and Leaders of the Civil War* (New York: Century Magazine, 1888), vol. 4, pp. 401–6.

If Buchanan has been the subject of only one previous biography, he is a key player in the biographies of several of his contemporaries. By far the best book in this context is Samuel E. Morison's *"Old Bruin": Commodore Matthew Calbraith Perry* (Boston: Little Brown, 1967), which has excellent coverage of Buchanan's service in the war with Mexico and during the expedition to Japan. Also useful are James M. Merrill's *Du Pont: The Making of an Admiral* (New York: Dodd Mead, 1986), and Frances L. Williams's *Matthew Fontaine Maury* (New Brunswick: Rutgers University Press, 1963).

Valuable secondary accounts of events in which Buchanan played a central role include Charles Todorich's history of the early Naval Academy: *The Spirited Years: A History of the Antebellum Naval Academy* (Annapolis: Naval Institute Press, 1984); Curtis Henson's study of American diplomatic efforts in the Far East: *Commissioners and Commodores: The East India Squadron and American Diplomacy in China* (University: University of Alabama Press, 1982); as well as Morison's biography of Perry.

The published literature for Buchanan's Civil War years is much richer. The most useful general work on the Confederate navy is J. Thomas Scharf's old but still invaluable *History of the Confederate States Navy,* first published in 1887 and reprinted in two volumes by the Ayer Company of Salem, New Hampshire, in 1988. Scharf makes some errors, but his book is still the best starting place for information about the C.S. Navy. The best modern history, by the Italian scholar Raimondo Luraghi, is *A History of the Confederate Navy* (Annapolis: Naval Institute Press, 1996). For a lively account of naval actions in the war, see R. Thomas Campbell's two books, *Gray Thunder* and *Southern Thunder,* both published by Burd Street Press of Philadelphia in 1996. A good introduction to the administrative difficulties of the Confederate navy is available in Joseph T. Durkin, *Stephen R. Mallory: Confederate Navy Chief* (Chapel Hill: University of North Carolina Press, 1954). For information about the Confederacy's shipbuilding and ironclad programs, see William N. Still Jr.'s many books and articles, especially *Confederate Shipbuilding* (Athens: University of Georgia Press, 1969) and *Iron Afloat* (Columbia: University of South Carolina Press, 1971).

Andy Warhol once said that every American has fifteen minutes of fame. Buchanan had two: one in Hampton Roads in 1862 and one in Mobile Bay in 1864. For accounts of the Battle of Hampton Roads, see William C. Davis, *Duel between the First Ironclads* (Baton Rouge: Louisiana State University Press, 1975); and Gene A. Smith, *Iron and Heavy Guns* (Fort Worth: Ryan Place Publishers, 1996). On the Battle of Mobile Bay, see Chester Hearn, *Mobile Bay and the Mobile Campaign: The Last Great Battles of the Civil War* (Jefferson, N.C.: McFarland, 1993).

~~ *Index* ~~

Acme, 8, 11, 13
Adams, Henry, 103
Albany, USS, 86
Alden, James, 212–13
Algiers. *See* Barbary States
Allen, William H., 26
Alligator, USS, 26
Alonzo Child, 191
Anacostia, USS, 137
Annapolis, 10, 30, 40, 45–46, 49. *See also* Naval Academy
Aulick, John H., 94, 96–98, 120

Bainbridge, USS, 64
Ballard, Henry E., 18, 19–20, 43–44
Baltic, CSS, 184, 192, 205, 207
Baltimore, USS, 29–32, 38
Bancroft, George, 67–71, 74, 77, 79, 81
Banks, Nathaniel, 203–4
Barbary States, 12–13, 15–16, 19–20, 38
Barron, Samuel S., 117
Bassett, Henry D., 184
Beagle, USS, 26
Beaufort, CSS, 157, 161, 166–67, 230
Bell, John, 135
Benjamin, Judah P., 123–24
Bent, Silas, 113
Bigelow, Abraham, 117
black codes, 227
blockade: of CSA, 151; of Mexico, 84; of Mobile, 181, 207–8
Bonita, USS, 88–90
Bragg, Braxton, 187, 197
Breckinridge, John C., 135
Breese, Samuel, 90
Brooke, John M., 152–53
Brooke rifle, 199

Brooklyn, USS, 212–13
Brown, John, 135
Bryan, Joseph, 53–55
Buchanan, Alice Lloyd (FB's daughter), 46, 129, 175, 222
Buchanan, Ann Catherine Lloyd (FB's wife), 37–38, 40, 42–43, 50, 64, 146, 221, 222–23, 225, 231; family life, 45–46, 74, 94, 115, 129; financial troubles, 45, 79–80, 225, 228
Buchanan, Elizabeth (FB's daughter), 46, 129, 222
Buchanan, Ellen (FB's daughter). *See* Screven, Ellen Buchanan
Buchanan, Franklin: appearance, 1; birth, 8; chief of Bureau of Orders & Detail, 147–48, 149–50, 151; children of, 45–46, 74, 115, 129, 136, 175, 222, 227; in China, 24, 106, 108–11, 134; as college president, 228–30; as disciplinarian, 29, 38–39, 42, 43, 54–55, 66, 71, 76–77, 78, 85, 92–93, 111–14, 180, 192–94; family life, 46–47, 80, 94, 115, 129; feud with French Forrest, 194–97; financial troubles, 45, 53, 64, 79–80, 225, 228; founds Naval Academy, 71–82; health, 119–20, 122, 128, 172, 174–75, 176, 220–21; intolerance for drunkenness, 39, 55–57, 75, 78, 91; in Mexican War, 83–93; as midshipman, 7–8, 10–27; mission to Japan, 96–106, 107–8, 124; in Mobile, 179–218, 224–25, 230; political views of, 129–33, 135, 226–27; as prisoner, 221–23; resigns from U.S. Navy, 1–2, 137–38, 196; on Retirement Board, 115–27; and slavery, 50, 130–33,

Buchanan, Franklin (*continued*)
139–40, 226; on CSS *Tennessee*,
191–219; on USS *Vincennes*, 51–66;
on CSS *Virginia*, 155, 156–70;
wounded, 168, 217–18
Buchanan, Franklin Jr. (FB's son), 46,
129
Buchanan, George (FB's father), 8–9,
130
Buchanan, James, 130, 135
Buchanan, Laetitia McKean (FB's
mother), 8–9
Buchanan, Letitia McKean (FB's
daughter), 46, 129
Buchanan, Mary Tilghman (FB's
daughter), 129
Buchanan, McKean (FB's brother), 47,
116, 222; in Battle of Hampton
Roads, 163, 168–70
Buchanan, Nannie (FB's daughter). *See*
Meiere, Nannie Buchanan
Buchanan, Rosa (FB's daughter), 129
Buchanan, Sallie (FB's daughter). *See*
Screven, Sallie Buchanan
Buchanan, USS, 234
Buchanan House (at USNA), 82, 234
Budd, George, 33–36
Bull Run, Battle of, 143, 148
Butler, Benjamin, 203–4

Calhoun, John C., 41
Carter, R. M., 221
cat-of-nine-tails. *See* punishment
Chancellorsville, Battle of, 196
Chapman, James, 112
Chauncey, Isaac, 17–18
Chauvenet, William, 70–72
Chesapeake, USS, 9
Chickamauga, Battle of, 197
Chickasaw, USS, 217
China, 24, 106, 108–11, 134
City Point, Virginia, 223
Claxton, Alexander, 47–49
coal. *See* steam propulsion
Confederate Navy: manpower, 186–87,
199–200; organization, 147;
resources, 148–50, 184, 185; strategy,
150–55
Confucius, USS, 109
Congress, USS, 160–70
Conner, David, 85

Conrad, Daniel, 208, 210, 215, 218–21
conscription, 186–87, 200
Constellation, USS, 38–39
Constitution, USS, 47–49
Cumberland, USS, 160–64, 166, 173,
209

Dahlgren, John A., 3, 137
Daugherty, Philip, 112–13
Davis, Jefferson, 151, 154, 174, 176, 181,
204, 224; visits the Rest, 227–28
Davis, Joseph, 224
Decatur, Stephen, 13
Decoy, USS, 27
Delaware, USS, 43–44
Doane, Francis C., 31–32
Dobbin, James C., 116–17, 126
Dorothea, 23–24
Douglas, Steven A., 135
Douglass, Frederick, 41–42, 178
Drayton, Percival, 217
Duer, John, 112–14
Du Pont, Samuel F., 38, 43, 54, 70, 73,
93–94, 96–97, 134; in Civil War,
149, 151; as midshipman, 18; and
Retirement Board, 116–26; and
secession crisis, 139–40, 143, 145

eastern shore of Maryland. *See* Talbot
County
Eggleston, John R., 165
emancipation, 226. *See also* slavery
Erie, USS, 19, 34–35
Exmouth, Lord, 15

Farragut, David Glasgow, 18, 144–45,
175, 192, 203; in Battle of Mobile Bay,
210–19; concern for FB, 220–21, 223
Farrand, Ebenezer, 185, 194, 224
Ferret, USS, 26
Fields, Barbara, 132
Fillmore, Millard, 95, 99–100, 105
Fisher, Nancy Hardcastle, 234
flogging. *See* punishment
Florida, CSS, 180–82
Foote, Andrew H., 117
Forrest, Dulaney, 12–13
Forrest, French: feud with FB, 194–97; in
Civil War, 149, 153–54; in Mexican
War, 90
Forrest, W. S., 219, 221

Fort Acachapan, 90–91
Fort Gaines, 179
Fort Lafayette, 221–23
Fort Morgan, 179, 188, 205; in Battle of Mobile Bay, 209–18
Fort Morgan, USS, 221
Fox, Gustavus, 192
Fox, USS, 26
Franklin, USS, 18–20, 134
Frémont, John C., 130
Fulton, USS, 149

Gaines, CSS, 205, 207, 213
Garrison, William Lloyd, 42
Germantown, USS, 81, 83–93, 199; characteristics of, 85
Giraud, Pierre, 219
Girault, Arsène Napoléon Alexandre, 72, 75–76
Glorie, 152
Goldsborough, Mary Eleanor, 49
Goldsborough, William T., 49, 124, 133
Graham, William A., 95–97
Grant, Ulysses S., 190, 197, 203, 223
Greyhound, USS, 26
gunnery. *See* ordnance
Gunnison, CSS, 198
Hampton Roads, Battle of, 160–68, 222, 227, 230
Hargous, Louis S., 61–63
Harpers Ferry raid, 135
Harrison, George W., 213
Hartford, USS, 210, 212–19
Hastings, H. P., 60
Heath, John, 16–17
Henshaw, Harold, 63
Hicks, Thomas H., 144
Higgins, James, 229–30
homosexuality: in U.S. Navy, 57; at Maryland Agricultural College, 229–30
Hooe, Robert E., 56–57
Hornet, USS, 28–29, 34
Houston, Sam, 122–23
Humphreys, Joshua, 12
Huntsville, CSS, 189–90

Inman, William, 94–95

Jackal, USS, 26
Jackson, Andrew, 43

Jackson, Thomas J. (Stonewall), 196
Jacob Bell, 182
Jamestown, CSS, 157
Japan, U.S. mission to, 95, 99–106, 107–8; ceremony in 105–6, 108; negotiations with, 103–5
Java, USS, 8, 10–17, 23, 69
Johnston, James D., 185, 200; in Battle of Mobile Bay, 209–18, 220
Johnston, Joseph E., 175–76, 177, 207
Johnston, Robert E., 64
Jones, George, 72
Jones, Thomas ap Catesby, 125, 173, 189, 198; at Naval Gun Foundry, 186, 199, 202; on CSS Virginia, 153–58, 168–69

Kamehameha III, 111
Kayama Yezaimon, 103–6
Kelley, John, 97–98
Kennedy, Edmund P., 28–29
Kennedy, John P., 96
Kennon, Beverly, 27–28
King, Darius, 73–74

Lackawanna, USS, 213, 216
La Peña, 86–87
Lazoretto Hospital, 8
Leadbetter, Danville, 198
Lee, George Washington Custis, 228
Lee, Robert E., 151, 177, 190, 196–97, 203, 207, 223
LeRoy, William, 219
Lew Chew (or Loo Choo). *See* Okinawa
Lily, USS, 35–36
Lincoln, Abraham, 135, 145, 175; attends wedding, 136; declares blockade, 151
Livingston, Edward, 43
Lloyd, Ann Catherine (FB's wife). *See* Buchanan, Ann Catherine Lloyd
Lloyd, Edward VI (FB's father-in-law), 40–42
Lloyd, Edward VII (FB's brother-in-law), 45–46, 129, 188; and slavery, 130–31, 226
Lloyd, Sally (FB's mother-in-law), 40, 46
Lloyd, Sarah Scott (FB's sister-in-law). *See* Lowndes, Sarah Scott Lloyd
Lockwood, Henry, 71–72

Lockwood, John A., 72, 80
Long, Andrew K., 44
Lorino, Baptista, 229–30
Louis Philippe, 43–44
Lowndes, Charles, 37, 49, 92
Lowndes, Sarah Scott Lloyd, 37, 49

Mackenzie, Alexander Slidell: in Mexican War, 90; as midshipman, 12, 14–15; in *Somers* mutiny, 69–70
Maffitt, John H., 180–82
Magruder, John B., 158
Mahon, Thomas, 55–56
Mallory, Stephen D.: as advocate of ironclads, 151–52, 154–55; as Confederate SecNav, 146, 150, 157, 174, 176, 184, 185, 187, 194–95, 206; as U.S. Senator, 117, 123; praises FB, 174, 178
Manhattan, USS, 217
Marcy, Samuel L., 70–72
Marcy, William L., 70–71
Marshall, Humphrey, 95, 98, 106–7
Marshall, John H., 55
Maryland Agricultural College, 228–30
Maury, Dabney, 221
Maury, Matthew F.: and Retirement Board, 119–21, 126; in Civil War, 149
Mayo, Isaac, 144–45
McCauley, Charles, 117, 125, 152
McClellan, George B., 176, 178
McClintock, James R., 188
McKean, Thomas (FB's grandfather), 8
McKean, William, 70
McLane, Robert M., 107, 108–11, 113
McLaughlin, Augustus, 78
McRae, Colin, 186
Meade, George Gordon, 204
Meiere, Julius E., 136, 175, 183–84
Meiere, Nannie Buchanan (FB's daughter), 46, 129, 136, 175
Memphis, Battle of, 176
Merrimack, USS. *See Virginia,* CSS
Metacomet, USS, 220
Mexican-American War, 83–93
mines. *See* torpedoes
Minnesota, USS, 169–70
Minor, Charles L. C., 228
Minor, Robert D., 159, 163, 167–68, 170, 174
Mississippi, USS, 152; described, 51–53; in Far East, 95, 98, 102–4; in Mexican War, 86, 92

Missouri Compromise, 41
Mitchell, John K., 183, 197; as head of Bureau of Orders & Detail, 197, 200, 202, 208
Mitchell, Lise, 224
Mobile, Alabama: Battle of, 203, 208–19; blockade of, 207–8, CSN squadron in, 182–83, 189–90; FB's defensive plan for, 189; strategic significance of, 179
Modena, Duke of, 20
Monitor, USS, 170–71, 172
Monongahela, USS, 215
Montgomery, James E., 176
Morgan, CSS, 205, 207, 213
Morison, Samuel E., 102
mosquito squadron, 27
Mullany, J. R. Madison, 213

Nashville, CSS, 184, 190
Natchez, USS, 33–36
Naval Academy, 2, 93, 134; curriculum, 71–72; description, 73; exams, 81; faculty of, 72–73, 75–77; founding of, 68–71; regulations of, 74–75
Nicholson, William B., 34

Ochiltree, David, 75–76
O'Dougherty, Dennis, 14
officer education, 13, 18, 22–23, 25; at Annapolis, 68–78, 80–82
Ohio, USS, 53
Okinawa (Lew Chew), 100–102, 106–7
Oliver, Henry, 225
Ontario, USS, 38
ordnance: in age of sail, 11, 44, 85, 86, 102; in Civil War, 153, 160, 168–69, 186, 194, 198–99, 210, 212–13, 216–17
Ossippee, USS, 219

Page, Robert, 207–8, 220
Palmer, James, 219, 221
Parker, William H., 160, 166–67, 173–74, 230
Patrick Henry, CSS, 157, 165, 227
Patterson, Daniel T., 44
Pawnee, USS, 136
Peacock, USS, 19, 27
Pendergrast, Austin, 166, 169
Pendergrast, G. J., 117
Pennsylvania, USS, 23, 156

Perry, Matthew C., 2, 24, 81; and discipline, 111–14; in Far East, 95, 98, 100–108; in Mexican War, 85–93; and Retirement Board, 117–19, 125, 127
Perry, Oliver Hazard, 8, 13–14, 16–17, 29, 85
Petersburg, 64
Phillipi, USS, 213
Pierce, Franklin, 99, 116, 129, 131
Pierce, Joseph, 193–94
piracy: in Caribbean, 22, 25–29, 33–36; in Mediterranean, 12, 15–16, 38, 57–58
Plymouth, USS, 97–98
Poinsett, USS, 66
Polk, Leonidas, 187
Porter, David, 26
Porter, John L., 152
Port Royal, S.C., 151
Powhatan, USS, 107, 111
Pratt, Thomas, 123–24
Pratt Street massacre, 1–2, 137
Princeton, USS, 86
privateering: in 1820s, 25–26; in Civil War, 150–51
Prometheus, USS, 17–18
punishment, 29; legislation concerning, 54–55, 111, 115–16; FB's use of, 38–40, 43, 92, 183–84; FB's dispute with Perry concerning, 111–14

Raleigh, CSS, 157, 165
Ramsay, H. Ashton, 159–60, 163
Reconstruction, 225–31
Rest, the, 52, 93, 115, 121, 230–31; described, 49; is destroyed, 197; is rebuilt, 225
Retirement Board, 93, 111, 131; deliberations of, 115–19; reaction to, 119–27
Richmond, USS, 213
Richmond, Virginia: in 1862, 146–47; in 1865, 223–24
Ridgely, Charles, 33–36, 81
Rousseau, Lawrence, 149
Rowly, Josias, 44–45
Rush, Richard, 18
Russell, William H., 179
Ruth, 32–33

San Juan Bautista. *See* Tabasco
Santa Anna, Antonio López de, 60, 65

Saratoga, USS, 101
Schenck, Robert, 95
Scott, Winfield, 85, 86, 129
Screven, Ellen Buchanan (FB's daughter), 46, 129, 227
Screven, George, 227
Screven, Sallie Buchanan (FB's daughter), 45–46, 129, 227
Screven, Thomas F., 227
Sea Gull, USS, 27
secession crisis, 135–36, 144–45
Seddon, James, 187
Selma, CSS, 205, 207, 213
Semmes, Raphael, 66, 144–45, 148–49
Seven Pines, Battle of, 176
Shaler, William, 16
Shark, USS, 35
Sharp, U. S. Grant, 234
Shaw, John, 14–15
Sherman, William T., 203–4
Shubrick, William, 117, 124, 143–44, 145
Sigel, Franz, 203–4
Singapore, 97
slavery: emancipation, 226; FB's attitude toward, 130–33, 226; in Maryland, 131–33, 226; as political issue, 129–31; at Wye House 41, 50
slave trade: external 36, 41, 58; internal, 132–33
Smith, Charles R., 55–56
Smith, William, 166, 169
Soley, James Russell, 148
Somers, USS, 66, 69–70, 84, 113
Southern Republic, 191
Spencer, Philip, 69–70
Spitfire, USS, 86–87
Stanton, Edwin, 223
steam propulsion, 27, 52–53, 84, 102, 109, 151, 159–60, 190–91
Stewart, Charles, 18–19, 54, 60, 63, 70
Stockton, Robert S., 55
Stribling, Cornelius, 117
Stromboli, USS, 86
Stuart, J. E. B., 177
submarines, 187–88
Suffern, 44
Susquehanna, USS, 152, 156; in Far East, 94, 96–98, 100–111; in Civil War, 198; punishment on board, 112–14
Swain, Edward A., 198

Tabasco, Mexico, 87–92
Taiping rebellion (China), 98, 108–11
Talbot County, Maryland, 37, 40–42,
    49–50, 129, 131–32, 135, 138–39, 225–26
Tattnall, Josiah, 173–74, 175–76; court
    martial of, 177–78
Taylor, Zachary, 84
Teaser, CSS, 157
Tecumseh, USS, 210
Tennessee, CSS, 184, 189; in Battle of
    Mobile Bay, 208–18; characteristics
    of, 190–93, 194, 199, 207–8; crew of,
    199–200; crosses Dog River bar,
    201–2, 203
Terrier, USS, 26–27
Texas Navy, 116
Thompson, Charles, 32
Thompson, Waddy, 61–63, 65
Thompson, William, 113
Toombs, Robert, 122–23
torpedoes, 179, 198, 211–12
Toucey, Isaac, 126, 134
Tredegar Iron Works, 153
Tripoli. *See* Barbary States
Truxtun, USS, 86
Tucker, John R., 150, 157, 227
Turner, Nat, 73
Tuscaloosa, CSS, 189–90
Tuxpan, Mexico, 86–87, 138

Union, USS, 66
United States, USS, 14, 19, 43–44

United States Naval Academy. *See*
    Naval Academy
University of Maryland. *See* Maryland
    Agricultural College
Upshur, Abel, 54, 56, 62
Upshur, George P., 93

Vancouver, 96
Vesuvius, USS, 86
Vicksburg, Mississippi, 188, 197
Vincennes, USS, 51, 58–66, 199; charac-
    teristics of, 53
Virginia, CSS, 149, 152–53, 172, 194–95,
    204, 209; in Battle of Hampton Roads,
    159–71; design, 153, 157, 159; destruction
    of, 175, 177–78
Vixen, USS, 87–90

Ward, James H., 72
Warrior, HMS, 152
Washington, USS, 19
Weasel, USS, 25–28
Welles, Gideon, 1–3, 136–38, 143–45,
    192, 196, 220, 223, 234
Wharton, Arthur D., 217
whipping. *See* punishment; slavery
Wild Cat, USS, 26
Williamson, William P., 153
Winder, Charles S., 49, 125
Winder, Edward S., 49
Winder, Elizabeth Lloyd, 49
Wye House, 40, 45–46, 123, 129

About the Author

Craig L. Symonds is professor emeritus at the U.S. Naval Academy and the author of eleven books, including *The Naval Institute Historical Atlas of the U.S. Navy* (1995) and *Decision at Sea: Five Naval Battles that Shaped American History*, which won the Theodore and Franklin D. Roosevelt Prize in 2006. He and his wife live in Annapolis, Maryland.